CONTEMPORARY
REFORM RESPONSA

CONTEMPORARY REFORM RESPONSA

by

SOLOMON B. FREEHOF, D.D.
Rabbi Emeritus, Rodef Shalom Temple, Pittsburgh

THE HEBREW UNION COLLEGE PRESS

1974

Library of Congress Cataloging in Publication Data

Freehof, Solomon Bennett, 1892-
  Contemporary Reform responsa.

  Includes index.
  1. Responsa—1800-   2. Reform Judaism. I. Title.
BM522.36.R368   296.1'8   74-23748
ISBN 0-87820-108-4

CONTENTS

Foreword   IX
Introduction   1
1   Dedication of a Synagogue   9
2   Selling Synagogue to Black Muslims   13
3   Joint Building for Synagogue and Unitarian Church   18
4   Homosexual Congregations   23
5   Quarreling Family and Bar Mitzvah   27
6   Father's Name Forgotten   32
7   Ark Open During Services   37
8   Translating Torah Reading Verse by Verse   40
9   Church Use of Synagogue Building   44
10   Composition and Size of the Sabbath Candle   49
11   Weekday Use of Sabbath Candlesticks   53
12   United Jewish Appeal at Kol Nidre   57
13   Candle Lighting at Kol Nidre   60
14   The Pregnant Bride   67
15   Visiting Israel   69
16   Sterilizing the Feebleminded   74
17   Marrying the Sterilized   78
18   Divorce for a Doubtful Marriage   82
19   Two Adoption Problems   86
20   Naming Child of an Unmarried Mother   91
21   Wedding Without a License   98
22   Ownership of Sefer Torah   107
23   Torah in Museum Case or in Ark   110
24   Posul Torah in the Ark   114
25   Fasting if Torah is Dropped   117
26   Hebrew Letters on Chaplain's Insignia   120
27   Lady's Pants Suits   123
28   Statuettes in the Synagogue   127
29   Substituting for Christians on Christmas   131
30   A Dubious Conversion   136
31   Reconverting an Ex-Nun   141
32   Adoption by Cohanim   145
33   Convert Buried in Christian Cemetery   151
34   Study of Foetal Material   155
35   Disinterment Due to a Labor Strike   160
36   Burial on the Holiday After a Strike   163
37   Which Body to Bury First   165
38   Cremation Ashes Buried at Home   169
39   Position of the Body in the Grave   172
40   Lights at Head of Coffin   177

41   Refusing to Handle an Infectious Body   181
42   Burial in His or Her City   185
43   Some Burial Duties   189
44   Congregational Charge for Funerals   193
45   Funeral Service for Non-Members   196
46   Funeral Service for Ex-Members   200
47   Burial of Fallen Israeli Soldiers   205
48   Caesarean on a Dead Mother   212
49   Bequeathing Parts of the Body   216
50   The Vandalized Cemetery   224
51   Family Disagreement Over Cremation   228
52   Visiting the Cemetery   232
53   Exchanging a Tombstone   236
54   A Convert and Jewish Burial   240
55   Copyrighting Books   245
56   To Dissuade a Would-Be Suicide   253
57   Garnisheeing Wages   260
58   Rabbinical Tenure   263

Inquiries:
1   Questions from Israel on Proselytism   269
2   Extra Shroud for Cohen   276
3   Oath of Office   279
4   Grandson and Grandfather   281
5   Plantings or Flowers on the Grave   284
6   Spices and Passover   287
7   Earthquakes   290
8   Asking Pardon of the Dead   293
9   The Falashas as Jews   297

To the honored memory of

HENRY E. KAGAN

and

JACOB M. ROTHSCHILD

Colleagues and Comrades

FOREWORD

In publishing this, Dr. Freehof's fifth volume of Reform Responsa, the Alumni Association again honors itself.

Solomon Freehof is a recognized giant among his peers. During a significant portion of his illustrious rabbinate he has been committed to building a bridge between the liberal Jew and the legal tradition of our Fathers.

In every age certain rabbis have been singled out by their generation for consultation on matters of halacha. Rabbi Freehof has occupied this special place for our generation. His Responsa reflect a liberal consciousness tempered by a deep knowledge and respect for the Jewish legal tradition.

Even in retirement Rabbi Freehof continues an ongoing dialogue with our past to the enrichment of his colleagues and fellow Jews everywhere. May the questions continue to be posed and may our beloved colleague be granted strength to respond.

Rabbinic Alumni Association of
Hebrew Union College-Jewish Institute of Religion

Samuel E. Karff
Chairman, Publications Committee

INTRODUCTION

In the late autumn of 1973, the Union of American Hebrew Congregations celebrated its hundredth anniversary. The commemorative convention of the Union took place in New York rather than in a resort city, because New York is the headquarters of the Union and it was deemed appropriate that the House of Living Judaism be open to the delegates who came from all over the United States and Europe.

In recognition of this important anniversary of a great organization, composed of close to eight hundred congregations, the New York *Times* commissioned one of its writers to research and write an article on the progress of American Reform Judaism during these hundred years. The article was researched and written and occupied a large space in this respected newspaper. The author did not devote much time to the history of the past century, but centered all his writing upon one theme, namely, the new relationship between Reform Judaism and *Halacha,* the traditional Jewish law. The question that the reporter asked of virtually everybody whose opinions he published was whether Reform Judaism is coming closer to Orthodoxy by accepting again as valid the traditional Jewish law.

Most of the answers were a qualified affirmative. If this judgment is correct and Reform is truly moving closer toward Orthodoxy, then this constitutes a surprising phenomenon. It is contrary to the general spirit of our times. These are times when all Orthodoxies are suffering erosion and losing strength. The most strictly disciplined of all churches is confronted with resignation of hundreds of its priests and the closing of its schools. Jewish Orthodoxy itself can hardly be said to be growing stronger, in spite of the Yeshivos recently established by pious Chassidic immigrants. This, then, would seem to be a time when people are moving away from strictly disciplined Orthodoxy. It would be strange if, contrary to this social current, Reform Judaism is returning to it or to something like it.

We must therefore ask ourselves whether this supposed approach to Orthodoxy is actually a fact. A good way to test it would be by a study of the fine and justly popular Sabbath Manual published this year by the Conference of Rabbis. What does the manual say about work on the Sabbath, which is one of the central prohibitions in Jewish law? It says, in effect, that if a person can avoid work on the Sabbath, he should do so. No heavy household work should be done on the Sabbath. But the book makes no attempt to enforce the strict prohibitory Sabbath laws. The person who would follow this book would surely have a warmer Jewish home, but would still be in the eyes of Orthodox

Jewish law a *M'chalel Shabbas,* a violator of the Sabbath.

Then how much of an approach is this? Would Orthodoxy consider it as praiseworthy and welcome it? An analogous gesture of approach was made a few years ago in England. A Reform congregation felt that without denying the validity of civil divorce, there should also be a Jewish type of divorce, a modern form of *get.* A formulation of a modern *get* was made and immediately the Orthodox *Bes Din,* which had hitherto largely ignored the Reform and the Liberal movement, burst into indignation and denunciation. They said that the so-called Reform *get* was a falsification, a snare and a delusion, and that people must be warned against it. Why did they not accept this as a friendly gesture? Why did they react so violently? This anger is not an exceptional reaction. Exactly the same reaction occurred when Conservative Judaism tried to liberalize the divorce laws on a traditional basis. Evidently there is something in these rapprochements which is particularly hateful to the Orthodox.

The official English Orthodox indicated the reason clearly. They consider these modifications of Orthodox observances by non-Orthodox groups as a form of deception or dishonesty. But why? May not a group be free to select which observances appeal to them? The Orthodox answer is forthright and clear: Certainly not! You have no right to choose. All of the six hundred and thirteen commandments are Divinely revealed and it is not for anyone to decide which commandment he will observe and which he will not observe. "Be as careful with a minor commandment as with a major commandment, because you cannot know God's reward for the respective commandments" (*Ethics of the Fathers,* 2:1). There is a clear-cut logical philosophy behind Jewish Orthodoxy. All the commandments are God-given. We are mandated to obey them all. No one may presume to choose between them.

Reform Jews, no matter what ceremonies they may readopt, must frankly admit that they do not and cannot accept the basic philosophy of Orthodoxy that all of the inherited commandments are God-given and inescapably our duty. As a matter of fact, we are glad that certain inherited commandments have fallen away such as, for example, those that led to the inferior status of women or to the isolation from our fellow citizens.

Nevertheless, these changes and readoptions of older ceremonies must be judged, not only from the Orthodox point of view, which would consider them deceptive or trivial, but from our own point of view. We know ourselves and we know our colleagues. We know that our intention is not to deceive and not to toy with tradition. We earnestly intend to strengthen Jewish life. What is our own understanding of the motives behind our new tendency toward the readoption of certain historic ceremonies? This question is not too easy to answer because much of our motivation is a half-unconscious one. We are influenced by the changing spirit of the times, without always being aware of the fact. Our Reform movement began in an age of philosophy. We are living today in an age of psychology. At the beginning of the Reform movement, observances and services were judged on the basis of whether they were logical or reasonable. Today we are not so much concerned with logical consistency as with emotional impact. In those days they asked of a ceremony, what does it signify? Today we ask, what does it do for us? Therefore there is, one might say, an almost subconscious preference for certain ceremonies because of their emotional impact.

But if we go further into the matter, we will see that behind our emotional preferences there *is* a sort of a doctrine. If we would list those observances that we adopt and then contrast them with those that we do not adopt, it would be noticed that we do not adopt, or are not likely to adopt, the ceremonial prohibitions, the restrictive negatives in the law, except, of course, those of direct moral impact. What we do increasingly accept are not even positive commandments, but one might say folk commandments, *Minhagim* that have emerged from the life of the people and are dear to the people. In fact, as Orthodoxy itself evolves in the Western world into "modern" Orthodoxy or "traditional" Orthodoxy, what is held to most tenaciously are folk observances such as *Yahrzeit*, Bar Mitzvah, glass-breaking at weddings, *Yizkor*, etc. It may well be that behind our readoption of such observances there is not so much theology as sociology. We are strengthening our folk feeling. We are "seeking our brethren."

It may well be, also, that our moves towards our brethren involve another type of reunion. This second reunion we may judge, not from the type of ceremonies to which we are now turning, but from the type of question that is asked of the Responsa Committee of the Conference. Every year in the last few years, between one hundred fifty and two hundred questions are asked of the Committee, and all these questions deal with the Halachic background of the problem presented by the inquirer. Our men want to know increasingly what is the reaction of the historic legal literature to the problems which confront them. This too is a reunion, a truly noble one. The great Halachic literature has been the chief self-expression and devotion of our people for eighteen hundred years. The Reform movement which had based itself first of all primarily on the Bible, now realizes that God spoke to Israel likewise through its many centuries' devotion to the study of the law. We are seeking a reunion with that grand expression of Jewish thought and feeling which is embodied in the vast Halachic literature.

So we may well say that our motive is rapprochement. Through the ceremonies we are now preferring, we are seeking a comradeship with the Jewish people. Through the questions that we ask, we are seeking a rediscovery of the creative minds of Jewry. These quests, of course, are not based upon a conscious doctrine. They are a feeling. But out of this feeling a doctrine will yet emerge. Somehow, some way, our thinkers will have to explain the term revelation in a way that is meaningful to the modern mind. Somewhere, somehow, our thinkers will find a harmony between discipline and freedom, between loyalty and individuality. Such a philosophy will not be imposed. It will emerge. It may well be that out of our instinctive present-day comradely mood, in reaccepting certain folk observances, in seeking to understand the thoughts and feelings of the legal literature, we will arrive also at a philosophy of our own. In the meantime, we live without a clear philosophy. We live on our actions and our observances; and the Talmud has said: "Let a man busy himself both with the Torah and with the commandments, even though he has not a fixed doctrine to guide him (*Af al pi she'lo lishmo*) because, though beginning in this way, without a doctrine, he will yet arrive at one." (*Pesachim* 50b).

1

DEDICATION OF A SYNAGOGUE

QUESTION:

Is there a fixed tradition and ceremony for deconsecrating an old synagogue about to be abandoned or sold and, following that, a ceremony of dedication of a new synagogue? (Asked by Rabbi Roland Gittelsohn, Boston, Massachusetts.)

ANSWER:

THE QUESTION that you ask about "deconsecrating" the old synagogue and dedicating the new one is especially interesting (in a negative way). There is almost no discussion of such dedications (and deconsecrations) in any of the codes. One would expect that from the earliest days there would be a well-established custom, with all its details and ritual firmly established by now. After all, Scripture devotes a great deal of space to the dedication of the Tabernacle in the wilderness and the eight-day dedication ceremony of King Solomon of the Temple in Jerusalem. Also there is a Psalm (#30) "A Song for the Dedication of the House"; and all eight days of Chanukah are a reconsecration feast for the Temple.

Now, inasmuch as the synagogue is deemed to be the substitute for the Temple (until Messiah's time) and since, indeed, the synagogue is called in the Talmudic literature, *Migdash Me-at,* "the small sanctuary" or "the small temple," one would imagine that by now there would be an established ritual for this event; yet there is none, and that is surprising.

As for deconsecration, a synagogue can be sold for any secular purpose, provided it is the synagogue in a *small* town where all the original contributors or their descendants are available to agree to its sale. Once it has been sold, it may be used for any purpose. In fact, a term analogous to "deconsecration" is used: *"Yotzo L'Chulin,"* i.e., it has now lost its holiness. See *Orah Hayyim* 153:9: "When the men of the village sell their synagogue, they may sell it as a permanent sale (i.e., an unconditional sale) and the purchaser may do what he wants with the building." However, the money received for the sale retains some sanctity and must be used for a sacred purpose such as buying Sefer Torahs, etc. (see *Orah Hayyim* 153:2). However, there is serious question in the law as to whether there is any permission at all to sell the synagogue of a large city. That is because the presumption is that visitors from distant countries may have come to the city and contributed to its building and, therefore, it cannot be sold without their permission which is unavailable. Hence one might say that the synagogue of a large city can *never* be "deconsecrated." But in recent years new decisions have faced the realities of the changing faces of the large cities, and based upon a landmark decision of Joshua Hoeschel of Cracow (1578-1648) in his responsa *P'ne Yehoshua,* (Vol. 1,

#4) and the recent decision of Moses Feinstein, chief of the Agudas Ha-Rabbonim, in his responsa *Igros Moshe* (*Orah Hayyim* #50), we now consider the members of a large urban synagogue as being as much its sole owners as if it were a small city; and therefore they may sell it, as mentioned above.

Just as there is no required ceremony for the consecration of a synagogue, so there is no ceremony of formal deconsecration. When the synagogue is sold and the Torahs removed, the building is just a building, and the purchaser may do with it as he wishes.

As to consecration, while there is no legally prescribed ritual, there can be no doubt that some such ceremony was frequently observed. We can judge this from certain incidental discussions in the Halacha. For example, Moses Sofer, the great Hungarian authority, in his responsa (*Orah Hayyim* 156) discusses the technical question of whether it is permissible to recite the blessing *She'echionu* at the dedication of a synagogue. The great compendium of Chaim Medini, *S'de Chemed,* in the section on "Synagogue," #45, discusses the rule "not to mingle one joy with another" (which is applied to the Orthodox prohibition of marriages on Chol Ha-Moed, which would be a mingling of the joy of a wedding with the joy of Yom Tov). He raises the question whether this principle of not mingling joys should not prohibit the dedicating of a synagogue on the holiday. So, clearly, they *did* have synagogue dedications. This is evidenced by these arguments in the Halacha; but as I have said, no fixed ritual ever developed in past centuries.

The article in *Ozar Dinim U-Minhagim* on dedication of the synagogue gives in detail the ceremony which was developed by Rabbi Lehmann when he dedicated the famous synagogue in Mainz, on the 24th of Elul, 1856. Evidently this was the first detailed record (cf. also *Meir N'siv,* Tel Aviv, 1966). I will mention the essence of it because you will see that it involves both the old synagogue and the new one.

The ritual was as follows: After the afternoon service in the old synagogue, the congregation recited Psalm 132; the rabbi preached a "sermonette of departure;" the elders took the Sefer Torahs from the Ark and carried them in procession to the new synagogue, led by the Rabbi, the Cantor, and the choir, and followed by the people in regular line of march. At the gate of the new synagogue, they recited Psalm 122 and the Cantor chanted, "Open to me the gates of righteousness," etc. The President then took the key and opened the door of the new synagogue. Those who carried the Torahs lined up on the platform in front of the Ark and they recited, "How lovely are Thy dwelling places," and Psalm 84. Then they marched around the synagogue with the Sefer Torahs seven times, as on Simchas Torah. Then they placed the Torahs in the Ark and the Rabbi preached a sermon of dedication and the people recited the Psalm of the Dedication of the House, Psalm 30.

The likelihood is that this ritual described here is so naturally suitable to the occasion that it must have been followed substantially for many generations. All that Rabbi Lehmann did, then, in 1856, was to write it down and elaborate it. At all events, this is practically the ritual that we follow; but since it has no definite Halachic mention in the codes, you may, of course, vary it to suit your needs.

2

SELLING SYNAGOGUE TO BLACK MUSLIMS

QUESTION:

> Two synagogues in San Francisco have merged and, therefore, one of the buildings is not needed and is available for sale. The building is situated in a Black area and an offer has been received for it from Muhammad's Mosque, a Black Muslim organization. Some of the members of the congregation object to the sale since the Black Muslims have frequently expressed themselves anti-Semitically. Is there any Halachic principle involved in selling the building to such an organization? (Asked by Rabbi Herbert Morris, San Francisco, California.)

ANSWER:

FIRST OF ALL, there arises the question whether a congregation really has, according to Jewish law, the full right ever to sell a synagogue building, since such a sale would be destroying or at least diminishing the sanctity of a synagogue. This basic question has received much discussion in the law and has resulted in considerable restrictions and limitations in the possible sale of a synagogue building. The discussion is found in the first place in the Mishnah, *Megilla,* Chapter 3, and then in the Talmud, *Megilla,* page 27 ff. Then the law finds its way into the codes and is discussed in the *Tur* and in the *Shulchan Aruch* in *Orah Hayyim* 153.

At the outset the Halacha makes a distinction between synagogues in villages and synagogues in large cities. The synagogues in small cities may when necessary be sold without much legal difficulty. But it is not so easy to permit the sale of a synagogue in a large city. The reason for the distinction is this: No synagogue can be sold without the consent of the members. In a village all who have contributed (or their heirs) are present and therefore have the right to agree to sell it. In the large cities to which many strangers come and where presumably many non-residents, visiting but not living in the city, have contributed to the building, these non-residents are deemed, as it were, part-owners of the synagogue and one can no longer know who they are to get their consent to sell. In a sense a synagogue in a large city belongs to world Jewry and so cannot be sold since consent cannot be obtained.

However a decision permitting the sale of a large urban synagogue was made in the sixteenth century by Joshua Hoeschel ben Joseph (1578-1648) Rabbi in Cracow (*P'ne Jehoshua,* I, 4). He said that in a large city where there are many synagogues, each synagogue really belongs to its own group of members, who can exclude non-members if they wish. Therefore each separate synagogue, even in a large city, is equivalent to a small-city synagogue and may be sold. It is on this basis that nowadays synagogues in large cities, when no longer needed, are sold. So this permissive line is followed through the law and, for example, in our day the great authority (head of the Agudas ha-Rabbonim) Moses Feinstein, in his *Igros Moshe, Orah Hayyim* 50, permits the sale of a large urban synagogue, especially when worship no longer takes place within its walls. Therefore there is no question that the Talmudic prohibition no longer applies and a congregation in a large city may sell its synagogue (*cf.* previous responsum).

There is an additional reason indicated in the pioneer sixteenth-century decision permitting the sale of the building. The synagogue in the city of Grodno about which Joshua Hoeschel wrote his decision was in ruins. A ruined synagogue is deemed to retain its original sanctity and must be protected. The members of the congregation had built a fence around the ruined synagogue to protect it from intruders who befouled it, but the fence was not adequate to save the ruins from being further defiled. Therefore Joshua Hoeschel said that since its sanctity was being destroyed by intruders, this was an additional reason why this large urban synagogue, despite the Talmud's negative opinion, could be sold.

There is no question that the synagogue building under present discussion which is now in a neglected neighborhood would undoubtedly be invaded, looted and generally defiled, and for that reason should certainly be sold to a tenant who would occupy and use it.

But the second question involved here is perhaps the more grievous one. To whom may a synagogue be sold?

This is really the question which is now being asked. A similar question was raised in the Mishnah and the Talmud and carried over into the codes. No synagogue may be sold for an unworthy purpose as, for example, a tannery (because of its evil smell), a bathhouse, etc. But even this is not a insurmountable obstacle, at least with regard to a small-town synagogue. If both the officers and the entire membership agree, they may sell it for an unspecified purpose. Nevertheless, there is obviously a hesitation about selling a synagogue for an unworthy purpose, since even in a small town it would require virtually unanimous consent of the entire community.

There is another indication that no sale should be made which is unworthy of the synagogue's sanctity. This example has no direct connection with the *selling* of a synagogue but with the *building* of a synagogue. It is permissible for a Jew to have a house built by the type of contract with a Gentile builder called "Ka-blonus," by which no time limit is established and the Gentile works on his own time, as it were. In that case, the building process may go on even on the Sabbath since it is not being done on that sacred day at the express command of the Jew. This Sabbath work is permissible for the building of a private house but is not permissible for the building of a synagogue because even the *appearance* of working on the Sabbath violates the sense of sanctity with regard to a synagogue.

Such feelings against selling the synagogue for an unworthy purpose or the violating of special religious sensitivity stand in the way of the sale of this synagogue to the Black Muslims who often are anti-Semitic.

Nevertheless, this synagogue should be sold and *must* be sold or its sanctity will be destroyed anyhow by intruders. Furthermore, it would be a distinct disservice to the Jewish community if the risk were taken of intensifying the anti-Semitic feelings of the Black Muslims by refusing outright to sell the building to them.

Perhaps the best solution would be somewhat in the line of the minority suggestion made by Rabbi Judah in the Mishnah (M. *Megillah*, III, 2) that while a synagogue may not be sold directly for an unworthy purpose (tannery, bathhouse, etc.) it may be sold to be used as a courtyard and then the purchaser can do with it as he wishes once it is sold. Therefore what should be done is this: The building should not be sold to the Black Muslims. It should be sold to some other purchaser. If he wishes to sell it to them, the building is no longer sacred and it is his property. But even so, there should be, as the Talmud suggests, virtually unanimous consent of the officers and members of the congregation.

3

JOINT BUILDING FOR SYNAGOGUE AND UNITARIAN CHURCH

QUESTION:

Our Temple Board of Trustees is presently considering the purchase of an existing Unitarian fellowship building with the understanding that the two groups would *permanently* share the same physical facilities. What would be the attitude of Jewish tradition and Jewish feeling to such an arrangement? (Asked by Rabbi Solomon T. Greenberg, Cincinnati, Ohio)

ANSWER:

THE BOARD OF TRUSTEES of the synagogue are to buy the building, but the Unitarians are to worship in it permanently. Does that mean that the Unitarians still have some ownership in it, or does it mean that they are the permanent guests of the congregation? Will the services of both groups be held in the same auditorium?

If the Unitarians are to worship in the building permanently, then the building continues to be what it was previous to the proposed purchase, a place of regular non-Jewish worship. It is true that the Unitarians are not Trinitarians, but neither are the Muslims. The question therefore would be equivalent to asking whether (if it were at all conceivable) a synagogue may buy a mosque with the understanding that the Mohammedans should permanently have the right of worship there. Furthermore, if both congregations use the same hall for their worship, what will be done with the Ark and the Scrolls of the Law during the Unitarian worship? Will they be removed? Under special military conditions, we did have joint chapels for Catholics, Protestants and Jews, and the sacred articles of each were removed during the services of the other. This was understood by all three groups to be a special wartime arrangement. But would such an arrangement (removing sacred symbols) be acceptable if it occurred in peacetime and every week?

Now as to the central question, that of ownership: It is, of course, due to the modern ecumenical spirit in America that such a question arises at all. There are plenty of discussions in the law in past generations as to whether a synagogue may buy a *former* church; also in modern times (in Reform and Conservative congregations) whether a synagogue may lend its building to a church for Christian worship in an emergency (cf. *Reform Jewish Practice,* Vol. 2, pp. 36-44). But that a synagogue should also have *permanent* non-Jewish worship in its building has been totally unheard of.

If, as is here proposed, the Unitarians have a permanent right to worship in the building, then the Jewish ownership of this house of worship is not exclusive nor complete. But does Jewish tradition make any clear statement that a synagogue must be completely and permanently the property of the community?

With regard to the ownership of a cemetery there is a definite requirement that it be owned permanently (*Bitzmisus*). But there is no clearly stated requirement that a synagogue must be so owned. Nevertheless, the law clearly implies that the ownership of the synagogue by the community should be permanent and outright.

Thus the law is clear that members of the community must compel each other to establish a synagogue (*Shulchan Aruch, Orah Hayyim* 150 ff.). This synagogue attains a permanent sanctity. Even if it falls into ruin, there are many ways in which even the ruins are deemed sacred. The building may not be used for any non-sacred purpose. Even if a man establishes a private Minyan in his house, he has no right to exclude any member of the community from worshiping there. In other words, a synagogue is communal and sacred. Menachem Mendel Auerbach (17th century) *Ateres Zekenim* to *Orah Hayyim* 150, says that especially in a small community the Jewish residents have a right to compel the building of a synagogue. Of course the law nowhere specifically says that this building must be permanently and exclusively the property of the community; but the very fact that there are severe restrictions as to how and when the building may be sold, if ever, and that an old synagogue may not be destroyed until a new one is complete, all these and similar laws clearly indicate that a synagogue is meant to be permanently a Jewish communal building in which every Jewish member of the community has the right of worship.

The *Shulchan Aruch* deals only with current and

practical laws and although the Christian church is not deemed idolatrous, nevertheless there are definite and current laws of avoiding too close a contact with church buildings. The *Shulchan Aruch* and the *Tur* sum up the law that a Jew may not even enter a church or stand within four cubits of its door(cf. especially the citation of Rabad in *Tur, Yore Deah* 142). Of course we do not feel that way at all today and we enter churches without hesitation for occasional joint services or for the weddings or the funerals of friends. But in the light of the former avoidance of the church building in the Jewish past, it would certainly be a shock to general Jewish consciousness if Jewish synagogue membere were expected every week, or many times a week, to come for Jewish worship to the building where non-Jewish worship is regularly held. The fact that Unitarians are not Trinitarians is as irrelevant as if this were a Mohammedan mosque, which is also Unitarian. It is a place of non-Jewish worship and to make it a Jewish *religious* requirement to enter it regularly is certainly contrary to Jewish feeling.

Besides, the very fact that it *is* Unitarian and not Trinitarian should cause us to hesitate even more. There are a number of Jews who leave Judaism and find it easier to become Unitarians than Trinitarians. There are a number of mixed marriages in which the Jewish partner, not wishing to have a Protestant pastor or Catholic priest officiate, will purposely choose a Unitarian minister. It is certainly unwise, therefore, and even dangerous on our part, so to blur the distinction between Judaism and Unitarians, as this suggested proposal would do, and thus tend to encourage these unfortunate defections from our faith and our people.

If it were understood that the building was definitely a synagogue and that the Unitarians were our guests who would occasionally be permitted to have services there, it would be acceptable; but if Unitarian services are regularly held in this building, what would happen on Easter when it coincides with Passover, or at Christmas when it happens to coincide with Chanukah? To whom would the auditorium belong? Even if the Easter service which would be largely attended occurred in another room, would that be a desirable situation? Clearly the whole arrangement, which tends to declare publicly that these two forms of worship are not particularly different from each other, would be a definite loss for Judaism.

Let the community do as all Jewish communities have done for two thousand years. Let it build its own synagogue, no matter how humble, which may become our own sanctuary, dedicated to our worship and to our fellowship.

4

HOMOSEXUAL CONGREGATIONS

QUESTION:

A rabbi on the West Coast, the Regional Director of the Union of American Hebrew Congregations for Southern California, organized a congregation of homosexuals. He said, "These are people facing their own situation. They have become a social grouping." Is it in accordance with the spirit of Jewish tradition to encourage the establishment of a congregation of homosexuals? (Asked by Rabbi Alexander M. Schindler, President of UAHC.)

ANSWER:

THERE IS NO QUESTION that Scripture considers homosexuality to be a grave sin. The rabbi who organized this congregation said, in justifying himself, that being Reform, we are not bound by the Halacha of the Bible. It may well be that we do not consider ourselves bound by all the ritual and ceremonial laws of Scripture, but we certainly revere the ethical attitudes and judgments of the Bible. In Scripture (Leviticus 18:22) homosexuality is considered to be "an abomination." So, too, in Leviticus 20:13. If Scripture calls it an abomination, it means that it is more than a violation of a mere legal enactment; it reveals a deep-rooted ethical aversion. How deep-rooted this aversion is can be seen from the fact that although Judaism developed in the

Near East, which is notorious for the prevalence of homosexuality, Jews kept away from such acts, as is seen from the Talmud (*Kiddushin* 82a) which states that Jews are not "under the suspicion of homosexuality." In other words, the opposition to homosexuality was more than a Biblical law; it was a deep-rooted way of life of the Jewish people, a way of life maintained in a world where homosexuality was a widespread practice. Therefore homosexual acts cannot be brushed aside, as the rabbi on the West Coast is reported to have done, by saying that we do not follow Biblical enactments. Homosexuality runs counter to the sancta of Jewish life. There is no sidestepping the fact that from the point of view of Judaism, men who practice homosexuality are to be deemed sinners.

But what conclusion is to be drawn from the fact that homosexual acts are sinful acts? Does it mean, therefore, that we should exclude homosexuals from the congregation and thus compel them to form their own religious fellowship in congregations of their own? No! The very contrary is true. It is forbidden to segregate them into a separate congregation. The Mishna (*Megilla* IV, 9) says that if a man in his prayer says, "Let good people bless Thee, O Lord," the man who prays thus must be silenced. Bertinoro explains why we silence the man who says, "Let the *good* praise Thee." He says it is a sin to say so because the man implies that only righteous people shall be in the congregation. The contrary is true. He adds that the chemical "chelbena" (Galbanum) has an evil odor; yet it is included in the recipe of the sacred incense offered in the Temple in Jerusalem. Bertinoro bases this idea specifically on the statement in the Talmud (*Kerisus* 6b) where the Talmud uses the example of the presence of ill-smelling Galbanum in the sacred incense as proof for the following statement: "No fast-day service is a genuine service unless sinners of Israel are included among the worshipers." That is to say that if we were self-righteous and considered the community to be entirely composed of noble people, we would then be far too smug and self-satisfied for a truly penitential fast-day service. That is why Maharil, in the 14th century, followed the custom of saying before the Kol Nidre that we must pray side by side with the sinners. This has become our Ashkenazic custom before the Kol Nidre prayer and, in fact, it has become a universal Jewish custom since Joseph Karo, the Sephardi, mentions it as a law in the *Shulchan Aruch, Orah Hayyim* 619:1 (and compare the *Be'er Hetev* to the passage). In other words, not only do we *not* exclude sinners, we are actually forbidden to do so; they are a necessary part of the congregation. That is the significance of the law in the Mishna that we silence the reader if he says, "Let only the righteous praise Thee."

This throws light on the present situation. We do not exclude them. We are forbidden by our tradition to do so. They are excluding themselves; and it is our duty to ask, why are they doing it? Why do they want to commit the further sin of "separating themselves from the congregation"?

Part of their wish is, of course, due to the "Gay Liberation" movement. Homosexuals, male and female, faced with laws which they deem unjust, are fighting in behalf of their rights and, therefore, are in the mood to extract formal recognition from all possible groups. If they can get the Union of American Hebrew Congregations to acknowledge their right to form separate congregations, it will bolster their propaganda for other rights. In fact, the press recently carried a demand on the part of women homosexuals for a separate congregation of their own. (I believe these were Christian women.)

It seems to me, also, that it is not unfair to ascribe an additional motive for their desire to be grouped together, to the exclusion of others: In this way they know each other and are available to each other, just as they now group together in separate bars and saloons in the great cities. What, then, of young boys who perhaps have only a partial homosexual tendency, who will now be available to inveterate homosexuals? Are we not thereby committing the sin of "aiding and abetting sinners" (*M'sayye Yedey Ovrey Averah*)? (b. *Aboda Zara* 55b)

To sum up: Homosexuality is deemed in Jewish tradition to be a sin, not only in law but in the Jewish way of life. Nevertheless it would be a direct contravention of Jewish law to keep sinners out of the congregation. To isolate them into a separate congregation and thus increase their mutual availability is certainly wrong. It is hardly worth mentioning that to officiate at a so-called "marriage" of two homosexuals and to describe their mode of life as Kiddushin (i.e., sacred in Judaism) is a contravention of all that is respected in Jewish life.

5

QUARRELING FAMILY AND BAR MITZVAH

QUESTION:

The father and mother of the Bar Mitzvah boy are divorced and they hate each other. The child shares his mother's hatred for the father. Now the boy is to be Bar Mitzvah. The father insists upon his rights as the father to participate in the service. But if the Rabbi promises to honor that right, it is certain that the Bar Mitzvah would not take place. Furthermore, the paternal and the maternal grandfathers also demand a share in the service. Since it was impossible to reconcile the various parties, the Bar Mitzvah was conducted without the father being permitted to participate, but instead the Rabbi himself read at the Bar Mitzvah the part that the father reads. Was this procedure proper? What is the law in this situation? (Question from Rabbi Philip Bernstein, Rochester, New York)

ANSWER:

SURPRISINGLY ENOUGH, considering the popularity of Bar Mitzvah, there is almost nothing in the classical legal literature on the details of this ceremony. Of course the age of thirteen is mentioned in the "Ethics of the Fathers." But there is no recorded legal basis for the Bar Mitzvah service as it developed in the Ashkenazic lands, namely, that the boy is called up to the Torah, that the father makes a specified blessing, that there is then a family celebration, "Seudah," after the services. The *Shulchan Aruch,* the classic code, has virtually nothing at all on the Bar Mitzvah service as we know it. Its only comment on it is by Isserles to *Orah Hayyim* 225:1, who merely mentions the fact that when a boy is Bar Mitzvah his father comes up to the Torah and recites the blessing, "Praised be Thou, Who has rid me of the responsibility." The only classic authority who believes that it is an actual legal requirement for the Bar Mitzvah boy to be called up to the Torah is Mordecai Jaffe in his *"Levush."* (See *Be'er Hetev* to the passage.) But Isserles himself is uncertain whether the ceremony has actual mandatory standing because he suggests that when the father recites the blessing, he shall leave out the words "Thou, O Lord, King of the Universe" (*Shem v'Malchus*). These words are always omitted when a blessing has dubious legal standing. This is due to the fear of taking the Name of the Lord in vain by reciting a needless blessing.

Since Bar Mitzvah has such shaky foundations, so that it is not certain whether it is an actual commandment or not, and since, therefore, so little is said in the classic codes about Bar Mitzvah, it becomes especially difficult to determine details involved in the ceremony, the father's rights, the grandparents' rights, etc. But perhaps we may find some guidance in this vague situation by finding a parallel in some other commandment involving father and son. Let us consider, for example, the commandment of the redemption of the first-born child (*Pidyen ha-Ben*). This definitely has the status of a commandment, an inescapable Mitzvah. It is rooted in Scripture in a number of places. See for example Numbers 18:14-16. It is positive commandment #393, and occupies a whole large section in the *Shulchan Aruch* (*Yore Deah* 305).

Now with regard to this well-established Mitzvah, the rights and the status of the father are absolutely clear. The redemption is a duty *incumbent* upon the father and upon no one else. If the father dies or neglects the duty, the son, when he grows up, must redeem himself. An interesting discussion of the father's right and duty in the redemption is given by Chaim Sofer in his responsa, *"Macheney Chaim,"* Volume III, *Even Hoezer* 75. A grandfather asked this question: His son-in-law is away on business and cannot be home in time to redeem the child on the thirtieth day. May the grandfather (who asks this question) take the place of the son, in consideration of the Talmudic principle (*Yevamos* 62a) that "the son of a son is considered his son"? The response of Rabbi Sofer is that only the actual father (or in later years the child himself) has this right and this duty. The grandfather *may* do so but not because he is the grandfather; he may do so only if the son appoints him by wire as his agent, and the son could appoint anyone as his agent. In this (except, of course, for the mention of telegraph) he follows the exact decision of the Taz (David b. Samuel Halevi, who lived in the 16th-17th century) at the end of Section 11.

By the way, the dictum quoted from *Yevamos* that a son's son is considered his son is paralleled in the

Palestinian Talmud (*J. Yevamos* 6:6) by the statement
that the *daughter's* son is not considered his son; but
both sayings have no relevance to *Pidyen ha-Ben* or
Bar Mitzvah, but refer to an entirely different matter,
namely, the question of when a man is deemed to have
fulfilled the commandment of "increase and multiply"
if his son or daughter dies and leaves him grandchildren.

At all events, judging by these laws of the redemption of the first born, the father's duty and right are
virtually absolute and unless he appoints an agent legally, the redemption cannot be fulfilled by any other
person, grandfather or not. If we have the right to
make an analogy between the redemption and the Bar
Mitzvah (since they differ so in their status) it would
seem that the father's right cannot be dispensed with.

As a matter of fact, the father does have a special
right in the case of a Bar Mitzvah to consider himself
indispensable. It is the duty incumbent primarily upon
the *father* to teach his son Torah. This can be seen in
the case of a divorce where the children may be in the
mother's custody, but the divorced father may claim
the custody of the sons after the age of six because it is
his duty to teach them Torah (cf. *Even Hoezer* 82:7).
And it is the father, therefore, who, Isserles says, must
recite the blessing, "Blessed be He Who has rid me
of this responsibility . . ." So we may well say that if
anyone can claim indispensability at the Bar Mitzvah
service besides the boy himself, it is the father. There
is, of course, no mention at all of grandparents in the

meager discussion of the sparse Bar Mitzvah reference in the *Shulchan Aruch*.

But the essential fact remains that, unlike *Pidyen ha-Ben,* Bar Mitzvah is not one of the recorded *Mitzvahs* and has dubious legal standing except that it has become a beloved ceremony arising first among the Ashkenazim. Therefore it is impossible to make definite decisions about anybody's rights in the matter. In this particular case, therefore, since the Bar Mitzvah would not be held at all if the father participated in it, it is better that it was held without him, for although he has more right than any other adult to be present, his right is nevertheless not a mandatory right but one of Minhag, of custom.

As for the Rabbi's solution of reciting the father's part in the service, that was not only a good and a practical solution, but also it is justified by the Talmudic dictum (b. *Sanhedrin* 19b) that he who teaches a child Torah is to be considered symbolically as his father. The law constantly speaks of reverence for father and for teacher and, in fact, in *Yore Deah* 242:1, the law is stated that one must honor one's teacher even more than one's father. Certainly the Rabbi, the teacher, has the right in an emergency such as this to act *in loco parentis.*

6

FATHER'S NAME FORGOTTEN

QUESTION:

A man wishes to memorialize his parents and grand-parents. On the memorial plaque in the synagogue the names are given in Hebrew fashion; thus, for example, Mordecai ben Isaac. Unfortunately, no one remembers the Hebrew name of his grandfather's father. Can the Halachic tradition guide us in finding a way to record this name in traditional fashion? (Asked by Rabbi Saul M. Diament, Saskatoon, Saskatchewan, Canada)

ANSWER:

THE QUESTION that is asked here has many reverberations in the Halachic literature. The legal tradition insists upon documents carrying a man's name together with his father's name. Of course, our present type of *family* name as identification is only a century and a half old. Jewish tradition ignores this modern type of family name and insists upon the old method of naming the man by giving his name and his father's name.

This traditional method of naming is of primary importance in certain official documents, especially in the documents for marriage and divorce, *Ketubos* and *Gittin*. The greatest importance of all is placed upon the exact naming in a *Get* because, due to a faulty identification of the man or woman, there could be a remarriage in adultery and illegitimate children. Therefore, in the laws of *Gittin* there is a great amount of discussion of the proper and exact traditional naming of the man, of the woman, and even the witnesses (see *Even Hoezer,* especially from #129). The various problems involved in the names in the divorce document (*Shemos Gittin*) is one of the large subdivisions in the legal literature.

Even after modern family names became the rule, it was always possible to carry out the traditional insistence upon using the father's name in legal documents. This was because when a person is called up to the Torah, he is always called up by his traditional name (his own name and his father's) and so the man's traditional name is known to him and also, presumably, known to the community in which he lives.

But this traditional method of naming has run into new difficulties in recent generations. First of all, even in certain Orthodox congregations, people are now no longer called up by name to the Torah, but are merely told beforehand when they are to come up. In fact, as early as a century and a quarter ago, Jacob Ettlinger, Rabbi of Hamburg, protests against the growing custom in Germany of calling people to the Torah without using their name and their Hebrew patronymic (see *Binyan Zion,* II, 172). Furthermore, there are thousands of Jewish men in every part of the world who have never been called up to the Torah at all and so have never heard their Hebrew name. There are thousands of Jewish men who were never even given a Hebrew name, or if they had been given a Hebrew name at their circumcision, never learned to know it. So the question which is now raised in this enquiry goes beyond the special case mentioned. We are dealing with a widespread situation. It is now a general problem as to how the Hebrew documents can be properly written nowadays, when such a large proportion of modern Jewish men do not know, or have never had, a Hebrew name.

Actually this question had come up centuries ago, not of course because of the special modern situation, but because of special circumstances under which even in those days when Hebrew names were universally used by Jews, a Jewish name in certain special cases was nevertheless totally unknown. For example, if a man is converted to Judaism, how could he be called by a Hebrew patronymic? His father was a Gentile. Or if a person were a foundling and no one knew his origin, how could one write his name in a Hebrew document? In these special cases, the *Shulchan Aruch* answers as follows: A proselyte is called "a son of Abraham" because Abraham our father was considered the father of all proselytes. See Asher ben Yehiel, Responsa 15:4 and *Even Hoezer* 129:20. Some say, also, that foundlings should also be named by Abraham as father, but this is disputed. (Cf. Isserles, *Orah Hayyim* 109:2).

In modern times the question of using the father's name has come up quite often. For example, Oshrey in his tragic responsa from the Kovno Ghetto during Nazi times (*M'Ma'amakim,* Vol. III, #11) discusses how an adopted child should be called to the Torah, whether by his father's name or his adopted name. So also, Moses Feinstein in *Igros Moshe, Even Hoezer* 99. In *M'Ma'amakim,* the name of the father is still known. In *Igros Moshe,* the name is no longer known. In this latter case, Moses Feinstein makes a cumbersome answer, namely, that the actual document should read: "So and so, the son of one whose name is forgotten and is called after So and so, who raised him." But, he adds, in order not to embarrass the person involved when he is called up to the Torah, he should simply be called up by the name of him who raised him. The same question is dealt with fully by Gedaliah Felder in his *Yesodey Yeshurun,* Vol. II, p. 158 ff.

It must be understood, however, that the problem of giving a father's name for a memorial tablet is not a *legal* requirement. A memorial tablet, a plaque or board is in no real sense a legal document such as a *Kesuba* or a *Get.* Therefore, if there is a desire to use a father's name, there are a number of possibilities available.

1. If the family is a family of Cohanim, he can be called, assuming, for example, that his name is Judah, "Judah the Cohen," or, in its well-known abbreviation, "Kohen Tzedek," i.e., K-Z (i.e., the well-known name of "Katz"). Or if the family is a Levitical family, his name can be "Judah Segan Leviah," i.e., S-G-L (the origin of the name "Segal").

2. If the family is neither Cohen nor Levite, the man may be named after his *mother* (if his mother's name

happens to be known). The Talmud (*Shabbas* 66b) mentions that in spells and incantations uttered in a man's behalf, his name is given with his *mother's* name. In fact it is still a modern custom when special prayers are uttered for a man (say in time of sickness) he is named in the prayer, not after his father, but after his mother. This practice is explained by the verse in Psalm 116:16, in which the psalmist prays for help and says: "I am Thy servant, the son of Thy handmaid," (i.e., "I am my mother's son").

3. If the family is neither priest nor Levite, nor is the mother's name known, there is still a third possibility. It has long been the custom in Jewish families to name a child after a deceased grandparent. Since, therefore, the son's name is known, we may assume that there is a fair probability that he was named after his father's father. Of course, this is not sure; it may be that he was named after his mother's father. However, it is a fair presumption. Thus, my name is Zalmon Dov Ben Yitzchok Zvi, and my father's name is Yitzchok Zvi ben Zalmon Dov. This may be counted as a fair probability.

4. If in this family the name "Abraham" appears frequently, then the name may be selected as the grandfather's patronymic, since there are cases in the law where this is the patronymic of choice.

5. There is still another possibility. Although the name of the grandfather's father is not known, it is not impossible that his grandfather or his great-grandfather is known by name. This could be if, for example, this ancestor were the author of a book. If this grand-

father, whose father's name is unknown, has a grandfather or a great-grandfather or even a great-great-grandfather whose names happens to be known (either as an author or for some other chance reason) then this man may be named after this ancestor, since the rule is clear in the Talmud (*Yevamos* 62b) that grandchildren are legally equivalent to children; and the later commentaries say that this applies up to four generations. See all references given in Gedaliah Felder, Vol. II, p. 185.

To sum up: Although great emphasis is placed in the law on the father's name, this strictness applies only to legal documents, not to memorial tablets. Therefore there is considerable leeway, and any one of the above suggestions may well be adopted if appropriate.

7

ARK OPEN DURING SERVICES

QUESTION:

The local congregation has the following custom: The Ark is opened at the beginning of the Friday night service and remains open during the entire service. Is this practice justified by tradition? (Asked by Rabbi Richard A. Zionts, Shreveport, Louisiana)

ANSWER:

THE QUESTION of when the Ark is open is not strictly a matter of law. For that reason there are variations in customs on this matter. Some congregations close the Ark immediately after the Torah is taken out to be read. Others keep the Ark open during the entire time that the Torah is read. This latter custom has given rise to legal discussion which has some bearing on the question asked here.

It is a law that when the Torah is being carried, all present must rise. From this custom many have developed the practice of remaining standing if, after the Torah is taken out, the Ark remains open, because the other scrolls are visible. This custom of remaining standing as long as the Ark is open is the subject of discussion among the authorities. The matter is dealt with to some extent in *Reform Responsa,* page 43 ff. To *Yore Deah* 242:18, the Taz (Samuel of Ostrow) records the fact that some people stand while the Ark is open. But, he adds, there is no legal necessity to do so. However, two premier Hungarian authorities, Meir Eisenstadt and Moses Sofer, both say that the people should stand as long as the Ark is open. Eisenstadt, in *Panim Meiros,* Volume I, 74, and Moses Sofer, in *Chatam Sofer, Choshen Mishpot,* 73, in fact say that it is actually *forbidden* to sit down as long as the Ark is open. Furthermore, the important later authority, Jechiel Epstein, in his *Aruch Ha-Schulchan,* to *Yore Deah* 282, par. 13, says that whenever people rise at the open Ark, the whole congregation should do so also, although this custom is not a law.

Thus it is clear that many eminent authorities insist that the whole congregation should remain standing as long as the Ark is open. Clearly, from this point of view, it would be preferable if the Ark in your congregation were not open during the entire service.

However, since to remain standing is not strictly a law, a modern Reform congregation might not be impressed with the requirement to remain standing as long as the Ark is open. Yet there is another consideration which would appeal to a modern congregation. It is a custom, which we in Reform congregations also observe, that at certain solemn moments in the High Holiday services, the Ark is opened and the congregation stands. If the Ark is open all year, then this impressive action on the High Holidays is not only physically impossible, but even if the Ark is then closed in order to open it, the ceremony has lost its solemnity because it is a commonplace in this congregation for the Ark to be open.

However, inasmuch as all that I have mentioned above is not strict law, then it would be advisable to be careful in trying to change it. If, for example, the congregation insists that this local custom is precious to it, then a *minhag* which has persisted for a long time, and which is not patently absurd, always has a respected status. If, however, the congregation will not mind the suggested change, then for the reasons stated above, it would be advisable to change it in conformity with the practice of most congregations.

8

TRANSLATING TORAH READING
VERSE BY VERSE

QUESTION:

A colleague conducts the public Sabbath reading of the Torah services in the following way: He reads a verse or a part of a verse and then gives the English translation of that portion of the verse, and so continues to the end of the Torah reading. Is such a practice justified by tradition? (Asked by Rabbi Fredric Pomerantz)

ANSWER:

BEFORE ANSWERING the question as to the bearing of the legal tradition on this matter, we might consider first the general effect on the congregation of this type of reading. To fragmentize the reading in this way can certainly break down the majesty and the sweep of many a great Biblical passage. Since our people are not expert in Hebrew, this judgment would apply especially to a powerful Biblical passage in English, whose poetic effect is destroyed by breaking it up into separate phrases. Furthermore, some members of the congregation have already expressed themselves that this sort of fragmentation destroys the solemnity of the worship service, converting the Torah reading into a sort of

Sunday school classroom exercise in word-for-word translation.

However, the above-mentioned judgments are matters of taste and matters of taste are always debatable. The rabbi might well feel that the practice which he has adopted increases the sense of intimacy between pulpit and pew, and that if it *does* create a classroom atmosphere, that is not too bad either. Is not the Torah meant also for instruction? But aside from this debatable matter of taste, is there anything in the traditional literature which might provide some guidance in the matter?

There seems to be a strong preference in the law, going back to the time of the Mishnah, *Megillah* IV, 4, that the Torah reading should be continuous and uninterrupted. The law is that while you may skip from section to section in the reading of the prophetic portion, you may not skip in the reading of the Torah from one chapter to another. By the way, we in our Reform synagogues do not observe this limitation in our reading on Yom Kippur afternoon. At that service we do break up the Torah reading, omitting parts which we deem irrelevant to the main theme. However, the law is in itself quite definite and it is so stated in the *Shulchan Aruch,* in *Orah Hayyim* 144:1.

However, there is an apparent justification for the method here referred to, of reading part of a verse and then giving the translation. The law itself makes provisions for the translation and, indeed, the translation was given verse by verse; a verse of the Hebrew and then a verse of the translation. In fact, it was required that the reader from the Torah should not read more than one verse at a time from the Torah to the translator (M. *Megillah* IV, 4). You could read more than one verse at a time from the Prophets, but not from the Torah, because the translations from the Torah (upon which laws are based) had to be exact and precise. Reading out more than one verse at a time might lead to an imprecise translation or a mere paraphrase; which is not harmful in the case of the Prophets, but wrong in the case of the Torah, where every word used may affect actual religious practice.

Yet even this reading of the Torah verse by verse to the translator had its definite restrictions, all of which were carefully stated. First the translation referred to in the Talmud and in the *Shulchan Aruch* did not mean translation into *any* language. It referred exclusively to the Aramaic language, which to some extent shared the sanctity of the Hebrew. This is evident from the fact that the Talmud requires every man to prepare for the Torah reading by studying on Friday the Scriptural portion twice, and the Targum, the standard Aramaic translation, once (*Berachot* 8a). This Aramaic translation which was common in the practice of ancient days is no longer permitted nowadays, and the Torah must not be interrupted for it (see *Shulchan Aruch, Orah Hayyim* 145:3). The reference is given to the responsa of Solomon ben Aderet, from whom the *Shulchan Aruch* took the reason that people do not understand Aramaic nowadays anyhow.

Now even with regard to this semi-sacred Aramaic translation which had a certain status, there were definite restrictions. First that although for the Aramaic translation the reading may be broken up verse by verse, it was not permitted to break up a verse, but only a *complete* verse of the Hebrew must be read to the Aramaic translator. There was a still further restriction: The reader of the Hebrew may not serve as the translator; he must be a separate person (see *Shulchan Aruch* 145:1). The two functions of reading the Hebrew and translating the Hebrew were to be kept strictly apart, in order that the people should not be misled into thinking that the translation is actually found in the Torah (*Orah Hayyim* 145:1). But, of course, this last objection would hardly be applicable to the reader today (i.e., not to have the same man do the Hebrew and the translating). Our people are not likely to imagine that the English is found in the Torah as they might have imagined in the past that the Aramaic was found in the Torah.

To sum up: While, of course, it is a matter of judgment and taste as to whether breaking up the Hebrew of the Torah to translate it phrase by phrase destroys or does not destroy the majesty of both the Hebrew and the English section, beyond this debatable question of taste it is clear that tradition took great pains to keep the reading of the Hebrew consecutive. Permission to break it up was made only for the semi-sacred Aramaic translation, and even there only complete verses could be given to the translator. Some of the restrictions of the past are hardly applicable today, nor do we need to take them with strict literalness, especially in a liberal congregation. Nevertheless we should bear in mind

the general intention to keep the Torah reading uninterrupted and thus dignified and effective.

9

CHURCH USE OF SYNAGOGUE BUILDING

QUESTION:

Is it proper for a synagogue to rent its facilities, including
the Sanctuary, for a temporary period, to a Christian
church for the conduct of classes and services at times
not in conflict with the synagogue's own schedule of
services? (Asked by Rabbi Joshua O. Haberman, Washington, D.C.)

ANSWER:

IT HAS BECOME a well-established Reform practice that
the synagogue quarters have been lent to Christian
congregations for services and for Sunday school if, for
example, the Christian church had burnt down or a new
church building was not yet completed. Also, Reform
congregations established institutes for the clergy in
which ministers of all denominations are invited to be
present in the synagogue Sanctuary for study. If, therefore, the question asked was concerned with ascer-
taining the *Reform* Jewish practice, the question need
not have been asked at all. The matter has been decided
for a generation now in actual Reform practice. The
question, therefore, must go beyond Reform practice
and is clearly meant to reach into the moods and de-

cisions of Jewish legal practice and the feelings of most Jewish people on this matter.

At first blush, the idea of Christian worship in a traditional synagogue would seem bizarre or even deeply disturbing to an Orthodox congregation. Yet, actually, a study of Jewish law on the matter contradicts what might be an instant, negative reaction to the question. Let us consider the law on the most extreme basis first. Suppose this were a Catholic or a High Church Episcopalian congregation: Part of their worship involves the presence of crosses and crucifixes. Would not this be shocking to a traditional congregation, perhaps, such objects even temporarily being set up in the synagogue?

Of course it is worthwhile mentioning that during the Second World War, in the military, the same chapel was used for Catholic, Protestant and Jewish services. The respective, specifically religious objects were either removed or covered up for the services of the other denominations. The decision to agree to such a triple use of the chapels was agreed to by the Jewish Chaplaincy Commission which was composed of Reform, Conservative and Orthodox rabbis. But, of course, this was under war conditions and the necessities of military life, and therefore no general conclusion can be drawn from that specific experience.

The question is whether under normal peacetime conditions it is permissible at all to have such objects as crucifixes in the synagogue. It is to be understood (and discussed later in this responsum) that Judaism does not believe Christianity to be an idolatrous religion. Nevertheless, such objects as crucifixes, etc., are deemed to be idolatrous objects and the prohibition of their use is fully discussed in the *Shulchan Aruch*. May, then, such objects deemed by the law to be idolatrous be placed in the synagogue, even for temporary use?

The Talmud (in *Avoda Zara* 43b) speaks of the most sacred synagogue in Babylon (called *Shev V'Yashiv*). It was the most sacred because, according to tradition, the exiled King Jehoiachin took earth from the Temple in Jerusalem for the foundation of this synagogue in exile. In this synagogue there were statues of the emperor. Yet the most famous of the Babylonian scholars worshiped there without hesitation. Elijah Mizrachi (1455-1525) the great Turkish authority, says in his code, *Kenesses Hagdolah, Orah Hayyim* 151 (the reference in *Reform Jewish Practice,* Vol. II, p. 44, in which the present discussion is briefly dealt with, has the *Orah Hayyim* reference erroneously as 192) that if idols had been placed in the synagogue, it would not invalidate the synagogue for Jewish worship after the idols are removed. The *Mogen Avraham* to *Orah Hayyim* 154 (end of paragraph 17) explains Benvenisti's statement as follows: The building itself has not been dedicated to idolatrous use, or worshiped as such. Therefore when the idolatrous objects are removed, the room can be used for Jewish worship.

Of course Jewish sentiment might be somewhat disturbed by the fact that the objects were put into the synagogue at all. Therefore it would be less disturbing if the denominations were of the type of Baptists or

Congregationalists, etc., who do not use crucifixes or can do without crucifixes in their services. In that case there would certainly be no objection in the law to their using the synagogue building or the Sanctuary itself.

Yet there is another objection to be considered: When a Jewish congregation lends its school facilities to a Christian church, it is aiding the teaching of Christianity. Have we the right to do so, or is it proper to do so? There is a considerable amount of law against the teaching of the Torah to non-Jews. There were many reasons for this. It often happened that those Gentiles who studied Jewish law would pervert what they learned and use it for anti-Semitic purposes. Most of the prohibitions of such instruction by Jews is based upon the statement in *Hagiga* 13a: "We do not give over the words of the Torah to Gentiles." However, the bulk of the legal opinion is that the objection, to the extent that it is valid, applies only to rabbinic law; but the Bible, which Christians revere, can be taught to them. See fuller discussion in *Reform Jewish Practice,* Vol. II, p. 72 ff. Since, therefore, most of church school instruction (certainly in Protestant schools) is a study of the Bible, there can be no objection to assisting this instruction by providing facilities for it.

Of course it may be objected that the Christian Sunday Schools interpret the passages in the Bible in a Trinitarian sense, which certainly from our point of view would be erroneous. Have we the right, then, to help them teach their Trinitarian interpretations of Scripture?

To this question it is important to note that the

greatest authorities in Jewish law, such as Rabbenu Tam (see the *Tosfos* to *Bechoros* 2b, s.v. *Shema*) authorities say that when Christians use Trinitarian expressions or add saints' names, they really mean to refer to God; in other words, they are basically monotheists. This is embodied in the law by Isserles (see *Orah Hayyim* 156).

From the point of view of traditional law, we must come to the following conclusion: Even if objects like crosses, etc., are brought into the synagogue, the synagogue remains untainted after they are removed, although from the point of view of people's feelings, it would be better if the renting were confined to those denominations who do not use crucifixes, etc. As for aiding in Christian instruction, it is mostly Biblical and even when the verses are interpreted in Trinitarian fashion, they really mean God. Therefore it is not objectionable.

10

COMPOSITION AND SIZE OF THE SABBATH CANDLE

QUESTION:

The Chaplaincy Corps (of the military) supplies candles for Sabbath worship in the chapels and also, now,
for Sabbath worship in the homes of married military
personnel. Does Jewish law require that the candles
be of some specific composition (as the Catholics require that their candles be at least fifty-one percent of
beeswax)? Furthermore, since the services in the chapels
are fairly brief and are over while the candles are still
burning, may broken parts of candles be used so that
they may go out (of themselves) by the time the services are over? May, also, soldier-families cut up larger
candles so that they go out before the family retires?
(Asked by Aryeh Lev, Director, Commission on Jewish
Chaplaincy.)

ANSWER:

THERE IS A GREAT DEAL of discussion in the legal tradition as to what substances may and may not be used
for the Sabbath light. All this is found in the second
chapter of Mishnah *Sabbath,* in the well-known section
Bameh Madlikin and in the Talmud, *Shabbas,* 21a ff.
Of course all the discussion in that section on what may
or may not be used for wicks, and what may or may

not be used for the fuel (which oils, etc.) refers, not to our present-day candles, but to their oil lamps which were (in simplest form) a container of oil of some kind with a wick floating in it.

The motivation of the Catholic Church requiring over fifty-one percent of beeswax in the candles used in Catholic services is a spiritual one. The pure beeswax symbolizes the pure body of Christ (*Catholic Encyclopedia,* Vol. I, p. 347). But it is clear that the requirements of Jewish law, as given in Mishnah, Talmud and later codes, have no spiritual or symbolic intent at all, but are based on purely practical reasons. For example, most of the materials forbidden to be used as fuel are forbidden because of their evil smell, which might cause a person to leave the room or, at worst, in disgust to extinguish the light of the Sabbath, which is forbidden. The objection to certain wicks is that they are too coarse or too hard to suck up the liquid fuel internally; the fuel just runs up their outer surface and chars it, and thus causes it to throw off sparks. It is evident, then, that the only objection to any material constituting the Sabbath light is a practical one, not a religious one. See the discussion in Talmud, *Shabbas,* 21a, and in *Orah Hayyim* 264.

As for our modern-day candle, at first blush it would seem that it should be forbidden entirely because among the materials which the Mishnah and the Talmud forbid is wax, but all the commentators make it clear that it is only the melted wax that is prohibited in the old type of lamp. If it is made, as our candles are, as a cylinder of wax around the wick, it is permissible.

See Rashi, at the bottom of *Sabbath,* p. 20b, and also the *Shulchan Aruch, Orah Hayyim* 264:7. Hence the matter is clear enough. As long as the candle has not an evil smell, as long as it does not keep on producing sparks, there is no objection to the material used.

Now as to the other question about the danger of the light burning too long after the services are over in the chapel, or after the family has retired in the home. It must be noted that although the extinguishing of light and fire is completely forbidden on the Sabbath, there are some exceptions. One may put the light out if the brightness of the room prevents an invalid from falling asleep (*Orah Hayyim* 278). Also it is permitted to cover the light if its flame may endanger the building. The Mishnah (*Sabbath* 16:7) speaks of endangering "the beams of the ceiling." A cover may be put over the light, not to extinguish it, but to keep the flame from doing any damage. Of course there must be enough air under the covering for the flame to continue burning (*Orah Hayyim* 277:5). So you could cover the light in the chapel or in the home with a porous dome like the dome that we use to keep toast warm, or like a kitchen collander. In other words, you may shield the light to keep it from doing damage, provided you do not extinguish it (cf. *Be'er Hetev*).

Is it permissible to use smaller candles or parts of candles so that they may burn out before the people leave the chapel or the people at home retire? This question depends on a larger question, namely, whether there is a minimum duration period for the Sabbath lights to burn. There is such a minimum duration period, for example, for the Chanukah lights. The Chanukah lights were originally kindled at the door of the house so that passers-by could see them. Therefore the duration period of the Chanukah lights was fixed in relationship to the street traffic. The Chanukah lights should not be lit before sunset, *nor later* than the time when pedestrian travel has ceased in the streets ("till the footsteps have ceased in the street") (*Sabbath* 21b, *Orah Hayyim* 672). After this latter period (i.e., when pedestrian traffic ceases) the proper time is considered past and thereafter secular use may be made of the Chanukah lights. See also *Responsa Rashba,* #170.

Is there such a definite time limit set for the Sabbath lights? There is a time set for the *beginning* of the lighting of the Sabbath lights. It should not be before sunset (*Orah Hayyim* 261:1). But if one wishes "to add from the profane to the holy," i.e., to begin his Sabbath observance sooner, the lights may be lit earlier. See Isserles to *Orah Hayyim* 261:1 and 2; also 263:4. But nowhere in the law does it say, as it does about Chanukah, what the *end* time limit is. Therefore it may burn an hour or two or three, or all night if that is desired. There is no period at which, as with Chanukah, one can say "its proper time is past." However, the *Kitzur Shulchan Aruch* (75:2) says they should burn at least till the meal is over. This is not very long. Therefore it makes little difference how large or how small the candle is.

As for broken parts of candles, there can be no objection to these either. It is, of course, preferable to have a whole loaf of bread for the *Motzeh,* or a full cup of wine for the *Kiddush,* but nowhere is any prefer-ence expressed for a complete, unbroken candle. After all, the original Sabbath light was just a dish of oil and a wick.

To sum up: Any material, except ill-smelling or inefficient material, may be used in the Sabbath candle. It may be covered to protect it from damaging the chapel after the services are over. There is no objection to using a small or a broken candle, since there is no fixed time limit as to how long the Sabbath light must burn.

11

WEEKDAY USE OF SABBATH CANDLESTICKS

QUESTION:

> During the recent coal strike in England, the electricity was cut off and people lived by candlelight. The ques-tion arose whether it is against Jewish tradition to use on weekdays, candlesticks or candelabra which have always been set aside for the Sabbath. (From Rabbi John D. Rayner, London, England)

ANSWER:

SINCE ANCIENT TIMES it was the custom to set aside special things for Sabbath use. The Talmud speaks of the setting aside of garments, special foods, etc., and it is known, of course, that all through the ages people had special clothes for the Sabbath and, of course, candlesticks and candelabra, etc. (see T. *Shabbas* 114a and also *Shulchan Aruch, Orah Hayyim* 262, which speak of special tablecloths and garments, etc., specially set aside for the Sabbath). The question is, here, whether these Sabbath objects may be used for weekdays.

There is a clear law with regard to the *opposite* question, namely, that certain weekday objects may not be used or even handled on the Sabbath. Such objects such as utensils, tools, etc., that belong to weekday work may not even be touched on the Sabbath. This is, of course, the law of *Muktza*. Thus, for example, an empty purse may not be touched on the Sabbath because it is *Muktza M'shum Basis;* i.e., it is the container or the "basis" for money (see especially the laws of *Muktza* in *Orah Hayyim* 310). But there is no law as far as I know of the reverse nature, namely, that that which is set aside for the Sabbath is not to be handled on weekdays.

The question would not be asked at all if it had not arisen in the minds of some people; and whenever such a question arises, there is always some sort of reason for it. Perhaps it arose because the kindled Sabbath light itself may not be used for a weekday purpose; that is to say, you may not use a Sabbath light to study by (see the various limitations to this law in *Orah Hayyim* 275). But that prohibition of using the Sabbath light for a non-Sabbath purpose was based on the fear that the light might be trimmed or adjusted in some way if one needed more light. This would violate the Sabbath law against kindling the light. In other words, the actual law is that the burning Sabbath light may not be used for a non-Sabbath purpose *on the Sabbath* (lest the Sabbath be violated by trimming the light). But that does not mean that the Sabbath light or the Sabbath candelabra, etc., may not be used *on weekdays,* when there is no danger of violating the Sabbath by trimming or adjusting the light.

In addition to this negative proof that there is *no law* against the use of Sabbath appurtenances, there are also certain indications in Talmudic statements of an Aggadic nature which also may indicate that there is no objection to the use of Sabbath objects on the weekday. While Aggadic statements may not be used as proof for Halachic decisions, nevertheless they are sometimes used as an auxiliary argument.

We are told in the Talmud (*Beza* 16a) that Shammai used to set aside a very fine steer to be slaughtered for Sabbath. Then if he would find a still finer steer, he would substitute the finer one for the original one. Now, if there were any objection in the law to using on weekdays something that had been especially set aside for the Sabbath, the Talmud would almost certainly have raised the question: How could Shammai use that first steer on weekdays? There is a second Aggadic indication in this matter: The Palestinian Talmud (J. *Peah* 8:8) speaks of Naomi's suggestion to Ruth (Ruth 3:3) to "put on thy raiment upon thee," and the Talmud asks: Was that not strange advice? Was she, then, unclothed? The answer is that Naomi told her to put on her *Sabbath* garments to make a good impression on Boaz. Now, if on a harvest day which was certainly a weekday there had been any objection to wearing the Sabbath garments, the Talmud would certainly have mentioned it. So these two Aggadic statements of Shammai and of Naomi and Ruth indicate at least that when these narratives were told it did not strike any one of the rabbis that there could be any objection to using on weekdays something especially set aside for the Sabbath.

To sum up: There is definite objection to using on the Sabbath weekday utensils, especially those involving work (i.e., those involving the iaws of *Muktza*) and there is also an objection to using the Sabbath light itself, *on the Sabbath,* for such non-Sabbath purpose as study, which would involve adjusting the light. But there is no objection mentioned in the law against using the appurtenances of the Sabbath on weekdays, and this negative is implied clearly in the two Aggadic narratives mentioned,

12

UNITED JEWISH APPEAL AT KOL NIDRE

QUESTION:

In a number of smaller communities the custom has grown up to hold a meeting for the United Jewish Appeal during the *Kol Nidre* service, when there is usually the largest attendance. Should the request for such a meeting be granted by the congregation, or should it be resisted? (Asked by Rabbi Fred V. Davidow, New York.)

ANSWER:

ALL THE LAWS of the Sabbath as to the prohibition of labor, business, etc., apply also to the Day of Atonement which is called *Shabbas Shabbason*. Therefore the question is whether a meeting, whose purpose is to raise money, may be held on the Sabbath (and, therefore, also on the Day of Atonement). The answer depends on what sort of business it is. A man may not plan certain procedures in his own business on the Sabbath, even if he does not handle any money, but is merely working out in his mind certain business procedures.

The Talmud (B. *Shabbas* 150a) cites the verse in Isaiah (58:13): "If thou turn away thy foot because of the Sabbath from pursuing thy business on My holy day, nor speaking thereof." The Talmud emphasizes the words, "thy business," and says that it is only "thy" personal business that may not be planned on the Sabbath. But communal business may be planned. One Rabbi says: "Plans for a *Mitzvah* may be calculated on the Sabbath." Another says: "We may determine upon charity for the poor on the Sabbath." All this is codified by Maimonides (*Hilchos Shabbas* 24:5). He says: "We may calculate calculations for *Mitzvos*, we may set charity for the poor, and go to the synagogue to attend to public affairs on the Sabbath." Thus there developed over the centuries the auctioning off of the various honor-duties (*Mitzvos*) on the Sabbath, and this practice is defended by the latest authority, Yechiel Epstein (*Aruch Ha-Shulchan, Orah Hayyim* 306:16). So there is no question that meetings for congregational business and in behalf of charity may be held on the Sabbath. See the full list of references in *Reform Responsa* (i.e., Volume I) page 46 ff.

What applies to the Sabbath applies, therefore, also to the Day of Atonement. In fact one might say that a meeting in behalf of charity fits especially well with the mood of the Day of Atonement, since on the High Holy Days, in the greatly revered prayer *U'Nasana Tokef*, the chief protection of man against the misfortunes that might befall him are given as Repentance, Prayer and *Charity* (*Teshuva, Tefilla, Tzedaka*).

Thus there can be no traditional objections to a meeting for charity at the *Kol Nidre* service. Nevertheless, there are a number of dangers involved, or at least difficulties to overcome. First, while supporting charity is an acceptable aim, the method of getting pledges at such meetings, the competition, the urging, the shaming of people can certainly be flagrantly violative of the mood of the Day of Atonement. Therefore such a meeting can be permitted only if it is conducted without any bullying or hectoring, but proceeds with the calm dignity appropriate to the Day of Atonement. Another important consideration is the undue lengthening of the service. Frequently in the codes, when certain additions or interpolations are spoken of at the public service, there is concern expressed that the congregation may be unduly burdened (*Mipne Tirchas Ha-Tzibbur*). It must be seen to that if such a meeting is conducted, it should be fairly brief. Perhaps most importantly, it should not be permitted to interrupt the proper sequence of the service. If the meeting is to be held, it should be held before the service actually begins, i.e., before *Kol Nidre*.

Because of all these dangers, namely, spoiling the mood of the service, burdening the congregation by undue length of the service, and breaking up the sequence of the service, the suggestion to hold such a meeting should be received with caution.

Of course if there is already an established custom to have such a meeting at the *Kol Nidre* service, then the fact that it has become a custom is in itself of some standing in the law. But whether, by now, it is a prevalent custom or not, the dangers mentioned above should be carefully avoided. If they are avoided, then it can be safely said that there is no objection in Jewish law that such a meeting for this charity be held at the *Kol Nidre* services.

13

CANDLE LIGHTING AT KOL NIDRE

QUESTION:

The congregation has an established custom of conducting a candle lighting ritual at the late Friday evening service. It is now planned to have such a candle lighting ritual at the *Kol Nidre* service (or is it, perhaps, already an established custom?). An official of the congregation objects to this Yom Kippur Eve ritual. It is not clear whether his objection applies just to this year, when Yom Kippur fell on the Sabbath or whether he objects to the candle ritual for any Yom Kippur. Should such a ritual at *Kol Nidre* be established or, if already established, should it be continued? (Asked by Rabbi Albert A. Michels, Sun City, Arizona.)

ANSWER:

THE OBJECTIONS of the officer of the congregation should be taken seriously, especially if his opposition to the candle ritual is shared by many members of the congregation. Even if there could be very little objection to such a ritual in a Reform congregation, nevertheless if a considerable portion of this congregation objects to such a ritual, even without justification, then it is wiser not to institute such a ritual if it does not already exist as a congregational custom.

This concern for the feelings of the congregation,

regardless of whether they are justified or not, is based upon the well-known caution in the Talmud (*Pesachim* 50b) namely, that if people *believe* that something is forbidden, then even though actually it is permitted, you may not declare it permitted in their presence. In other words, we must be careful not to shock the religious sensibilities of people, even though they may not be justified. If, therefore, there is no such established custom at present in the congregation, and such a custom is now contemplated, then one must judge, carefully, the sentiment of the congregation in this matter.

However, the feelings of the congregation, pro or con, are not the basic consideration. They are only the grounds for caution. The question can best be decided objectively, i.e., according to law and tradition. Should such a custom exist (or continue to exist)? As to the actual law, the Halacha in the matter, there is no question that the custom of lighting candles at a late Friday evening service after dark is violative of the traditional laws of Sabbath rest. However, this lighting of candles in the synagogue has, by now, become a well established custom in Reform synagogues and our people have come to accept it. Our rabbinate, also, favors the ritual on the ground that its spiritual benefits outweigh the fact that it is violative of the laws of Sabbath work. The question now is: Should this established custom carry over to Yom Kippur also?

We mentioned above the possible sensitivities of people who accept the kindling of candles late Friday night but nevertheless object to it on Yom Kippur.

Beyond the necessity of considering their sensitivity to the matter, we must now ask ourselves objectively: Do the laws of Sabbath rest apply more strictly to the Day of Atonement, since that is called "The Sabbath of Sabbaths"? As a matter of law, the laws of Sabbath rest apply also to the Day of Atonement (of course, even if it occurs on weekdays). See *Minchas Chinuch,* commandments 316, 317. But one may well say that the laws of Sabbath work apply, not more strictly, but *less* strictly to the Day of Atonement, since in the days of the old Jewish state, violation of the Sabbath was punished as a capital crime by the courts (*Sekilla*); whereas violation of the Yom Kippur laws of rest were not punished by the courts, but left to the punishment from heaven (*Karres*).

More specifically, the Sabbath lights belong properly in the home, on the table, not in the synagogue. The Mishnah (M. *Sabbath* 2:7) says that when a man comes *home* from the synagogue, he must ask the household, "Have ye kindled the lights?" There is, therefore, no strong legal reason for having these home lights kindled in the synagogue, as has become our modern Reform custom. On the other hand, the lighting of candles in the *home* on Yom Kippur is only a custom which varies in different cities (see *Orah Hayyim* 610:1). But lights in the *synagogue* on Yom Kippur are virtually mandatory; not only the memorial light (*Neshama* light) but lights in general are to be multiplied in the synagogue on the Day of Atonement (*Orah Hayyim* 610:4). Of course those lights were meant to be lit before dark. However, it can be stated that on the basis of tradition the kindling of lights on the Sabbath belongs primarily in the home, and the kindling of lights on *Kol Nidre* belongs primarily in the synagogue. Therefore, as far as tradition is concerned, we can say that if the custom had developed in Reform congregations to have a candle lighting ceremony only on *Kol Nidre,* that would be much more in consonance with tradition than our present custom of lighting candles on Friday night in the synagogue.

To sum up: If the ritual of candle lighting on *Kol Nidre* has not yet been established as a congregational custom and it is a question of initiating it now, then careful consideration should be given to the sentiment of the congregation on this matter. If there is no strong feeling against it in the congregation, and especially if it is already a custom of the congregation, then it is evident that lighting candles at *Kol Nidre* can find much more justification in the tradition than lighting them in the synagogue on Friday night, which is already an established custom with us.

14

THE PREGNANT BRIDE

QUESTION:

The bride was found to be pregnant before the marriage ceremony. Should this fact cause the marriage ceremony to be postponed or perhaps to be cancelled altogether? (Asked by Vigdor W. Kavaler)

ANSWER:

THE ORDINARY and immediate common-sense reaction would be that the marriage should certainly take place and, for the sake of the unborn child, the sooner the better. However, there are certain obstacles in the legal tradition with regard to this simple solution. As well may be imagined, in the course of human experience such situations, namely, that the bride was pregnant before the wedding ceremony, have occurred many times in the past. Therefore there is considerable law on the matter which must be considered when we are confronted with a circumstance such as the one described. Of course, some of the situations dealt with at length in the past are no longer applicable today; but for the sake of completeness they should be mentioned.

The word "engagement" which we use today meant something much different and much more legally binding in the time of the Mishnah and the Talmud and for a number of centuries thereafter. What we today call "engagement" is simply a promise, often merely verbal, to marry at some future date. But in the past this "engagement" was marked by a ceremony and documents. It was called *Erusin* and was virtually a marriage in every respect except sexual relationship. The betrothed woman, *Arusa,* stayed in her father's house until the *Nissuin* when she was brought to the house of the groom and the marriage then completed and consummated. But before that she is "betrothed" and, in the full legal sense, the man's wife. If, therefore, she became pregnant during that period, this occurred while she had the actual status of a married woman. If, then, it was proved that during this betrothal period she was impregnated by some stranger, the husband-to-be (who was actually her "betrothed" husband now) would not be permitted to live with her and the marriage would have to be called off. Of course if, contrary to the law, the husband-to-be himself was the man who impregnated her, then that is largely their own affair, except that he must rewrite her marriage document describing her no longer as a virgin.

There is much in the law concerning complaints by the groom that he was deceived and his bride was not a virgin. But if he was in her parents' house with her during the betrothal period, he could no longer make such a complaint (Mishnah *Kesubos* 1:5).

All this was based upon the legal fact that the engagement in the past was actually a full betrothal, virtually a marriage. But this no longer applies today and has not applied for many centuries. Nowadays we combine the betrothal (*Erusin*) and the *Nissuin* in one ceremony with two sets of blessings under the *Chuppah*. Therefore our modern engagement is merely a promise to marry and not a legal betrothal, and if the bride becomes pregnant during the engagement, it is not as his wife that she has become pregnant and so there is no basic objection to his marrying her if he wishes to. So the *Be'er Hetev* (Judah Ashkenazi of Tiktin) to *Even Hoezer* 68, paragraph 2, says that nowadays the whole ceremony takes place under the *Chuppah* (i.e., before the *Chuppah* she was in no sense his betrothed wife). If, therefore, it is found that she is not a virgin, she is nevertheless permitted to marry the husband-to-be because the immorality took place before the wedding (i.e., she was not in any sense his wife).

However, there is still another obstacle in the law against a pregnant bride being married. If a woman is pregnant, she may not marry another man for twenty-four months after the child is born (*Even Hoezer* 13:11 ff., based on *Yevamos* 42a). This is for the protection of the child. The fear is that if she marries while she is pregnant, or after the child has recently been born, her milk will dry up if she becomes pregnant again and the child will suffer from malnutrition. The law, then, becomes complicated, namely, as to whether a divorced woman is in duty bound to nurse the baby of her former husband (or give it to a wet nurse).

There is an interesting modern case in the responsa of Moses Feinstein, the present head of the Agudas Ha-Rabanim, in his *Igros Moshe, Even Hoezer* #32.

The case is as follows: The bride is pregnant by some man other than the engaged groom. The groom, nevertheless, wants to marry her. They agree that as soon as the child is born they will put it up for irrevocable adoption through the courts. The child therefore will have someone else to nurse it and take care of it. Need this couple, therefore, wait the twenty-four months of lactation? Moses Feinstein answers in the negative and permits the couple to marry. An analogous case two centuries earlier was decided in the same way by Ezekiel Katzenellenbogen, Rabbi of Altona, 16th-17th century, in his *Kenesses Yechezkel,* #73. So in this case here, if the child will be born normally and will need to be nursed, other arrangements can be made to take care of it, either to feed by formula or to put the baby up for adoption, as in the case mentioned above.

There is, of course, one final element involved here. I understand (from the verbal discussion of the question) that both bride-to-be and groom-to-be acknowledge that the child is theirs. In that case, the law is clear enough that the safety of the child will be considered assured since it is their child and the law is that they may marry. So the *Be'er Hetev* to *Even Hoezer* 13, at the end of his paragraph #17 says: If he and she both agree that it was with him that she had sexual intercourse, and that she was impregnated by him, then we have no ground for suspicion that she was also immoral with others and there is no reason to fear that her lactation will be spoiled (therefore they may be married at once). So too, Moses Sofer (*Chatam Sofer, Even Hoezer* 27) gives the following case: An engaged girl who was pregnant stated that she was impregnated by her fiance. He denied it but when he was told that if she was impregnated by someone else, she will have to wait twenty-four months before she can marry this fiance, thereupon he changed his statement and admitted that he had impregnated her but had been too ashamed to admit it. Are we to believe him? Moses Sofer reluctantly comes to the conclusion that we do believe him but must impress upon him the importance of telling the truth in this case. After doing so, we permit him to marry her at once.

To sum up: Our modern "engagement" is not the classic "betrothal." Therefore the engaged bride is not really (in the legal sense) a wife; and if she becomes pregnant before the marriage, there is no requirement in the law for him to refuse to marry her. As for waiting twenty-four months of lactation, more recent decisions permit other provisions for the nursing of the child. Finally, since both acknowledge that it is *their* child, then, while there is the general objection in the law to sexual relationship between unmarried people, now that it has occurred and they wish to marry, they may do so. Thus the requirements of common sense in this matter are fully justified by the legal tradition.

15

VISITING ISRAEL

QUESTION:

A couple saved for years to visit Israel for a month. But now they plan to use the money for the college expenses of their children. Have they the right to do so? Is it not a supreme, religious duty to go to Palestine? (Asked by Rabbi Allen S. Maller, Culver City, California.)

ANSWER:

A PERSON nowadays may want to go to the land of Israel and consider his visit to be a moral obligation. In that case it is a matter for him to decide as to how important this is to him in comparison with other uses for his money. But the question here is a deeper one than a sense of group commitment or pride. It is a question of religious duty. Is it a *religious* duty to go to Palestine and does one violate any religious duty if one fails to do so?

This question of whether it is a religious obligation to settle in the Holy Land has been discussed since the Middle Ages and, interestingly enough, has become again from the Halachic point of view the subject of a rather heated discussion in our day. The Chassidim, especially the Satmar group, who consider themselves the most completely and uncompromisingly religious of all Jews, are also bitterly opposed to the modern state of Israel. It is therefore necessary for them (and for those who are like-minded) to come to terms with this religious question. Because of this deep concern on the part of these anti-modern-Israel Orthodox Jews a considerable literature has grown up on this subject. The most important is the collection by Moses Bloch in three volumes of a work called *Dovev Sifse Yeshenim,* in which he gathers all the opinions of the Orthodox rabbinate of the last hundred years against a modern Jewish state and the plans to establish it. The very first letter in the first volume is typical and representative. It is by the famous scholar Jacob of Lissa, addressed to the pioneer protagonist of religious Zionism, Rabbi Zvi Hirsch Kalischer. Virtually all the Orthodox arguments on the anti-Zionist side of the question are marshalled here (as they are in the subsequent letters).

It is important in our attempt to solve this question of religious obligation to go through the law systematically. The basis of the law is the very last Mishnah in the tractate *Ketuboth* in which we are told that a husband can compel his wife to emigrate with him to the Holy Land. If she refuses he can divorce her without even giving her the money stipulated in her *Kesubah.* To which Rashi (in the Talmud, *Ketuboth* 110b) says this means a man may compel not only his wife, but his entire family to settle in the Holy Land.

However the Tosfos to this passage says that this law is not applicable today because it is dangerous to travel there (this was the eleventh century). The Tosfos further quotes Rabbi Chayim who gives a second reason why it is no longer a religious duty to settle there: namely, that there are so many important commandments which are applicable in the Holy Land and which a man may not be able to fulfill nowadays.

This negative point of view is contravened by many other authorities. Nachmanides counts settlement in the Holy Land as one of the Mitzvoh. Isserlein (14th century) in his *Pesakim* #88, acknowledges the great dangers of settlement, but says a man should judge whether he can endure and fulfill the commandments; and if he can, he should settle there. The Mordecai (Mordecai ben Hillel) 14th century, quotes the Tosfos as to the danger of travel and settlement and says that the law therefore is that a husband cannot compel a wife to go with him there. Caro (*Shulchan Aruch, Even Hoezer* 75, 4 & 5) first states the law definitely that a husband can compel a wife to settle in the Holy Land with him, but adds, then, "Some say it is dangerous and a man has no right to bring himself or others into danger; therefore (if the journey is short) from Alexandria eastward, he may compel his wife to go with him; but if they live west of Alexandria, he may not." Hayim Benvenisti (Turkey, 17th century) in his *Keneses Hagdola* to Bes Joseph, *Even Hoezer* 75, marshals all the arguments on either side and tends to agree with the above compromise opinion taken by Caro in the *Shulchan Aruch*.

There is an interesting discussion of the question from Prague at the end of the seventeenth and the beginning of the eighteenth century. It is a responsum by Jonah Landsofer in his *M'il S'daka,* #26. The cir-

cumstances are interesting enough to deserve mention.
A group of three men decided to settle in the Holy
Land and take with them their young children of the
ages of three and four. Many people raised the objection that they have no right to endanger the lives of
little children on this perilous journey. Landsofer answers that the commandment to settle in the Holy
Land is an eternal commandment. As for the danger,
that may vary from time to time and place to place
and must, of course, be considered when we discuss the
question as to whether a man can compel his wife to
go with him. But aside from the question of the rights
of his wife, if there is not too much danger, it will be
just as safe for the children as for the adults. A fair
statement of the law is to be found in the balanced
opinion arrived at in the *Be'er Hetev*, (Judah of Tiktin)
to the passage. He says, "Since the question of whether
or not it *is* a religious duty is a subject of disagreement
among the great teachers, it is clear, then, that a husband cannot compel his wife to move with him to the
Holy Land. Cf. also, *Igros Moshe, Even Hoezer* #102
(end) where he says that it is a Mitzvah only for
Palestinians to dwell in Israel, but there is no mandatory Mitzvah for others to live there.

Clearly the question of the religious duty to settle
in the Holy Land can be considered a *moot* question
in which, therefore, compulsion of husband against
wife cannot be applied. For completeness' sake it
should be mentioned that there is a great deal of
Halachic debate on the reverse of our question, namely,
whether a person already settled in the Holy Land may

emigrate in order to live in the diaspora. For a full discussion of this question see *A Treasury of Responsa,* page 167 ff., where there is an account of the responsum on this subject by Yom Tov Zahalon (1557-1638), Rabbi of Safed.

Returning to the case discussed here, it is not even a question of *settling* in the Holy Land but a question merely of going there for a brief visit. In that regard there is not, as far as I know, any authoritative opinion at all to the effect that a brief visit is to be considered as a religious duty.

Now as to the children, if it were a question of the study of the Torah, let us say it was a choice between the parents' going to Israel and the children studying in the Yeshiva, that question could possibly enter into the discussion. Isserlein cites the fact that in his day there was very little Talmudic study in Israel and that fact was used as an argument against settling there. But the secular education has no standing in the Jewish law (although under special circumstances it is *permitted*) and therefore college education, unlike Talmudic education, could not be weighed against settlement. Nowadays, of course, with the many Yeshivos there, there is a large Orthodox settlement from the Yeshivos in America, according to the recent Mizrachi official magazine. But these Yeshiva heads and Yeshiva students are confident that they can fulfill their religious duties all the better in Israel and hence follow the caution of Israel Isserlein.

But in the case mentioned, it is first of all not a question of *settlement,* but of a visit which is no particular Mitzvah; and secondly a question of secular education, which is of no concern in Jewish religious law. In this case, therefore, the parents can do as they wish.

16

STERILIZING THE FEEBLEMINDED

QUESTION:

A public social service organization in a southern state sterilized a feebleminded young girl who was a client of the organization. After the operation was performed, the mother of the girl strongly protested, on the ground that when the authorities suggested to the girl that she be sterilized, she did not understand what was being asked of her. The mother's protest soon became a public agitation. The question is asked: What is the attitude of Jewish law and tradition to this action and to the protest against it? (Asked by R. G., Tallahassee, Florida.)

ANSWER:

JEWISH LAW is quite definite about the status of the feebleminded (*Shota*) with regard to family relationships. (See the descriptions of the feebleminded in *Hagiga* 3b-4a). It is a definite law that a feebleminded person, like a person who is definitely insane, cannot legally contract marriage (b. *Yebamos* 112b; *Even Hoezer* 44:2). While the specific reason mentioned (in the Talmud) for the inability of the feebleminded to contract legal marriage is based on the fact that it is dangerous for a normal person to live with such a person, the basic reason must be that the express purpose of marriage is to procreate children. The law is clear that every man is in duty bound by Jewish law to marry and have children (*Even Hoezer* 1:1). While it is true that the great Polish legalist, Isserles, says that nowadays we do not insist that a man should not marry a woman who *cannot* bear children, nevertheless, the basic law remains that the purpose of marriage, its mandate, is to "increase and multiply." If, therefore, according to Jewish law a feebleminded person cannot legally contract marriage, it follows logically that they are not meant to have children. Since there may be no marriage for the feebleminded, they may not have children. Of course the law does not deal with or advocate procreation without marriage.

But this fact that the feebleminded may not have children is not necessarily any justification for the social service office to have sterilization performed on a feebleminded person. There is a general Jewish law dealing with sterilization. It is based on Leviticus 22:24, which declares that mutilated animals should not be brought to the altar as sacrifices. Then the verse concludes: "Thou shalt not do so in thy land," upon which the Talmud bases the clear-cut prohibition of any act of sterilization anywhere against animals or humans. So the prohibition is recorded in the law, *Even Hoezer* 4:12, 14. Therefore an observant Jewish doctor would be prohibited by Jewish law from sterilizing any human being or, for that matter, a Jewish veterinarian would be prohibited from performing a similar operation upon cattle or birds.

While the law seems absolute, there are some mitigations of it. Maimonides (*Issure Biah* 16:2, 6, 9) in discussing the further prohibition that a eunuch, i.e., a sterilized person, may not contract legal marriage, makes this distinction: that if it is because of the patient's sickness that a doctor sterilizes him or her, such a person *may* contract legal marriage. While some disagree with this statement of Maimonides (Tur, *Even Hoezer* 5) he remains a strong authority and most scholars agree with him on this matter. Furthermore, Isserles to 5:14 states that if it is a matter of health, the operation is permitted.

If, therefore, it could be demonstrated that it was for the physical and mental health of this feebleminded girl not to bear children, or not to have the responsibility of raising children, this might be a further mitigation of the general prohibition against sterilization.

There is also another possible permissiveness involved. The law against sterilization applies more strictly againt sterilizing males than sterilizing females, because the Biblical command to "increase and multiply" is understood to be directed at men. It is a *man's* obligation to marry. He commits a sin if he remains a bachelor. A woman commits no sin if she remains a spinster. Therefore the law states (*Even Hoezer* 5:12) that it is prohibited to administer a sterilizing medicine to a man, but a woman may take such a medication (cf. *Chelkas M'chokek ad loc.*). So one authority, Rabed to *Sifra Emor*, section 5, says that there is no objection to sterilizing a woman medically, but there is objection to sterilizing surgically. Furthermore, Yechiel Epstein, in the *Aruch Ha-shulchan* to *Even Hoezer* 5 (22) says that the sterilization of women is not forbidden Biblically but only as a cautionary measure (i.e., rabbinically) and then he says at the end of section 23, speaking here of both men and women, that if the operation is indispensable for the person's health, it may be done.

One of the legal scholars calls attention to the different forms of the verb "give" in both halves of the law. One may not "give" the medicine to a man, but it does not say "one may give" the medicine to a woman. It says "a woman may drink the medicine," which means "of her own accord," or "with her consent." In other words, the sterilization would be more defensible in the law if this feebleminded girl gave her consent, or if she cannot understand what is asked of her, if her parent or guardian gave consent.

To sum up: The law forbidding marriage to the feebleminded implies forbidding them to have children. However, the act of sterilization is forbidden by Jewish law, although the prohibition applies less strictly to women than to men. An exception to the prohibition may well be made when health is involved and effective consent is given. If these limitations are observed, it would be safe to say that Jewish legal tradition would not oppose sterilization of the feebleminded.

17

MARRYING THE STERILIZED

QUESTION:

A man undergoes vasectomy. His bride nevertheless agrees to marry him. May we officiate at such a marriage? Furthermore, what if the doctor declares it dangerous for the woman to bear children and she is sterilized? Should we officiate at such a marriage? (Asked by Dr. M. J. K., Vineland, N.J.)

ANSWER:

THE FIRST QUESTION asked is based upon the clear statement in Deuteronomy 23:3, that a man who is a eunuch may not enter the congregation of God, i.e., may not marry a Jew. In the definition of this physical state the law clearly adds that closing off of the duct which carries the seed constitutes rendering the man a eunuch (*Even Hoezer* 5:2). Thus the modern operation of vasectomy comes under the Biblical prohibition of *Kruss Shofcho*.

While the law seems clear enough, there are a number of exceptions which modify this law considerably. First of all, there is a limitation as to what is meant by a eunuch. The law is clear that a man is to be defined as a eunuch if his state is the result of an operation

(*Saris Adam*); but if the impotence is not the result of an operation but is the result of a birth defect (*Saris Chama,* made a eunuch "by the sun," i.e., by nature) then he is not forbidden to marry. In fact, Maimonides (*Issurey Biah* 16:2, 6, and 9) is still more permissive. He says that even if the man is made impotent by a doctor, due to the man's sickness which makes this operation necessary, even then he is not to be considered a eunuch who is prohibited to marry.

There is some doubt as to this permissiveness with regard to the man who is sterilized because of sickness. The Tur in *Even Hoezer* 5 says that Rashi and his own father (Asher ben Yehiel) disagree with Maimonides as to the admissibility of a man who has been sterilized because of sickness. Be that as it may, in the case which is before us the woman is sterilized because of sickness and (for other reasons which will now be mentioned) there is no objection to her being married. In fact, according to the commandment to "increase and multiply," there is no objection to her being married, since this is a commandment imposed upon the *male,* not upon the female. Therefore it is permitted for a woman to be sterilized (*Tosefta Yevamos* 8:4).

Another modification of the eunuch law should be mentioned. The rabbis emphasize the phrase in the Deuteronomy verse: "the congregation of the Lord." They explain this phrase as meaning the community of those who are born of Jewish parents. While proselytes are of course accepted as full Jews, nevertheless they are considered as being organized into a separate "congregation of proselytes" (*Kehal Gerim*). Therefore the law is clear that a sterilized man may marry a convert (m. *Yevamos* 8:2).

There is still another consideration. If the man now sterilized already was the father of a son and a daughter, then he is considered by the law to have fulfilled the commandment to "increase and multiply" and thereafter there is no objection to his marrying without the prospect of children. See especially Rashi to *Yevamos* 61b in which he says that in that case (since he already had a son and a daughter) it is not necessary to look for a wife who can bear him children (*Eyn Tzorich,* etc.).

Now the question is whether such a marriage between one or two sterilized people can be considered to be a valid Jewish marriage (*Kiddushin*). Maimonides in *Hil. Ishus* 4:10 says that if a man who is sterilized marries, whether he be born sterilized and thus technically he is not considered a *Saris,* or whether he is sterilized through human action, this marriage is to be deemed valid. The *Lechem Mishna* (Abraham De Boton) raises an objection against the decision of Maimonides that such a marriage with a sterilized person is valid. As a matter of fact DeBoton would accept, surprisingly enough, the validity of such a marriage only in the case of a person sterilized by *human* means and not by nature. The reason for this distinction of DeBoton is found in *Mishna Yevamos* 8:4, that such a marriage is valid because the man at one time *was* normal; in other words, he had *Sha'as Ha-Kosher,* just as in the case that is before us where the sterilized person was at one time fruitful.

A very interesting and full discussion of this decision of the Rambam (that such a marriage is valid) is given by Yair Chayim Bachrach in his *Responsa* #221, near the end of the responsum. His comment fits, almost precisely, the case in question here. He explains the Rambam must have considered this marriage valid on these grounds: First, she knows of the situation beforehand and consents and secondly, the operation made him unfruitful but has not made him sexually impotent. This is exactly the circumstance today with modern vasectomies.

But suppose she did *not* know of his condition before the marriage, would the marriage be valid? Bachrach in this responsum says "no;" but Jacob Reischer of Metz (*Shevus Ya'akov* 101) says that even if she did not know of it beforehand, this marriage is nevertheless valid and she cannot be freed from it without a *Get*.

Besides all these considerations, when the law discusses various blemishes in a husband for which a woman might be justified in asking for a divorce, they frequently mention the fact that there are many other reasons why a woman might want to remain married rather than being alone (*Kesuvos* 75a, *Tov l'meysav ton du*).

To sum up, while of course the purpose of marriage is children and such marriages as here described should not be encouraged, nevertheless one cannot say that such marriages are invalid and that we should refuse to officiate. We should bear in mind the fact that Moses Isserles was well aware of changes in the social mood from one era to another. In *Even Hoezer* 1:3 he says that nowadays we no longer stand in the way of marriages which will not result in children.

18

DIVORCE FOR A DOUBTFUL MARRIAGE

QUESTION:

A Jewish couple was married by civil ceremony in Russia and then they parted without any divorce. The man now lives with a Greek Orthodox wife. It is not clear whether the man formally became a Christian. The first wife wants to marry a Jewish man. Does she need to get a divorce (a *Get*) from the first husband before she can enter into a Jewish marriage? (Asked by Rabbi Josef Zeitin, Odessa, Texas.)

ANSWER:

THERE ARE A NUMBER of complex questions involved in this situation or else the question would not have been asked at all. First of all, is the original civil marriage between these two Jews in Russia to be considered a valid marriage which can only be broken by death or a *Get?* The second question is, if the marriage *is* a valid Jewish one and if this man is to be deemed an apostate (a *Mumar*), does he still have the right to give a Jewish *Get,* and then does she have to bother to get it from him?

As to whether that Russian civil marriage is to be considered a valid marriage in Jewish law is a rather open question. I do not have the books with me now, but I remember that it came up with regard to exiles from Spain in the period between 1396 and the final expulsion in 1492. Shimon Duran of Algiers had to decide the question whether a Jewish couple married even in a church could be deemed Jewishly married or not (Tashbetz, Vol. 3:47). The answer depended on whether the man gave her a ring and said the proper marriage words and, also, if the man *intended* the marriage to be a valid Jewish marriage. If the above conditions were met, then whatever words the priest may have uttered were merely irrelevant. The marriage was a Jewish marriage by the actions and the words and the intentions of the Jewish man to a Jewish woman. So it is with the civil marriage. If the man meant it to be a Jewish marriage and gave her a ring, then what the Russian judge may have said was of no intrinsic significance. But if the man had no such intention (of it being a Jewish marriage) then it was not a valid marriage and she would not need a *Get*.

There is also another consideration involved. In the case of those Marrano marriages, another necessary element was mentioned, namely, that there were other Jews present at the ceremony. Since a Jewish marriage requires at least two valid Jewish witnesses, it is this last element (which I might have mentioned above) which was used by the famous Rabbi of Kovna, Israel Elchanan Spector, in the case of such a marriage (*En Yitzchok, Even Hoezer* 47): A Jewish soldier and a Jewish girl had no proof that they were married. It may be that they just lived together as husband and wife; but if they lived later in a Jewish community and were known in that community as husband and wife, then the community itself became, as it were, witnesses to their being married.

Now let us assume (which is doubtful because of the requirements mentioned above) that this marriage *is* valid, does she need to get a *Get* from this particular person, who is now living with a Christian wife and who may or may not have converted to Christianity?

In answer to this, it must be stated that it is an open question in Jewish law whether one needs to get a divorce from an apostate. What is involved in the complicated debate (*Get Mumar*) is when he became an apostate, etc. This man may be an apostate or, at all events, he belongs to the category of "those who depart from the ways of the congregation," i.e., one who has purposely and consciously isolated himself from the congregation. So it is an open question whether she needs a *Get* from him.

Clearly it must be assumed that it is very difficult to get a *Get* from him, if it is not impossible to do so. And it is always our duty to deliver a woman from the state of being an *Agunah*. In this case, we should bear in mind that Moses Feinstein, the greatest Orthodox authority in America today, and the head of the Agudas Ha-Rabbonim, in order to free an *Agunah* who could not get a *Get* from her former husband, discovered that the marriage was conducted by a Reform Rabbi. On that basis (that there were no valid witnesses, etc.) he took the bold step of declaring the marriage invalid and the *Get* unnecessary (*Igros Moshe, Even Hoezer* #76). Now, if he declared a

Reform marriage conducted with all solemnity as invalid, in order to perform the *Mitzvah* of freeing an *Agunah,* how much the more may we do so with regard to a Russian civil marriage.

To sum up: The marriage itself is of doubtful validity, since we do not know about the man's action, the ring, his intentions, the presence of valid witnesses, etc. Also, we do not know whether the man is a *Mumar* or not. At all events, the woman is a helpless *Agunah* and it is our duty to liberate her from that state; and in the situation mentioned above, there are so many uncertainties that we may safely consider her free to marry again without a *Get.*

19

TWO ADOPTION PROBLEMS

QUESTION #1:

A woman divorced her husband. She divorced him in court but has not yet received her *Get*. She became pregnant and states that the child belongs to her lover. She gave birth to the child and her sister adopted him. The sister now wishes to circumcise the child and give it a Jewish name. Since she did not receive a *get* from her husband, the child could easily be considered a *mamzer,* and therefore the question of circumcision is involved and all the problems of *mamzeruth*. In fact, the mother asked if she could have a *Pidyen ha-Ben*. (Asked by Aryeh Lev, New York, New York)

ANSWER:

IT IS INTERESTING that Rabbi Soloveitchik said that he would hesitate about calling this child a *mamzer*. I wish he would publish his response. His students justly admire him, but he deprives the rest of us from seeing his answers in writing.

The persons who asked you the question assume a principle which is not correct. They assume that a *mamzer* is out of the general orbit of Jewish law and that, therefore, it is a question whether circumcision, etc., are required in his case. But the laws concerning the *mamzer* are actually entirely different.

A *mamzer* is restricted only with regard to certain specific marriage laws. He may not marry into a normal Jewish family, but on the other hand, he *may* marry a slave and thereby a *mamzer's* family can be purified (Kiddushin 69a). But beyond these two marriage laws, a *mamzer* is like all other Israelites and *all* the laws apply to him. For example, he can be a witness in a Jewish court (*Choshen Mishpot* 34:21, based on the debate in *Baba Kama* 88a and the Tosfos there). Also it is specifically declared that he must be circumcised even on the Sabbath (of course if it is the eighth day). In fact, Ezekiel Landau in his *Noda b. Yehudah,* II, *Yore Deah* 182, makes it as a general principle that a *mamzer* is in duty bound to obey all the commandments (with the marriage exception which I have mentioned). This statement of Ezekiel Landau's is well known. It is stated also by Isaac Lamperonti in his *Pachad Yitzchok,* under the word *mamzer.*

So there is no question about the child's being circumcised. That is mandatory (a *mitzvah*). Also there is no question about the *Pidyen ha-Ben,* except that with regard to the *Pidyen ha-Ben* certain difficulties may arise. It is the responsibility of the *father* to arrange the *Pidyen ha-Ben.* In this case, then, this man (the "lover") would have to acknowledge the child as his and arrange for his redemption.

QUESTION #2:

> A couple adopted a child. They do not know the source of the child. When they got the child the father had the boy circumcised for the purposes of *gerut.* Normally,

sometime later, a *Bes Din* is brought together and the child is given *mikveh* and it is a kosher Jewish child. There are no problems there. In this instance they slipped up on *mikveh*. It was never performed. Now the boy is 12½ years old and is being prepared for Bar Mitzvah. The parents are Orthodox Jews and they want to do what is right in accordance with law. However, they never informed this child that he was adopted. They still do not want him to know that he is an adopted child. They feel they may want to tell him at a much later age or never tell him at all. It is a forgotten matter in the family. The father is prepared to go to mikveh with his boy at this time on the excuse that they want to prepare themselves properly for the Bar Mitzvah at the synagogue. However, as far as this boy is concerned he is now a *bar-daas* and he must know that if it is for *gerut* he must have *kavanah*.

ANSWER:

THE QUESTION amounts to this: If a *tevillah* is not consciously declared to be a *tevillah* for the purpose of conversion, is it legally such or *must* the child be told that it is a *tevillah* for conversion? But if he *were* told he would find out what his adopting parents do not want him to find out, i.e., that he is an adopted child and born a Gentile.

Of course, if I were answering the question as a liberal, I would say that the *tevillah* is *not* indispensable; it can be omitted entirely; that Rabbi Eliezer in *Yevamos* 46a said that just as the patriarchs became Jews simply by circumcision and did not take the ritual bath, so if a proselyte is circumcised and does not take the ritual bath, he is a full Jew because of his circumcision. But, of course, such a decision would not satisfy an Orthodox rabbi, since the final state of the law is that a preselyte requires *both* circumcision and *tevillah*.

In that case, I would raise another question: This child is going to be bathed in order to complete, belatedly, the process of conversion. Does he need to be told the purpose of this *tevillah?* This depends on the larger question of whether *Mitzvos* need *kavanah,* conscious intention, or not. See the debate summarized in my *Responsa Literature,* page 259 ff.

But aside from the question of whether he needs *kavanah* for the *tevillah* to be legal, the law is very clear that if a proselyte takes a *tevillah* for any purpose other than consciously for proselytizing, that act of *tevillah,* even though not intended for this purpose, is nevertheless valid for proselytizing. The law is in *Yore Deah* 268:3, namely, that if a candidate for conversion does not take the bath for the purpose of being proselytized (as, for example, if the man takes the bath to be cleansed of a seminal impurity, or the woman candidate takes the bath for menstrual purification) then even so this bath is valid also for the purpose of conversion. Therefore if the father and the son go to the *mikvah* together and he does not tell the son that this bathing is for the purpose of completing the conversion, the bath is valid nevertheless for this purpose.

It should be noted, however, that Ezekiel Landau in his commentary *Dagul Mirvava* to the *Shulchan Aruch* (*ad. loc.*) says that when an *infant* is converted the *tevillah* must be consciously for the purpose of conversion (i.e., with *kavanah*). His reasoning is as follows: The true essence of the conversion process is the explanation by the *Bes Din* to the candidate of the commandments and their acceptance by the candidate. The ceremonial rituals are merely additions (necessary but not indispensable, at least with regard to the *tevillah*). Hence, the law is given in the *Shulchan Aruch* that if the *tevillah* is taken for any *other* purpose it is valid also for conversion. But this easement of the law cannot apply to an infant when converted because he cannot understand the explanations of the commandments and, therefore, the *tevillah* is not an "addition," but of the essence. Hence the *tevillah* in the case of the infant must be with *kavanah*. But in the first place, Landau's requirement of *kavanah* applies to the *Bes Din,* not to the candidate, i.e., the infant himself. Besides it refers only to the period of infancy, whereas in this case a boy on the verge of Bar Mitzvah certainly knows the meaning of the *Mitzvos*. Finally, Ezekiel Landau's statement is only a solitary one. In general we can rely on the law as stated in the *Shulchan Aruch* that the *tevillah* need not be for the express purpose of conversion in order to be valid for conversion. Therefore the boy need not learn that he was adopted and converted.

20

NAMING THE CHILD OF AN UNMARRIED MOTHER

QUESTION:

An unmarried mother desires that her child be given the usual type of Hebrew name: his personal name and the name of his father. However, the man whom the young woman declares to be the father denies that he is the father. Is there any way by which this child can be named in accordance with Jewish tradition with his personal name and a patronymic? (Asked by Rabbi Kenneth Segel, Pittsburgh, Pennsylvania)

ANSWER:

LET US FIRST take the extreme type of such a situation. Suppose that according to Jewish law this child is a bastard (*mamzer*). It need not be more than just stated that the Jewish definition of a bastard is much more liberal than that used in most legal systems. In Jewish law a child born out of wedlock is not necessarily illegitimate. Only such a child is illegitimate who is born of a relationship which cannot be legitimatized; as for example, the child of a married woman from a man not her husband. Since the woman in the case before us is unmarried, her child cannot be deemed illegitimate for that reason. Nevertheless it may be illegitimate for another reason. If, for example, her sexual relationship had been with a close relative whom she is not permitted to marry, this child would be illegitimate even though the mother is an unmarried woman. Therefore let us for the sake of completeness consider the extreme case, namely, that this child is in Jewish law illegitimate. Should it be named at all? Should any religious ceremony be performed in his behalf (assuming that it is a male child)? The law in Deuteronomy (23:3) states that a *mamzer* shall not enter the community even unto ten generations. This means that he may not marry into "the community" of priests, Levites, or Israelites (*Kahal Kohanim,* etc.). He may, of course, marry into the community of proselytes (*Kahal Gerim*) or freed servants, and such a marriage would be a legal and sacred Jewish marriage. In fact, the law recommends such marriages as a step in the purification of a *mamzer.* But other than the restriction placed on a *mamzer,* namely, not to marry into the three communities of Cohen, Levite and Israel, he is considered to be a Jew in every respect. For example, if the eighth day of his birth is on the Sabbath, he may be circumcised on the Sabbath. See *Yore Deah* 265:4 and also especially Jacob Reischer in his *Shevus Yaacov,* II, 82. He may be called up to the Torah. See *Orah Hayyim* 282:3, end of the note of Isserles. In other words, he is a Jew in every respect except for the above-mentioned marriage restriction.

In fact, the great Rhineland authority Maharil (Jacob Moelln of Mainz, 1367-1427) who may well be described as the prime source of our Ashkenazic customs, had the case of the circumcision of a *mamzer* which he had conducted in the vestibule of the synagogue with full rites except for the final blessing, which would imply that such should increase in Israel. So one may say in a summary that even if this child is illegitimate (a *mamzer*), the father being one of the forbidden blood relatives, even so he should be considered Jewish in every way and no traditional ritual should be denied him.

But this child is not to be considered a *mamzer.* Since the mother claims that a certain man is the father and since the man denies it, we may say that the child's paternity is not really known. In that case, the child belongs to the class called *shetuki,* "the silence," i.e., those of whom we cannot say who is the father. In such cases the law is according to Abba Saul (M. *Kiddushin,* IV, 1 and 2 and b. *Kiddushin* 74a) who says that if the child is a *shetuki* the mother is asked about the father of the child. If she says that the father was one whom she would have been permitted to marry (*L'kosher Nivalti*) i.e., not one too close in blood kinship and not a non-Jew, then she is to be believed and the child is not a mamzer.

We may assume, therefore, in accordance with the mother's statement that this is not the child of a father who is a forbidden blood relative and, therefore, this child is in every sense legitimate in the eyes of Jewish law. In the same section of the *Minhage Maharil* (*Hil. Milah*) in which Maharil spoke of the ritual circumcision of a *mamzer,* he also discusses the circumcision of a child born out of wedlock but legitimate (i.e., neither of a married woman by a man not her husband, nor from forbidden blood relatives). He speaks here of precisely the problem which is asked here, but unfortunately he does not give us a solution. He states, first of all, that he rebuked the *mohel* who wanted to leave out part of the Psalm, a praise to God for this child, and he made the *mohel* repeat the full ritual. But when it came to naming the child, the following difficulty arose (exactly as in the case of the question asked here). The man whom the woman said was the father, denied that he was. Therefore Maharil did not give the child that patronymic, since he said that to do so might shame an innocent man. Maharil does not then say what patronymic he *did* give the child. This is the essential point of our question.

But have we the right to choose any name we prefer? As a matter of fact, there *is* considerable latitude in the choice of a patronymic. The only exception to this freedom of choice concerns the divorce document (the *get*). In a *get* the precise naming is required, even to the embarrassing appellation, for example, of writing "Benjamin, the son of the apostate." But other than in a *get* there is, indeed, a wide latitude in the choice of a patronymic. A man may change his patronymic, and certainly the spelling of it, after his father's death; but if his father is still alive, he may do so only with his father's consent (cf. the references in Moses Feinstein, *Igros Moshe, Even Hoezer* #22, p. 340). The specific case with which Moses Feinstein deals here is that of Miriam, a learned Jewess, a Hebraist, whose father was a Christian. She selected for herself the patronymic

"Joshua" and signed herself in her Hebrew correspondence, "Miriam, daughter of Joshua." Feinstein decides that if that name has become current, it is actually now her name (except, of course, if it happens that a divorce document needs to be written for her).

Since, then, we are indeed free to choose a patronymic for this child, which name should we choose? A simple solution presents itself at once but, really, it is too simple and should be rejected. There has been established a custom that when special prayers are given in behalf of the sick or the otherwise unfortunate, that the person in behalf of whom the prayer is given is named, not by his patronymic but by his matronymic; thus, instead of "Jacob, the son of Moses," it would be "Jacob, the son of Sarah." The reason for this is the petitional sentence in Psalm 116:16, "I am Thy servant, the son of Thy handmaiden." In other words, this child could be named, "Jacob, the son of Sarah" (or whatever his mother's name is). The Talmud speaks of a man named "Mari the son of Rachel" (*Baba Bathra* 129a cf. Rashi). See also Ezekiel Landau to *Even Hoezer* 129:10 (*Dagul Mirvava*). But this simple solution must be rejected, because whenever this boy would be called up to the Torah, if he were called up in his mother's name instead of his father's, it would brand him for the rest of his life as having been born out of wedlock.

There is a better and a more considerate guidance in the Talmudic literature in this situation. There are a number of instances given in which children were named after people who were not their relatives. For example, in *Shabbas* 134a, we are told of a woman who lost two children because of the circumcision, and Nathan Habavli gave the mother advice to wait until the child was older, and her third child and her subsequent children survived the circumcision safely. Thereupon, the children were named "Nathan" after him, although he was no relative. So it was with the children who were named after Rabbi Eliezer, who solved a ritual question (as to blood) for a large number of women enquirers, and the children born were named for him (*Baba Metziah* 84b). Of course these children were given the name of the Rabbis, Nathan and Eliezer, as their personal name; but in an analogous case of Rabbi Yochanan (*Rosh Hashonah* 18a) we are told that the children were called "the family" of Rabbi Yochanan. So it is possible, on the basis of these precedents, to select a name that has no direct relationship to the paternity or the imputed paternity of the child. But is there any specific guidance as to which name to adopt as the patronymic?

The Talmud, in *Sanhedrin* 19b, refers to the fact that certain children were described as the children of Saul's daughter Michal, when actually they were the children of his other daughter, Merab. The Talmud explains this fact by saying that Merab bore those children but Michal raised them, and then the Talmud gives the following dictum: Whoever raises an orphan in his house may be considered its parent. Therefore if this child is given out for adoption (and since, anyhow, an adopted child is given the family name of the adopting family) he can be given the Hebrew patronymic of the head of the family which adopts him. If it is a fairly common Hebrew name, it would not necessarily point to him as the actual natural father. But if the name is unusual enough to point to him as such, the child can be named after the adoptive grandfather. Or, following the precedent of the various rabbis mentioned in the Talmud, the Hebrew name of any scholar greatly admired may be adopted; or, as we do with proselytes, who are called "the children of Abraham our father," the name of Abraham might be adopted as a patronymic.

Also there is another solution: When a man's father is an apostate whose name we will not call out when the son is called to the Torah, the son shall not be called up by his name alone, for that would shame him. He is called up as the son of his grandfather (see Isserles, *Orah Hayyim* 139:3; *Terumas Ha-deshen* #21). In *Orah Hayyim* 139:3, at the end of note, Isserles says a *shetuki* (one whose father is unknown) is called to the Torah by his own name, as the son of his mother's father. So, too, Ephraim Margolis in his *Shaarey Ephraim* 1:27, suggests that a *shetuki,* when called to the Torah, be called by the name of his mother's father.

The essence of the matter is this: Even if, in the strictly delimited sense of the Hebrew definition, the child is actually illegitimate, even so, no traditional rite may be refused to him. But since this child is not illegitimate, but just the child of an unmarried mother, he is entitled, of course, to every ritual of circumcision and naming, and the name is to be selected according to the various alternatives mentioned above.

21

WEDDING WITHOUT A LICENSE

QUESTION:

Two elderly people, both on Social Security, would like
to be married by Jewish law (by a Rabbi and under a
a Chuppah, etc.) but without taking out a marriage
license. The reason for their desiring to be married
without a marriage license was to avoid reduction in
the total of their Social Security. May the Rabbi officiate at this marriage? Is this mariage valid according
to Jewish law? (Asked by Rabbi Allen S. Maller, Culver
City, California.)

ANSWER:

THE QUESTION raised here may very well become an
important one. I have learned from a number of
sources that there are many elderly people now living
together without any marriage ceremony at all. The
reason that they are not formally married is the same
as given in the question, namely, to avoid reduction
in their joint Social Security. This couple, a religious-
minded couple, would not live together without some
marriage ceremony. There are undoubtedly other such
couples, so the question will very likely come up rather
often.

The specific question asked is whether this marriage
(if the Rabbi does conduct it) is valid according to

Jewish law. Of course it is. Jewish marriage is not dependent upon outside law, nor is it dependent upon the formalities of public ritual. Jewish legal literature is full of cases in which a young man in the presence of others gave an object of value to a young girl and said that the object was given for the purpose of marriage. If the girl accepts the object for this purpose and there are legal witnesses present, the marriage is certainly valid enough to require a *get,* a Jewish divorce, if it ever is to be dissolved. So considering Jewish law separately, if the groom gives an object as, for example, a ring, and pronounces the words which indicate that it is for the purpose of marriage, and there were valid (kosher) witnesses present, this marriage is valid Jewishly and would require a *get* to dissolve it.

But the Rabbi and the couple are also citizens of the United States and are subject to American law. So it becomes important to ask: Would this marriage be valid in the eyes of the state? Let us say, for example, that the state (as many states do) prohibits the marriage of two cousins, a marriage which is permitted in Jewish law. A Rabbi officiating at such a marriage would be conducting a valid Jewish marriage but a non-valid state marriage. Should a Rabbi officiate at such a marriage when there is such a conflict of laws?

As far as I know, there has been no discussion of this conflict in American-Jewish legal literature. It has been discussed in England by the Anglo-Jewish legal scholar, H. S. Q. Henriques, in his book, *Jewish Marriage and English Law,* London, 1909. In England many immigrants came from eastern Europe, where the state exercised no control over Jewish marriage, and the sole evidence that the marriage had taken place was the Jewish marriage document, the *kesubah*. English law accepts the *kesubah* as evidence. Then, also, there were some marriages conducted by Rabbis, in England, which would be invalid in English law (such as a marriage of an uncle and niece) but were valid by Jewish law. These were called in Jewish parlance a *shtille chuppeh* (a silent or a private marriage ceremony). Henriques does not say that such a marriage is invalid, but he says (page 53): "Though valid, such marriage should not be encouraged, being in direct contradiction to the spirit of modern legislation." He adds further that it would lead to many abuses, such as desertion, etc.

Until you raised the question, I do not remember reading anywhere in our American-Jewish literature, any question of a *shtille chuppeh,* that is to say, a marriage without legal license or validation.

It must now be mentioned that an important practical question, from the point of view of the Rabbi, must first be settled. Is the Rabbi violating the state law by officiating for a couple who do not have a marriage license? I have received various legal opinions on this matter. The majority opinion seems to be that it is a violation of the law so to officiate. Another opinion is that since our particular state (Pennsylvania) gives some recognition to common law marriage, a Rabbi officiating at such a marriage might *not* be considered culpable. But even the latter opinion (as to common law marriage) is debated on the ground that common law marriage is recognized only as a man's acknowledgment of a *present* situation, but not as a prepared-for status. Therefore it would be wise for the Rabbi, before officiating at such a *shtille chuppeh,* to inquire from legal authorities whether or not he may be violating the law of the state.

So far the conflict between the two legal systems has been discussed from the point of view of state law; i.e., what attitude the state will take to a marriage without its permission (license). But now we must ask the other question, from the point of view of Jewish law: What is the attitude of Jewish law to a marriage conducted contrary to the laws of the state? Is there not the well known principle in Jewish law, *dina d'malchusa dina,* that the law of the state is valid in Jewish law?

Of course this principle applies primarily to civil matters, taxes, business law, etc., but not to ritual matters. If the state imposes a tax on the entire community, it is a valid mandate in Jewish law that the tax must be paid. But the principle does not apply to spiritual and ritual matters. If, for example, the state would prohibit the Jewish method of slaughtering animals (as has happened in certain countries) or the holding of religious services on Saturday (as might happen when Church and State are one) in such matters we do not say that the law of the state is valid in Jewish law. On the contrary, we would (as a matter of conscience) resist the law of the state in all such religious matters.

Now marriage and divorce are deemed spiritual

matters in which the law of the state does not apply. Thus if a couple is divorced by civil law, they are not yet considered divorced in Jewish Orthodox law, but must also receive a Jewish divorce (*get*). Nevertheless, even in this case, in practice (if not in theory) Jewish law takes cognizance of civil law. In actual practice in America, a *get* is not granted by Jewish authorities unless the couple has first received a divorce from the state courts. But as far as I know, there has been no discussion in the United States of the interrelationship of Jewish law and state law in regard to marriage.

Although the principle of *dina d'malchusa dina* does not apply to such matters as marriage and divorce, there is a directly relevant way in which it *does* apply in the particular marriage which is the subject of this inquiry. As has been mentioned, the principle of *dina d'malchusa dina* applies in civil matters. In the discussion of this principle it has been frequently stated that not every fiscal law by the ruler of the state (the law was developed during the period of monarchy) was deemed valid in Jewish law. If it was an unfair tax placed only upon the Jews, or if it was some willful notion of the king, such decrees, although fiscal, were not valid in Jewish law. It was only such valid laws which applied equally to all citizens which were deemed valid in Jewish law.

Now it is evident that the Federal regulations governing Social Security are just and equal laws promulgated by authorized legal bodies, and as such, are deemed absolutely valid in *Jewish* law. Therefore since this marriage ceremony is being conducted without a license for the purpose of evading or contravening the just and legal regulations governing Social Security, such an arrangement must be deemed illegal, even from the Jewish point of view.

To sum up: Considered separately, as a Jewish ceremony, the marriage in question would be valid and would certainly require a Jewish divorce to dissolve it. It may, however, be an illegal action by the Rabbi who officiates, if the law of the state requires a recording and information of every marriage conducted. Furthermore, it is questionable whether such a marriage would be accepted as valid by the state. Finally, since the Social Security legislation is a civil matter, its laws are valid in Jewish law. Therefore from the *Jewish* point of view, the Rabbi may not assist in contravening the laws of Social Security.

22

OWNERSHIP OF A SEFER TORAH

QUESTION:

In the city in question there were two congregations, one of which was unable to maintain itself. Most of its members joined the other congregation as individual families. (It was not a formal merger.) These individuals turned over to the larger congregation the various religious articles belonging to the defunct congregation, including some *Sefer Torahs*. Now a woman who had once belonged to the defunct congregation, but who now belongs to another in another city, demands that one of the *Sefer Torahs* given to the larger congregation be restored to her. Her reason is that her father had donated this Torah in memory of her mother, and that the members who had now joined the larger congregation had no right to turn this Torah over to it. The Rabbi of the larger congregation suggested that she speak to those members of the now-defunct smaller congregation and ask them for that *Sefer Torah*. She did so but they did not wish to give it to her. The question is: What rights of ownership does this woman have in this *Sefer Torah*? (Asked by Rabbi Sidney Ballon, Nassau Community Temple, West Hempstead, New York)

ANSWER:

THE QUESTION involved here has, tragically, become highly relevant these days, due to the fading of our inner cities. The defunct congregation spoken of here may have faded for other causes than the decay of its environment, but the problem involved is the same as the one now widely relevant, namely, who has the right to dispose of the sacred objects of a defunct congregation.

Since there is a claimant in this case (i.e., the daughter of the donor of the *Sefer Torah* in question) her rights should be considered first of all. In general, the question of the ownership of a Sefer Torah under the circumstances mentioned has come up in various forms rather frequently in the legal literature. By and large the various opinions expressed over the centuries have come to a fairly clear consensus.

On the face of it the situation is completely covered by the rules in the laws of *Zedaka* in the *Shulchan Aruch, Yore Deah* 259. There it is stated as a general principle (Section 1) that a donor may change the purpose of the gift, or the recipient of the gift. But this right to change the recipient or the purpose exists only before the gift has come into the hands of the proper officials (*Gabaim*). If, for example, a donor sets aside money for one charity and still has possession of the money which he has set aside, he may change his gift to any other charitable purpose; but if he has already turned the money over to the officials (in this case, the officers of the synagogue) he or she can no longer change the purpose or the recipients (see *Yore Deah* 259:1).

By this general rule it would seem obvious that since the Torah was in the possession of the synagogue to which her father had given it, she, her father's daughter, no longer has the right to give it to any other recipient. Yet it must be stated that this general negation of her rights to change purpose or recipient is in itself weakened by two considerations: First, there is at least one opinion (Israel Rapaport, *Mahari Ha-Kohen, Yore Deah* #47) that all synagogues are to be of equal status and, therefore, giving to one synagogue after intending to give it to another is not deemed to be, by this one authority, an invalid or non-permitted change. The only question in this case would be whether she still has any rights of ownership at all in this Torah, once it had been given to the synagogue.

The other mitigation of the rule (prohibiting any change after it had been officially received) is the custom mentioned by a number of scholars, that in certain communities it had become an established custom for people to have *Sefer Torahs* written and to deposit them in the synagogue, remembering always that it is *their Sefer Torah,* and without at all intending to transfer the ownership to the synagogue. According to this custom, then, the Torah, although used in the synagogue, is deemed to be still the property of its original owners and they can take it, sell it, or give it to somebody else. See this custom of retaining ownership as described in the Responsa *Shearis Yoseph* by Joseph B. Mordecai, Aldorf, 1767, Responsa #41. He describes this custom of retaining ownership of the Torah and agrees that the owner had the right to sell it for a debt. The other description of such a custom is much older. In the Responsa of Joseph Colon (*Ma-*

harik, 1st edition, #161, near the end; in later edition, p. 173, column 2) the questioner likewise describes such a custom in which people gave or rather lent the Torah to the synagogue and carefully insisted that they still owned it.

To this situation Joseph Colon (Italy, 15th century) who is one of the prime authorities, gives the following answer which has become, one might say, classic: He says, once the Torah has been used in the synagogue and had the mantle on it, it is sacred and belongs to the sanctuary and cannot be sold or transferred, except by the decision of the officers of the community. In this case, the membership of the congregation, therefore, are the only ones who have the right to transfer the Torah. As for the statement of the questioner to Maharik that they had the custom of retaining ownership of the Torah, he dismisses this argument. He says no custom is valid enough to overturn a law unless it is a widespread custom and one established by scholars (*vatikin*).

This opinion of Joseph Colon is repeated almost exactly by the sixteenth-century Polish authority, Solomon Luria (Maharshal) in his Responsa, #15. The case of this questioner is almost precisely the case in this question asked today, namely, the sons of the man gave or loaned the Torah and now are moving to another city and want to give or loan the Torah to the synagogue in this other city. Solomon Luria is even more specific in his answer than Joseph Colon. He says that once the mantle was on the Torah, it can no longer be returned or be sold even if the man who gave it claims he never intended to give it outright. Such a claim would be valid only if before he gave it, he declared formally, in the presence of two witnesses, that he is not giving the Torah as an outright gift, but is merely loaning it to the congregation. If he had not made such a formal declaration previously, then now that the Torah had been used (once the mantle is put upon it) he may never take it back, whatever may have been his unspoken intention. The opinion of these great authorities is repeated by Joseph Caro in his *Bes Joseph* to the *Tur, Yore Deah* 259 and also by Joel Sirkes (ibid.). Isserles to *Yore Deah* (ibid.) comes substantially to the same conclusion.

If, then, it is clear that the donor or his descendants do not have the right of the disposal of this *Sefer Torah,* who does have the right? The law speaks of "the seven good men of the city" (as we say today, "twelve good men and true") (*sheva tuvey ha-ir,* i.e., the officers). Sometimes it speaks of the membership (*b'nay ha-ir*). In either case, we have the right to assume that those who decided to carry over their congregational life to the congregation which now has the Torah, include what was left of the officers and many of the members. They are the ones (and the only ones) who have the right of disposal of the sacred objects. In fact, they were consulted by the claimant and they decided to give the Torah to your congregation. Their decision is valid. Moreover, their decision is strengthened by the fact that they did not sell the Torah, but gave it to another congregation, thus maintaining its sanctity.

If they had decided to give the Torah to the claimant, this decision would also have been valid, since she intended to place the Torah in another congregation and thus its sanctity would not be diminished. But they decided otherwise. Perhaps they wanted to avoid the danger that all the other original donors of sacred objects might now claim their gifts and thus the objects would be scattered. They wanted the Torahs of their former congregation to be in the congregation where they now worship. Whatever was their motivation, the decision was theirs to make.

To sum up, the situation is as follows: If there was a well-established custom in the community that people would loan *Sefer Torahs* to the synagogue with the express intention to keep their ownership of them, such a custom, if established in consultation with learned authorities, might have some validity. But even that is doubtful. Further, if the woman's father had made a specific declaration that the Torah in question was not given outright to the synagogue, but was only a loan so that it could be read in the services, only then could it now be reclaimed. But since this Torah has now been transferred to the larger congregation by the majority and perhaps also the officers remaining in the now defunct congregation, this transfer is a valid act. The weight of tradition is on the side of the opinion that this Torah may not be removed from the synagogue in which it is now placed.

23

TORAH IN MUSEUM CASE OR IN ARK

QUESTION:

The congregation was given one of the Torah scrolls from Czechoslovakia. This Torah was repaired by the Commission in Great Britain. Some members of our congregation would like to have this Torah kept in a display case with other ceremonial objects. Others would like to keep it in the Ark. Which is preferable? (Asked by Rabbi Albert Lewis, Grand Rapids, Michigan)

ANSWER:

ACCORDING to Jewish law and custom, the Torah must be held in great honor; hence the important question involved here is: Which of the two settings would be of greater honor for the Torah? There is a rule (*Megillah* 26b, *Yore Deah* 282:10) that when a *Sefer Torah* is no longer usable, it must be disposed of in an especially honorable way. It must be placed in an earthenware urn and buried in the cemetery beside an honored scholar. In other words, it is the mood of tradition that if a Torah is no longer to be used because it is unfit, then, like the no-longer used body of a person who has died, it must be honorably buried. Therefore, it would seem to me that if this Torah is *posul,* then it should be decently put away and not openly displayed.

However, if the term in your letter "repaired by the Commission" means that the Torah has been corrected and is no longer *posul,* then there are other objections to its being displayed in the ceremonial case. Among all the sacred objects in Jewish worship, the Torah is by far the most sacred. The other ceremonial objects are only "auxiliary to holiness" (*tashmishey kedusha* or *tashmishey mitzva, Orah Hayyim* 154). Even the Ark itself is called "holy Ark" only because it contains the Torah (*Orah Hayyim* 154:1). There are questions even as to whether printed Bibles or Talmud volumes may be kept in the Ark together with the Torahs. If you put the Torah in a museum case with menorahs, Pesach dishes, pewter Purim plates, etc., you are demeaning its unique status by declaring it to be one more ceremonial object among others.

There is also another objection to putting it in the display case. The law requires (*Berachoth* 25b, *Yore Deah* 282:8) that if the *Sefer Torah* is kept in a room in some private house, then people's demeanor in that room must be especially careful and circumspect. Now, this museum case may be (as it is in many congregations) in the entrance lobby. How can we be sure that people in a crowd, coming and going, will keep a dignified demeanor and be careful with their speech? We might well say that putting the Torah in a case in a building lobby puts an unfair restriction upon the speech and demeanor of members of the congregation.

Besides the decorum to be observed in a room where

a Torah is kept, and besides the respectful disposal of
a Torah when it is no longer usable, the chief manifestation of respect for the Torah is during the ceremony
of the public reading of the Scriptures in the services.
If, then, the Torah is kept in the Ark and is being
taken out on occasion for public reading, there can be
no greater honor given to a Torah than that. First of
all, even if people are walking around the building
during parts of the service, they are required to come
in to the synagogue to see the Torah taken out (cf.
Maharil, *Hilchos Kerias Ha-Torah*). When the Torah is
taken out, everyone present, and that means the entire
available congregation, must stand while the Torah is
being carried from the Ark to the reading desk and
later when it is carried back from the reading desk to
the Ark. The reason for standing is worth noting. The
Talmud, in *Kiddushin* 33b, discusses the verse in Leviticus 19:3: "Stand up in respect of a gray-haired man."
And the Talmud says, "This is the basis of the law
that when a scholar comes by, you must stand up in
respect for him. How much more must we stand up in
respect for the Torah."

And as for exhibiting the Torah, this is provided for
at the beginning of the Torah Reading by the Sephardim and at the close of the reading by the Ashkenazim. The mitzvah of *hagbeh,* raising the open Torah
to show to the people, is a most honored one (*Orah
Hayyim* 134:12).

It is clear that putting the Torah in a display case
would merely equate it with other ceremonial objects,
whereas it should be considered the *most* sacred of all

religious objects. Also, it would require special decorum in the lobby of the Temple. But putting it in the Ark and having it read gives the Torah the continual honor of the presence of all the congregation, of their respectful rising, and the honored display in the ceremony of *hagbeh*. Clearly, then, since we presume that this is a corrected Torah which can be used in the reading, the Ark is the honorable and proper place for it.

There is a proverb given in the *Zohar* (III, 134a) that everything depends on fortune, even the Torah in the Ark. An Ark may contain a half dozen Torahs. One of them, no better than the rest, will have the "good fortune" of being read every Sabbath. Another, equally good, will be read only as the extra Torah, on a holiday. Still another, as good a Torah as the others, will only be carried around once a year in procession on *Simchas Torah*. So one might say of this Torah about which you ask that once it had the good fortune of being a beloved object in a historic congregation. Children kissed it as it was carried in procession. Men were honored to be called up to recite a blessing over the reading from it. The congregation that had cherished it has long since been martyred and has now disappeared. Let its "fortune" now be restored, and let it be read in reverence during your congregation's worship.

The collection of scrolls from which your scroll comes was in the care of my late classmate, Rabbi Harold Reinhart, and was kept in his synagogue in Kensington (London). He showed me the collection a number of years ago, and I observed that quite a number of these scrolls were very large and obviously very heavy. If this scroll which you have received from this collection is too large and heavy to be conveniently handled for the public reading on Sabbath and holidays, then at least give this scroll a permanent place in your Ark. Whenever the Ark will be open for the Torah reading, the congregation will rise in respect for all the scrolls in the Ark and this scroll, now permanently rescued from captivity, will thus be honored among them.

24

POSUL TORAH IN THE ARK

QUESTION:

A Torah scroll had been in a fire and was declared by a scribe (*sopher*) to be *posul* and beyond repair. The scroll has sentimental and historical significance to the congregation. May it be kept in the Ark with the useable *Sepher Torahs?* (Question by Rabbi Samuel Weingart, Champaign, Illinois)

ANSWER:

THERE IS A GREAT DEAL of material in the Law with regard to the status and the disposal of a *posul Sepher Torah*. Some of the statements in the law seem at first glance to contradict other statements and, therefore, the legal situation of the *posul* Torah needs to be analyzed.

The Talmud in *Ketuboth* 19b (in Rashi) says that *Sepher Torahs* and other books that are unfit may not be kept. This appears as a fixed law in the *Shulchan Aruch,* 279:1, which says that every *Sepher Torah* must be proofread (*mugah*) every thirty days. It must either be corrected if erroneous or put away (*yigonez*). And the question is, what does "put away" mean? It is, of course, an established custom that a *Sepher Torah* that is *posul* is buried in an earthen jar in the grave of a scholar (*Orah Hayyim* 154:5). This seems clear enough. So on the face of these laws, all unfit *Sepher Torahs* should not be kept in the Ark but should be buried.

Yet actually this is not the law because of variations in the definition of the word *"posul,"* "unfit." For example, a Torah may be unfit for reading, yet can easily be repaired. If when it was being read, the Reader found an error, another Torah is taken out, and this *posul* one is *put back into the Ark*. Or the Torah may be unrepairable and yet one of its five books is in perfect shape and, therefore, retains its holiness (cf. Isserles to *Orah Hayyim* 143:4). As a matter of fact, a *Sepher Torah* is considered holy if even less than that is still good. So Rashi to *Sabbath* 115b indicates that if there are eighty-five consecutive letters, it is holy. So there is still holiness to a *posul Sepher Torah*. If that is the case, there are strong objections to burying and thus destroying a sacred book with God's name in it.

Thus it has happened that the custom arose to keep the *posul Sepher Torahs* in the Ark. The first justification was from the Talmud in *Baba Basra* 14b, namely, that in the ancient Ark of the Tabernacle and the Temple there were not only the two tablets of stone, but also the broken fragments of the tablets that Moses smashed. *Sepher Chassidim* (perhaps the earliest source on this matter) in section 934 (Margolis edition) says that the custom is on that basis of the broken tablets to keep *posul Sepher Torahs* in the ark. But the passage in *Sepher Chassidim* seems to indicate that separate sheets (*yeriot*) were buried.

Upon this basis a continued chain of authorities permit keeping the *posul Sepher Torah* in the Ark. The classic authority, Ezekiel Landau, in his *Nodeh b. Yehudah,* Vol. I, *Orah Hayyim* 9, says that there is no objection on the ground of holiness of the Ark to keeping a *posul Sepher Torah* in it. But he is inclined not to permit it for a practical reason: The people might forget and take that Torah out to read in the service. This objection, however, is put aside by Elazar Spiro (the Hungarian Chassidic authority, "Der Muncaczer"). In his *Minchas Elazar,* Vol. III, #52, he agrees with Landau that the *posul* Torah may be kept in the Ark but he brushes aside the danger of the Torah being taken out by mistake by saying that the wrapper tied around the Torah can indicate which is which. So, also, the great German authority, Jacob Ettlinger, in his *Binyan Zion,* I:97, likewise permits. In fact, the *Mogen Avraham* to *Orah Hayyim* 154:8 simply says that it is the custom to put *posul Sepher Torahs* in the Ark.

Some useful references on this matter are to be

found in the footnotes of Margolis to the *Sepher Chassidim,* passage mentioned above, and a full treatment of the subject is provided by Gedaliah Felder in his fine handbook *Yesodeh Jeshurun,* II:142 ff.

In general it may be said that it is a well-established custom based on a continuous permissive line in the law that *posul Sepher Torahs* may be kept in the Ark

25

FASTING IF TORAH IS DROPPED

QUESTION:

One of our oldest members was carrying the Scroll back to the Ark. He got a dizzy spell and fell on the floor with the Torah in his arms, in front of the Ark. What is Jewish tradition and what should a Liberal congregation do with regard to fasting if the Torah has fallen? (Asked by Abram E. Salas, Curacao, Netherlands, West Indies.)

ANSWER:

THIS CUSTOM of fasting when the Torah is dropped is not, in any strict sense, a law. It is not given in the *Shulchan Aruch* by Joseph Caro, or in the Ashkenazic notes of Moses Isserles. It is not found in the previous code, the *Tur.* Neither could I find any reference on this question in *Sha'arey Ephraim,* the well-known book which specializes in all questions of the Torah reading. Clearly, then, this is not a requirement of Jewish law. In fact, the only mention of it in connection with the

Shulchan Aruch is in the commentary, *Mogen Avraham* to *Orah Hayyim* 44:5. The *Shulchan Aruch* there speaks of what should be done if the *Tefillin* are dropped; to which the *Mogen Avraham* comments that fasting, if the *Tefillin* are dropped, is perhaps the reason for the *custom* that people fast, also, if the Torah is dropped. (By the way, even with regard to the *Tefillin*, if they are dropped while they are in their bag, is is not necessary to fast at all.) At all events, the custom of fasting when the Torah is dropped is a sort of an outcome of a popular analogy. Chiefly it seems to have sprung up as an extension of an actual law. There is a law that whoever sees a *Sefer Torah* burnt up must make a tear in his garment (*keriah*) as he would do at the death of a close relative. If, therefore, one should show signs of mourning if a Torah is burned, then one should, perhaps, at least fast if *Tefillin* or the Torah is dropped. This must have been the unconscious reasoning which led to the custom.

However, although it is not a legal requirement (since it is not given in the codes) nevertheless discussion of it is found in the Responsa Literature. The fullest discussion of it is found in the Responsa *Bes Yitzchok* by the famous Rabbi of Lemberg in the last century, Isaac Shmelkes (in Volume II of *Yore Deah* of his responsa, #165). The specific question that he was asked was: If it was on the Sabbath when the Torah was seen to be dropped, how shall one fulfill the custom of fasting, since one may not fast on the Sabbath? In answer to this question, he cites other authorities, among them two famous Sephardim, Daniel

Terni, Rabbi of Florence, Italy, in the 18th-19th century, and Chaim J. D. Azulai, the famous Palestinian emissary who lived in Italy about the same time as Daniel Terni. Daniel Terni's work is called *Ikrey Hadat* (the reference given is *Yore Deah* 26); Azulai's responsa, *Chaim Sho-Al*, #12. Cf. *Sheyurey Beracha, Yore Deah* 340:19 and *Shulchan Aruch, Yore Deah* 340:27. The *Kitzur Shulchan Aruch* gives it as an established practice; #28, paragraph 12, refers to *Birche Josef*, #44.

The strictest view is that the one who drops the Torah must fast a succession of three days after the Sabbath, Monday, Thursday, Monday; and that the whole congregation who were present should fast one day. Other opinions are that only the one who dropped the Torah should fast and the others need not fast. Since it is merely a custom, Isaac Shmelkes is lenient and says that those who find it difficult to fast should merely give charity. The whole subject is likewise discussed by Gedaliah Felder in his *Yosedey Yeshurun*, Vol. II, p. 106.

To sum up: Fasting if the Torah is dropped is not a legal requirement; it was never given as such in any of the great codes. As a custom which has spread among both Ashkenazim and Sephardim, there are various degrees of strictness suggested by those who describe it. In my own opinion, since this custom has no real legal status, nothing should be done by the entire congregation except, perhaps, by the man who dropped the Torah. Since he is not in the best of health and the Torah dropped because he had a dizzy spell due to his high blood pressure, he certainly should have no sense of guilt. If, however, he has some feeling of guilt or deep regret, let him fulfill the suggestion of one of the scholars who discussed the matter (above) who said that if the fasting is difficult, he should give some charity, preferably to the congregation.

26

HEBREW LETTERS ON CHAPLAIN'S INSIGNIA

QUESTION:

The lettering for the Ten Commandments on the chaplain's insignia is Roman lettering. If a request comes to change the letters to Hebrew letters, should this request be encouraged? (Asked bp Rabbi Aryeh Lev, New York)

ANSWER:

YOUR QUESTION as to whether there would be any objection if at some time the letters on the two tablets on the chaplain's insignia were changed from Roman numerals to the Hebrew letters, can be answered at once. In *principle* there can be no objection to such a change, but in practice it would be undesirable.

The question which is basic to the entire discussion is whether there is any sanctity in the Hebrew letters per se, i.e., just as letters. That the Hebrew writing in itself is *not* sacred is evident from the fact that the Talmud says of certain writings in Hebrew that they need not be rescued from burning on the Sabbath. See *Shabbas* 115b, which speaks of *kameyos* and *berachos:* "Even though they contain names of God, they may not be rescued from the fire on the Sabbath, but must be allowed to burn up, including the names of God they contain." In those days prayers were not permitted to be *written;* hence if written, the writing was not deemed to be sacred.

Of course, although the Hebrew letters are not sacred per se and the sacredness is dependent entirely upon what is written in them, nevertheless the written name of God, to be fully sacred, must be written in our square Hebrew letters. Thus the Mishnah in *Yadaim* 4:5 says that the written name of God is not sacred until it is written in our square Hebrew letters on parchment and with ink. In spite of this law, even the name of God so written is not always sacred. A *Sefer Torah* itself, if it is written by an apostate or a heretic, must be burnt up with all the names of God that it contains (*Orah Hayyim* 334:21).

This, then, is the law strictly stated. There is no sanctity in the Hebrew writing as such; the sanctity inheres only in the name of God written in Hebrew, and even that under certain circumstances (if written by a heretic) need not be rescued from fire.

However, while the above is strictly correct, there grew up in the passing of the centuries a noticeable sentiment to protect Hebrew writings in general. Perhaps this was due to the Kabbalah which taught that there was a sacredness in every Hebrew letter in the Bible and that all of them can be mystically woven

together to form names of God. You will notice, therefore, that while the Talmud says clearly that written
kameyos (spells) must be allowed to be burned up
and the Sabbath not violated by rescuing them, the
Shulchan Aruch in *Orah Hayyim* 334:14 repeats the
Talmudic rule that they should not be rescued, but then
adds: Some say that they *should* be rescued (in this
regard it quotes the *Tur*).

In general there has grown up a feeling against carrying any Hebrew writing into unclean places. An
example of this growing sensitiveness occurred with the
famous responsa anthology of *S'dey Chemed* by Chaim
Chiskia Medina. Although the title means *Pleasant
Fields*, some rabbis raised the objection that the word
S'dey, meaning "fields," could be misread as "Shaddai,"
and therefore the name of God. Hence the title should
not be used, lest pages from it be taken into an unclean
place. This objection was taken so seriously that there
was printed in one of the many introductions to the
anthology a fifty-page collection of defense opinions
entitled "Be'er B'S'dey," "The Explanation of the Word
S'dey." I am sure that people today would object even
to a Socialist paper printed in Hebrew letters being left
in or taken to unclean places.

Since, therefore, the chaplain's insignia on the chaplain's coat is carried around everywhere, there certainly
would be feeling against the fact if the chaplain's insignia had the Hebrew letters of the Ten Commandments instead of the Roman letters.

It is worth mentioning that the Talmud expresses
some concern about the king and the *Sefer Torah*. The

Bible says (Deuteronomy 17:19) that the *Sefer Torah* that is written in behalf of the king, he should read all the days of his life; and the Talmud, *Sanhedrin* 21b, cautiously says that he must read it in a place that is proper for the Torah to be read in. In other words, it should not be taken to an unclean place. The Talmud says further that he should not go with it into the bathhouse or into the toilet.

But as I said at the beginning, there is no strict law against it, although there would be definite Jewish feelings opposed to a possible desecration.

27

LADY'S PANTS SUITS

QUESTION:

The historic congregation in Curacao is constantly visited by vistors from American cruise ships. Many of the ladies, as is the modern custom, wear pants suits. Some of the traditional-minded members of the congregation object to this type of clothing as a violation of the Biblical prohibition of women wearing men's clothing. Rabbi Malcolm Stern, to whom they spoke, reminded them that in Morocco and elsewhere in North Africa, pants suits were the traditional garments of women. However, Rabbi Stern suggested that the status of the law be more fully discussed.

ANSWER:

IT IS EXTREMELY difficult to discuss the matter of modern women's clothing on the basis of Halachic precedent. After all, the social situation and the social mood have changed so drastically since ancient times that it is difficult for a modern man to grasp the relevance of these ancient laws. Nevertheless, the laws had a most worthy intention and deserve our understanding and even our acceptance, whenever that is possible for us.

The law stems from Deuteronomy 22, verse 5, which states: "A woman shall not wear that which pertaineth unto a man, neither shall a man put on woman's garments, for whosoever doeth these things is an abomination unto the Lord thy God." Now, why should men's clothing on a woman or women's clothing on a man be, as Scripture says, an "abomination?" Rashi explains it quite clearly. He says the change of clothing was in order that a woman could mingle among men, and that could only be for the purpose of adultery. Of course when one thinks of the complete separation of men and women in the earlier centuries, certainly a woman circulating in men's disguise among men might be justly suspect.

But can we truthfully say that today? It is true that there is a great relaxation of moral standards nowadays. But in spite of that, can we truthfully declare that a woman who wears a pants suit wears it with an immoral intent? If that were the intent, surely many of the modern mini-skirts and other such garments are much more provocative of sexual looseness.

We must therefore judge this particular garment on the basis of intent. As a matter of fact, this approach is justified by Jewish law. The oldest Halachic source, after Scripture itself, is the *Sifre,* and the *Sifre* on this passage (paragraph #226) says: "Does that mean that men may not wear colored cloth because women wear it? Certainly not. The key word is the Biblical word 'abomination.' If the garment is worn for the abominable purpose of secretly moving among the other sex, that is the 'abomination,' and that is the prohibition." So, too, the Talmud (*Nazir* 59a) says there is no "abomination" in the wearing of the garments, but only if they wear them in order to mingle in each other's groups. In other words, we must judge by the intent.

A further proof that we judge by intent was the relation of the Rabbi to the masking and hilarity of Purim. On Purim often men would dress in women's clothes and women would dress in men's clothes, and Rabbi Judah Mintz of Padua, in his responsum #17 says that there is no objection to it on Purim because there is no other intention involved but rejoicing. So Moses Isserles, the great Ashkenazic authority, discussing the dressing up on Purim in *Orah Hayyim* 696:8 says, "As for the custom to wear masks on Purim and men wearing garments of a woman and a woman wearing garments of a man, there is no prohibition in this matter since the intention is only joy." See also *Ozar Dinim u-Minhagim,* page 337, column 1. So the purpose of the type of clothing must always be taken into consideration.

There is also another way to consider the modern problem. The law forbidding a man to wear a woman's garments was extended to forbid a man to use any of the feminine devices of beauty culture. The *Shulchan Aruch* in *Yore Deah* 182:6 says that a man may not even pluck out one white hair from his black beard and he may not use a depilatory on his arm-pits. All these are forbidden because they are cosmetic devices of women. Nevertheless, the *Shulchan Aruch* itself says that where it is the custom for men to remove the bodily hairs, there is no objection to it.

In other words, we must judge these matters by what has become the prevailing custom. Rabbi Stern, therefore, was quite right in calling attention to the fact that wearing pants suits was the established custom of the North African women. Similarly, might we not be justified then in saying that the pants suit is no longer an exceptional garment worn by some bold woman to attract attention, but by now has become established as a normal type of women's garments, and therefore may be considered as no longer violative of the law in Deuteronomy?

As we said at the beginning, the whole mood of modern life is so different from the life in ancient times that it is hard to apply a law which was so deeply rooted in vanished moods and social attitudes. But this much we can say: If the garment is not for the purpose of, as Scripture says, "abomination," and if, also, it has become established as a woman's garment, then I believe that we can no longer object to it on Halachic grounds.

A similar decision on this question was arrived at by Obadiah Joseph, Chief Sephardic Rabbi of Tel Aviv. He says it is "better than miniskirts." (Published in *Or Ha-Mizrach,* Tishri 5733, p. 37. He cites the *Schach* and the *Bach* to *Yore Deah* 182.)

28

STATUETTES IN THE SYNAGOGUE

QUESTION:

Two small statues of marble, one of Moses and one of David (almost naked) have been offered to a Conservative synagogue. Should they be accepted and permanently displayed in the lobby of this synagogue? (Asked by J. R. Kohn, Tampa, Florida.)

ANSWER:

IN GENERAL the commandment, "Thou shalt not make any graven images," would seem to prohibit any sort of statuary. However, this general prohibition of representing actual objects in art is immediately delimited by the laws in the Talmud, *Avoda Zara* 43b and *Rosh Hashonah* 24b. There the prohibition is confined to such objects which were in the image of the Divine chariot or entourage as described by Ezekiel. Hence, lions, oxen, eagles and humans were the images which were actually prohibited. In fact, figures of humans were specifically and additionally prohibited. However, even in the cases of the prohibition of these images, the Talmud and the later codes (see especially *Tur* and *Shulchan Aruch, Yore Deah* 141 *passim*) prohibit only three-dimensional objects but not flat objects such as painting and embroidery, and certainly not sunken objects such as intaglio. In the Middle Ages, however, there was some prohibition by certain Franco-German authorities even to decorations of birds and flowers (even though these were not among the specific objects in the image of the Divine entourage and also were not three-dimensional). The reason given by Rabbi Eliakim, who ordered the removal of such decorations from the synagogue in Cologne (11th century) was that they would distract the worshiper. This concern that the worshiper would be distracted was evoked in the discussion of the lions, often three-dimensional, that were found in certain synagogues as decorations of the Ark. However, even in such a case the lion images were defended if they were not *above* the Ark where all the worshipers could see them, but down lower where they would not be seen and would not distract the worshipers.

Clearly these statues will not be in the main synagogue where worshipers might be distracted, but in the lobby where no worship takes place. So there would be no objection.

Now the question is: Is it proper, even if it does not distract worshipers, to have a statue altogether in a synagogue? To this it must be noted that it is an actual fact that in one of the most ancient synagogues in Babylon there was a bust of the monarch. This synagogue is discussed in the Talmud in *Megilla* 29a, *Avoda Zara* 43b, and in the letter of the Gaon Sherira (10th century) edition Lewin, p. 72. This synagogue which was called *Shev V'Yashiv* (a name whose meaning is debated) had a most honored origin. The Talmud says it was founded by the exiled King Jehoiachin himself, and he used sacred soil and stones from the Temple in Jerusalem for its foundation; and indeed when the question was asked where does the *Shekinah,* which follows Israel in its exile, come to rest in Babylon, the answer which the Talmud gives is that the *Shekinah* rests in this ancient synagogue, *Shev V'Yashiv.* Furthermore, we are told that the greatest of the early Babylonian Rabbis, Rav and Samuel, worshiped there. Evidently they had no objection at all to the presence of a statue of the emperor in the sanctuary. But the question (by implication) is asked in the Talmud: Should not such a bust or statue be prohibited on the ground that some misguided person might worship it? And the answer that the Talmud gives is that perhaps such a suspicion might arise if the statue were in private premises, but in a public place such as the synagogue, where all the people are together, we need have no such suspicion. So a historic synagogue founded by a king of Judea where the Shekinah reposed and where the great rabbis worshiped without demur, had a statue; and since it was in public, there was no suspicion that it would lead to idolatry.

So if a statue of a heathen king was permitted in this most sacred of ancient synagogues, then certainly it would be permitted to have a statue of the Jewish King David and of the great leader, Moses. The only possible objection would be that the statue of David is virtually naked. It is very likely Michelangelo's David, which is almost entirely naked. I would think that this then becomes a matter of taste; although, even here, it must be stated that in a public place (as, for example, a bathhouse) where many people are together, the matter of nakedness is not a matter of too strict a concern (see *Shulchan Aruch, Even Hoezer* 21:5, the note of Isserles). However, if the nakedness would offend the majority of the congregation, even if the statue is in the lobby and not in the synagogue proper and is of a Jewish king, it should not be displayed.

If the statue of Moses is a copy of Michelangelo's Moses, it has two horn-like projections from the head of Moses. This is based upon the ancient understanding of the verse (Exodus 34:29) that when Moses came down from Mount Sinai his face shone with rays of light, and the Hebrew verse is "Koran or ponov," in which the word "koran" which means "rays of light" was taken to mean the same as "keran" which means "horns." But there is no objection to this representation of Moses. Many Hebrew books with elaborate title pages depicted Moses in the same way.

In short, the answer is as follows: There is no basic objection to statues, especially in the lobby where they do not distract from actual worship. There may be a sense of impropriety in the nakedness of the David statue; that must be decided as a matter of taste. There is no objection to the statute of Moses.

29

SUBSTITUTING FOR CHRISTIANS ON CHRISTMAS

QUESTION:

The Men's Club of Temple Beth El, Detroit, substituted for Christian volunteer hospital aides on Christmas last year (1971). That year Christmas fell on the Sabbath and questions arose in the Detroit community as to whether it was proper for a Jewish congregation thus openly (and also with newspaper publicity) to violate the Sabbath. Since then, other Men's Clubs are planning to volunteer for such duties on Christmas. This has raised the wider question: first, as mentioned about the Sabbath and secondly, about the value or propriety of this sort of substitute volunteering. (From Rabbi Richard Hertz, Detroit, Michigan)

ANSWER:

THERE ARE ONE or two general statements which must be made before going into the detailed laws involved in this matter. First of all, the propriety of violating the Sabbath: It is of course obvious that most modern individuals, not only in Reform congregations but in others, do not, in their personal life, follow with any degree of strictness the laws of working, traveling, opening letters, etc., on the Sabbath. Nevertheless, there is a difference between what is done privately and what is done publicly. This difference has long been recognized in Jewish law. The building of a house by contract (*kablonus*) may go on any day of the week including the Sabbath, for the Gentile contractor works, not by day-by-day orders from the Jewish owner, but by his own orders. But while such Sabbath work would be permitted, let us say, outside of the city, in the city where everybody sees the work going on, it is prohibited (see *Orah Hayyim* 244).

The Responsa Committee of the Conference receives many inquiries about the propriety of the Sabbath observance in our synagogues. May we permit a caterer, preparing for a Bar Mitzvah meal, to prepare the meal on the Sabbath? May the congregation have its business meeting on Friday night? May the Gift Corner (Judaica Shop) be open for business on Friday night, etc., etc.? So whatever the personal observance of individuals may be, there is considerable sensitiveness as to public violation of the Sabbath by the congregation itself. The question therefore is, whether such activities as substituting on Christmas for hospital work, etc., would justify the various public violations of the Sabbath that might be involved in transportation, copying of records, etc.

First of all, it must be recorded that the motivation which led this Men's Club and leads other Men's Clubs to such help to Christians is a well-established and honored motivation since ancient times. There is both the negative motive to avoid ill-will (*m'shum eyveh*) and the positive one to increase comradely relationship (*mipney darche shalom*). See the full discussion of these two motives in Dr. Lauterbach's magnificent paper, "The Attitude of the Jew Towards the Non-Jew," *C.C.A.R. Yearbook,* XXXI, 186. The motivation therefore for these volunteer substitutes is not only worthy, it is also traditional.

But there is a more specific concern that this substitution takes place on Christmas. The Talmud (the beginning of Tractate on Idolatry, *Avodah Zara*) prohibits any association with the heathens on or within days of their holidays, lest we become involved in their worship, or lest the money that they earn in business dealings with us be contributed to the idol worship. These laws of non-association at the non-Jewish holidays are carried over in the *Shulchan Aruch, Yore Deah* 147; but it is a well established principle in Jewish law that these laws refer to actual idol worshipers; that Christians and Mohammedans are not deemed to be idolators in Jewish law, and therefore there is no objection to associating with them on Christian and Moslem holidays (see *Yore Deah* 147:12, especially the long note by Isserles). Furthermore, it has long become an unobjectionable custom to give gifts to Christians on their holidays. The great fifteenth century authority, Israel Isserlein (*Terumas Ha-deshem* #195) discusses the propriety of giving gifts on New Year's Day, which of course was a *religious* holiday (as he himself mentions) namely, the Christian Feast of Circumcision, eight days after Christmas.

Since the motivation of comradeship is traditionally praiseworthy and since there is no objection to associating with Gentiles on the days of their religious festivals, the question now arises: What sort of activity is most suitable for this expression of goodwill? The Talmud lists certain types of what we would call social service today, which it is our duty to do for non-Jews. This is discussed in the Talmud, *Gittin* 61a; namely, we sustain the poor of Gentiles, comfort their mourners, bury their dead as we do with fellow-Israelites; and in the Palestinian Talmud (J. *Gittin* 47c) there is added that in cities where Jews and Gentiles live together there is even joint collection and expenditure of funds, i.e., a sort of Community Chest. And all this social service referred even to idolators from whom in those ancient days Israelites were expected to keep away. Then how much more is it our duty to perform these social services for Christians who are not idolators at all and with whom we associate freely.

Now what should be the final question is: Which of these praiseworthy acts of social service and comradeship may be done on the Sabbath whenever, as occurred in 1971, Christmas falls on the Sabbath? First of all, any seriously sick person may be helped on the Sabbath and, in fact, it is considered a sin to hesitate and inquire whether to violate the Sabbath or not (see especially *Orah Hayyim* 328). It may be properly considered that sick people in the hospital are under the class of "seriously sick," and it is a duty to help them on the Sabbath. It is not only for the seriously sick that the Sabbath may be violated. The violation of the Sabbath is likewise permitted in order to rescue anybody from danger (see *Orah Hayyim* 329 and 330). Since saving people from danger permits the violation of the Sabbath, we can properly include our substituting not only for hospital workers, but also for firemen and policemen on these days, even if the days occur on the Sabbath.

However, it would not be proper (even though still comradely) to substitute in violation of the Sabbath for salesmen, postal clerks, etc. There is no objection and, indeed, it is comradely and in accordance with the spirit of Jewish tradition to substitute for *any* workers on their holidays, provided Sabbath violation by a congregation is not involved. But in those years in which Christmas comes on the Sabbath, it would be in consonance with Jewish tradition and the sentiment of the general Jewish community if these voluntary, comradely acts were confined to hospitals and to the institutions of public safety.

30

A DUBIOUS CONVERSION

QUESTION:

A woman came to me a year ago seeking instruction
in Judaism with a view to being converted. I gave
her the usual instruction. She is now ready for conversion. Her five-year-old son by her previous marriage
is registered in our Religious School. It turns out she
has been going with a Jewish man and wants to marry
him.

However, her previous marriage is not legally dissolved. Four years ago, she sued her husband for divorce. During the course of litigation, he was stopped
by a police officer for a traffic violation and pulled out
a gun and shot the police officer. The officer survived,
but her husband was apprehended and sentenced to 20
years in the Elgin, Illinois State Prison. Once in prison,
his attorneys argued that as a prisoner he was unable to
defend himself in court, that his civil liberties and con-
stitutional rights were being violated, and the Courts
subsequently refused to grant a divorce. Meanwhile,
this woman is living with the man she has been going
with because she seems to have no prospects of securing
an early divorce.

Does Jewish Law cover any controversy such as I
have described? What would this woman's status be?
I would be interested in any advice and information you
might have to offer. (Asked by Rabbi Richard C.
Hertz, Detroit, Michigan.)

ANSWER:

THE SITUATION which is here described is certainly a miserable one. As you properly indicate, it is very hard to know how to act here in harmony with the spirit of the Jewish legal tradition. The Christian woman whom you are converting has been "living" with a Jewish man. She is not divorced from her Christian husband because he is in the penitentiary for what virtually amounts to a life term. She has failed, so far, to get a divorce from him because his lawyers insist that being in the penitentiary, he cannot adequately defend himself. We may therefore assume that she is not likely to get a divorce from him in the near future.

The question therefore amounts to this: Is there in Jewish law a possibility of our considering her virtually divorced or free, since it is impossible for her actually to get a divorce? If that is possible (to consider or declare her free) then should you continue the process of converting her and then marry her Jewishly to the man she has been "living" with?

There is a whole mess of complications involved here. First, what is the status of a non-Jewish marriage as a legal institution in Jewish law? Are we concerned with those relationships? The concern of Jewish law with a non-Jewish marriage begins when a married non-Jew is converted to Judaism. What is the status of her Gentile marriage, now that she has become a Jewess? Basically a convert is deemed to be "a new-born child" (*Yebamos* 97b) and therefore her previous relationships do not exist. This would surely apply to her marriage relationships, since it applies even to her blood relationships. Theoretically these pre-Jewish relationships no longer exist for her and she would be permitted to marry a blood kin (of course, only if he converted and he, too, therefore would be "a newborn child"). However, this theoretical doctrine of the non-existence of a convert's previous relationships is not a practical fact in Jewish law because, as the Talmud says, (*Yebamos* 22a) if we permitted a convert to ignore these previous relationships, then the convert could say, "I left a religion of greater sanctity for one of lesser sanctity." Therefore we respect the validity of her non-Jewish marriage; she is a married woman.

It might also be mentioned that if this were a marriage between two Jews, i.e., a Jewish convict and his wife, there would be no way of voiding the marriage. If it were she who was confined (for example, in an insane asylum) there is in Jewish law a cumbersome method (consent of a hundred rabbis from three provinces) for *assigning* a divorce to her and thus freeing him to remarry. If the situation is in reverse and *he* is confined in an institution, there is no way of freeing her without his initiative. But as you know, traditional Jewish law is masculine oriented. As I have said, this is a Gentile marriage and, as far as Jewish practical law is concerned, Judaism respects its validity.

That being the case, according to traditional law the Jewish man may never marry her. In fact, even if she were never married to the convict and was an unmarried woman but lived with this Jewish man, he would not be permitted to marry her (Mishnah, *Yebamos* II, 8, and *Shulchan Aruch, Even Hoezer* 11:5). In other words, a man who lives with a woman in adultery may not be permitted to marry her even when she becomes free to marry him. However, if he *does* marry her, there are many opinions in the law that he may keep her as his wife. At all events, even if she will be finally divorced from her convict husband, it is at least *dubious* in Jewish law whether he should marry her. But if you were lenient and did marry her to him, they could remain married.

However, all this is still a theoretical question. According to the laws of the state of Michigan, this woman is a married woman, and if you officiated at a marriage, you would be compounding the crime of bigamy; so the question here cannot possibly be whether when her conversion is completed you should marry them. The laws of Michigan prevent that. Your question therefore actually must be: Shall you continue the process of converting her?

As to that question, the following must be said. Most of our conversions in the Reform movement (and, in fact, most conversions today in all branches of Judaism) are for the purpose of marriage. This very intention of marriage actually makes the conversion dubious in the eyes of Jewish law. A conversion, to be valid, must be purely for the sake of the conversion and not for any type of personal benefit. That is why we in the Reform movement had declared in "The Report of Mixed Marriage and Intermarriage" that hereafter we fully accept a conversion made for the purpose of marriage. However, according to traditional Jewish law, conversion for such a purpose has dubious standing.

Therefore we must come to the following conclusion: Since you cannot by Michigan law officiate at the marriage of this couple, and since even by Jewish law such a marriage is dubious, as has been mentioned above, then you are in fact converting this woman without the clear prospect of marriage. Therefore the conversion is traditionally, perhaps, more acceptable than many another conversion. We must, however, consider the fact that she is an unworthy woman, since "Children of Noah" are in duty bound to follow the laws of morality. On the other hand, since it is not alleged that she wantonly "lives" with other men too, she may be deemed to be a *pilegesh,* and therefore not actually sinful.

Perhaps you should proceed with the conversion and see what the future will bring. The husband may die or he may finally consent to divorce her. When that happens, you will have to decide whether the traditional dubiety about such a marriage (of a couple which has lived together) is a dubiety which you feel bound to honor or not. But that is for the future. For the present, the conversion may well continue.

31

RECONVERTING AN EX-NUN

QUESTION:

A Jewess had converted to Catholicism and had become a nun. Now she wants not only to return to Judaism, but to become a teacher of Judaism in a Jewish educational system. Should there be some special procedure for her reconversion? Should such a reconvert be permitted to become a teacher of Judaism under Jewish auspices? (Asked by Rabbi David Polish, Evanston, Illinois.)

ANSWER:

THE QUESTION of reconverts has come up rather frequently in recent years chiefly due to the decades of danger and oppression which European Jewry has had to endure. The questions generally were of the following nature: A boy who had been baptized by his parents for safety sake is now of Bar Mitzvah age. Should the rabbi permit him to become Bar Mitzvah? A young lady of a European Jewish family who had been baptized and raised as a Christian now wants to be married to a Jewish young man. Should such a marriage be conducted by a rabbi? Is there some preliminary reconversion needed, etc.?

It happens, of course, that in the traditional legal literature there is a great deal of discussion on the question of reverting proselytes, since experiences

analogous to those of the last few decades had occurred many times in the past, as for example the
conversions of Jews to Christianity in the Rhineland
during the Crusades, and three centuries later in Christian Spain. Many of these converts to Christianity returned to Judaism when things quieted down in the
Rhineland, or when they fled from Spain to Turkey
and North Africa. Most of the Halacha on the question
developed as an outcome of these events.

As far as I know there has been no systematic study
of the varying attitudes of the Halacha to reverting
apostates from era to era. But even at first glance it
would seem that in those countries where there was
comparatively little experience with mass conversion
and, therefore, with mass reconversion, the rabbis
tended to be stricter than in those countries where it
was important to encourage the great mass of ex-Jews
to return to the parental faith. This can be seen in a
contrast between the statement of Joseph Caro and of
Moses Isserles. There was no mass conversion in Poland and hence no great need for making it easy for
apostates to return. Therefore Isserles, to *Yore Deah*
268:12, mentions the rabbinical requirement for a reconvert to take a ritual bath and to promise loyalty
(*chaverus*). Of course he admits that this is not a
Torah requirement but only a cautionary rabbinical
requirement. But Joseph Caro to this section of the
Shulchan Aruch makes no mention at all of any such
a reconversion ritual. Nevertheless Caro in his *Bays
Joseph* to the *Tur does* make a reference, but it is entirely different from that of Isserles. He cites the de-

cision of Solomon ben Shimon Duran (Rashbash 89) who lived in North Africa after the first mass conversion in Spain in 1396 (and Caro himself was a refugee from the great mass conversion in 1492). Duran, as quoted by Caro, says it is wrong to require *any* ritual. Reconverts must not in any way be discouraged from returning.

However it is clear that there are a number of differences between the specific case asked about here and those referred to by Joseph Caro and his source, Solomon Duran. There is no discussion in these Spanish sources of any reconversion of Jews who had become monks or priests or also those reconverts who would want to become active and practicing teachers or Cohanim again in Judaism. While we have no references to the return of Jews who had become nuns or priests, we do have cases of Cohanim who reverted to Judaism. The question with regard to them arose immediately, as to whether they are entitled to the special sanctity which Judaism confers on a Cohen, to be called up to the Torah first, to bless the people at the Duchan. This reference is found, not among the Spanish Jews, but among the Rhineland Jews. Rabbenu Gershom, the "Light of the Exile," discusses exactly such a question, namely, whether a revert, born a Cohen, regains all his former Kedusha when he reverts. His answer (in *Machzor Vitri,* p. 96) is headed "Letter of peace" and urges that they should be restored to all their full sanctity and no one should ever remind them of their unhappy past. This answer of Rabbenu Gershom covers at least half of the question asked here;

not with regard to the status while Christian of some ex-Catholic priest or nun, but with regard to the desired status when returning to Judaism; i.e., a reconvert reachieving a sanctity or special religious status in Judaism.

There is still a further difference between the present case and the precedents of the past. The chief sources of the law arose in periods of oppression when Jews were driven into Christianity by fear of their lives. But it is not clear in this case whether this young lady lived under dangerous European conditions and fled into Christianity for fear of her life, as had happened to many. Even if she were a European, there was nothing to compel her to become a nun. If she did become a nun the presumption is that it was because of deep Catholic conviction. If there was such a deep Christian conviction in her and now when she returns she has a Jewish conviction so deep that she wishes to teach Judaism, this situation raises the question of her emotional stability. A teacher should be normal and balanced, and not subject to such sudden and extreme changes of conviction.

The situation therefore calls for caution. Even when the rabbi or the other Jewish authorities concerned become convinced that there is no emotional imbalance here, they should not accept her outright as a teacher of Judaism. This young lady is a person who had been deeply impressed with ritual procedures, and so it might be well therefore in her case to follow the counsel of Isserles, who suggests some ritual to impress the reconvert.

If this matter is supervised by a Reform rabbi, then there will necessarily be less ritual than if it were supervised by an Orthodox rabbi. An Orthodox rabbi would, as Isserles suggests, have her go to the *mikvah*. We do not generally require the *mikvah,* even for converts who are born Christians. But the other part of the ritual should surely be observed, namely, that in the presence of three, she should declare *divre chaverus*. She should make a statement under rather solemn circumstances that she will devote her heart and mind to the faith of her fathers. When this is done, we would then follow the mood of Rabbenu Gershom, never mention her past again and let her take up the sacred and priestly function of Jewish instruction.

32

ADOPTION BY COHANIM

QUESTION:

If a husband marries a widow with two children and adopts both children and the husband is a Cohen, are both children considered a Cohanim? (Asked by Dr. Jacob R. Marcus, Cincinnati, Ohio)

ANSWER:

IF THE WOMAN's first husband was a Cohen, then the children remain Cohanim, no matter how many times or whom she marries. If her first husband was not a Cohen and her second husband is a Cohen, this marriage does not affect the status of the children of a previous marriage. They are Israelites.

Of course, if she has children from this second husband and it is he who is the Cohen, then these children are Cohanim. But if the second husband is a Cohen and he *adopts* the children, does that change their status from Israelites to Cohanim?

This question, in this form, was never asked before, as far as I know, because Jewish law has almost nothing to say about adoption. To what extent are the adopted children the actual children of the adopting parent? The matter is discussed in my *Reform Responsa* (i.e., Vol. I, p. 200 ff.). The essence of the matter is this: Judging by the few Aggadic statements and one or two legal discussions, we can say that the children adopted are to be *considered* as much his children as the natural children; except, of course, that whether one is a Cohen, Levite or Israelite depends entirely on the *bloodlines,* and in this case upon the father's status. The rule is that in every marriage where no sin is involved, the status of the child follows that of the father (m. *Kiddushin,* III, 12). Therefore by blood these children are Israelites. Adoption cannot change it.

The question as to whether a child adopted by a Cohen becomes a Cohen because of this adoption can be discussed in another way. A fair analogy can be made between the status of such a child and the status of a proselyte (*ger*).

With regard to a proselyte, we are taught that it is our duty to love him and to give him every consideration. In fact, Maimonides in his famous answer to

Obadiah the proselyte said that (even though he, Obadiah, is not of Jewish descent) nevertheless when he prays he may always use the phrase, "our God and God of our fathers" (even though his fathers were not children of Israel). The reason is, as Maimonides says, that all the proselytes are children of Abraham our father. In fact, this is the law in the *Shulchan Aruch, Orah Hayyim* 199:4.

Nevertheless, although Maimonides would insist that a proselyte may use in his prayers the phrase, "God of our fathers," Maimonides would never dream of saying that because of that right the various special laws governing the proselyte should not apply to him. For example, Maimonides would never say that a proselyte, like any other Israelite, may *not* marry a *mamzer* (which actually he may) or that the proselyte may act as a judge in a case involving born Israelites (which, in fact, he may not). In other words, Maimonides would give the proselyte every *spiritual* equality with born Israelites, but he would not dream of giving him ritual or ceremonial equality which would be against specific law.

The same analogy applies to the priesthood. Since priests today have no longer kept up a careful record of their genealogy, they therefore are actually in Jewish law "priests by doubt" (*Cohen Sofek*). (Cf. *Mogen Avraham, Orah Hayyim* 457, paragraph 9.) This being the case, one might perhaps say that the child adopted by the priest should have all the rights of the priest, since the priest is only a "priest in doubt" and these priestly privileges are given him merely out of courtesy and custom (cf. *Responsa Isaac bar Sheshes,* #94). In that case, why should not an adopted child take up all these privileges which, after all, are only courtesy, not a strictly legal priestly right?

Nevertheless, while this would seem reasonable, no scholar of the law would say that this child adopted by a Cohen is henceforth forbidden to go to the cemetery, as a Cohen is forbidden; or that this child when he grows up may demand the privilege of being called to the Torah first, as a Cohen may demand. In other words, a child adopted by a Cohen has all the *spiritual* advantages (for example, the right to affection, sustenance, education) that a natural born child has; but he cannot claim the *ceremonial* privileges or restrictions which apply only to the Cohanim. If, for example, this adoption occurred in ancient times, no single authority would dream of saying that this child may eat the heave offering (*Terumah*) which is the test of priestly descent. The ritual uniqueness of a Cohen is purely a matter of bloodlines, and the modern doubts as to Cohen status are a matter of genealogy.

So the analogy with the convert is a close one. Just as a convert has all the rights of a Jew except certain special ones which depend upon actual bloodlines (such as a Jew being forbidden to marry a *mamzer*), so this child adopted by a Cohen has all the spiritual rights of a born child, but none of the ceremonial uniqueness of a born priest.

A further difficulty in this situation arises as follows: This adopted child grows up and is called up to the Torah. Since, as mentioned above, he cannot *claim* to be called to the Torah first as a right which belongs to Cohanim, one would imagine that it would be wiser not to call him up to the Torah with the title "Ha-Cohen" because often, when people would forget that he was adopted, they would ask him to come up first as a Cohen, or to go on the holidays to the *duchan*. Or he might be asked to preside at a *Pidyen ha-Ben,* all of which would be a considerable embarrassment, calling time and time again for uncomfortable explanations. He would constantly need to explain that he is adopted and not a Cohen by birth. Furthermore, it would be a life-long embarrassment to his parents, who may not want to be reminded all through their lives that this is not their son by birth.

Of course, not much harm would be done if he were called up first to the Torah, since there are some occasions when this is permissible. For example, if a Cohen (the only Cohen in the synagogue) came late to services and he is in the middle of his prayers when the Torah is being read, he may not be interrupted in his prayers in order to be called up first, which is the Cohen's prerogative. An Israelite is called in his place (*Orah Hayyim* 135:5). Isserles adds (based on *Maharik* #9) that if on fast days when they come to read the Torah the only priest present had not fasted, he cannot be called up to the Torah and, again, an Israelite is called up in his place. So if by chance this adopted person is called up to the Torah first, no harm has been done. Besides, Rabbi Jose in the Talmud says, "I know I am not a Cohen, but if I am called up to the *duchan,* I go" (*Shabbas* 118b). So while no great harm would be done, the situation might lead to uncomfortable explanations.

So even as far as the blessing of the community by the priest, there is this Talmudic precedent that it would not be so terrible a thing if a non-priest blessed the people. After all, in the daily service at the close of the *Shemone Esra,* before *Sim Shalom,* the reader reads the priestly blessing; and then, of course, it is an established custom that if for some reason a Cohen does not participate in the *duchan* (although it *is* a commandment) he can step out of the synagogue.

Perhaps the best solution would be in the community in which he lives and in which he is known, to be called up to the Torah, not as "Moses the priest, the son of Amram the priest," but as "Moses, the son of Amram the priest." This would be correct and as for cities in which he is not known, he need not claim to be a Cohen and so will have no embarrassment.

33

CONVERT BURIED IN
CHRISTIAN CEMETERY

QUESTION:

A woman converted to Judaism (with her daughter and her husband) is now dying of cancer and asks that when she is dead, she be buried in the Dutch Reformed churchyard, in the family plot or near the graves of her parents. Has she the right to make this request? Should the rabbi officiate at such a funeral? (Asked by Rabbi Elihu Schagrin, Binghamton, New York.)

ANSWER:

IT MUST BE CLEAR at the outset that this convert, who is now so dangerously sick, is a full Jewess. The fact that she is a converted and not a born Jewess does not lessen the permanence of her Jewish status. According to the law, if a convert returns to his original faith, he is a sinful Jew but still a Jew. We have here, therefore, the question of a Jewess who asks to be buried in a Christian cemetery.

On the face of it, there is no way for a rabbi to agree to this request. We make efforts to remove Jewish bodies which are buried in Christian cemeteries, to rebury them in Jewish cemeteries. How can we agree to having a Jew, then, buried in a Christian cemetery?

It is true that in general it is considered to be a Mitzvah to obey the requests of the dying, but not when these requests would violate the law. However, there are so many human reasons why one would wish to accede to the wish of a woman dying, racked with pain, that I must confess that one should try to see whether there is not some way in which we could ease her mental anguish and agree to her request to be buried beside her parents.

In the first place, a convert's desire to express her love and her reverence for her Gentile parents is not contrary to Jewish law. Even though as a general principle a convert is deemed to be "like a newborn child" and therefore is no longer related to the family into which she was born, nevertheless the Talmud itself says that this rule is not followed too strictly. Otherwise she could marry her Gentile brother (if he converted). The continuing bond thus implied in the Talmud with the non-Jewish family in which she was born is developed in later law, that a convert may certainly say *Kaddish* for her Gentile parents. See the references in *Recent Reform Responsa* (i.e., Vol. II) page 136, ff.

On the basis of the respect for one's family bond bridging the gulf between the different religions, we have permitted memorial plaques, etc. for Christian parents; and furthermore, in our Reform movement, we have also permitted the burial of close Christian relatives in the family plot in a Jewish cemetery. So while it is true that we have not yet discussed the question of a Jew (i.e., this convert) being buried beside her parents in the *Christian* cemetery, we have permitted the burial of the Christian parents beside their daughter in a family plot in the Jewish cemetery.

It must be further stated that we do not fail in Jewish law to ascribe a certain spiritual status to the Christian cemetery. The Talmud (in *Taanis* 16a) speaks of going to non-Jewish cemeteries on fast days (as well as to the Jewish ones) in order that we may feel humble and realize our mortality. The *Shulchan Aruch* (*Orah Hayyim* 579:3) speaks of going on fast days to weep in the cemeteries; and Isserles adds, "If there are no Jewish graves available, we go to Gentile cemeteries." So there is no objection, for example, if her Jewish friends went to the Christian cemetery for the interment.

Also, we must recall the famous passage in *Gittin* 61a that we sustain the Gentile sick and bury the Gentile dead, and the Tosefta adds, "We eulogize and comfort them." Rashi to the Talmudic passage makes the cautionary statement, "That does not mean we bury them with the Jewish dead in the Jewish cemetery." So, therefore, Rashi clearly implies that "for the sake of peace" we would bury a Gentile in the Gentile cemetery. See all relevant references gathered in *Reform Responsa,* (Vol. I) page 143 ff. If, therefore, this woman had not converted at all, it is clear that the rabbi could officiate at her funeral in the Christian cemetery.

But she *did* convert and she *is* a Jewess. Jewish tradition would be against burying a Jewess in a Christian cemetery (otherwise the question would not have been asked at all). Furthermore, the idea of a rabbi officiating for a Jewess in a Christian cemetery would not be a good precedent. It would encourage other converts to make similar requests.

I therefore suggest the following which is, frankly, a practical compromise: The rabbi should assure the woman that her requests will be fulfilled. He should officiate, certainly in the home or in the chapel. As for the interment, perhaps it would be better if that were done by the Dutch Reformed minister. There is perhaps some objection, too, to having a Jewess buried by a Christian minister, but in all likelihood the laws of that Christian cemetery may require that none but a Christian officiate. It would therefore end up as follows: The rabbi would officiate at this Jewess's funeral in the home or chapel, and because of the denominational difficulties (i.e., the rules of the cemetery) the Dutch Reformed minister would officiate there.

34

STUDY OF FOETAL MATERIAL

QUESTION:

The British government's Department of Health and Social Security is inquiring of the various religious groups as to their attitude regarding use of foetuses and foetal material for research. Would such use of the material be permitted by Jewish tradition? (Asked by Mrs. S. B. Rosenberg, Organising Secretary of the Union of Liberal and Progressive Synagogues, London, England.)

ANSWER:

IT IS UNDERSTOOD that the question is not whether abortion should or should not be permitted; in other words, whether or not the foetus, while in the body of the mother, may be destroyed or removed. The question of the *intentional* destruction of the foetus is a moot question in Jewish law, and the answer would depend upon many considerations as, for example, whether the woman was condemned to death (for a capital crime) and then the foetus might be destroyed before the mother was executed. It depends also upon whether the unborn child is endangering the life of the mother. These and other cases are cited under the heading "Abortion" in *Recent Reform Responsa,* p. 188 ff.

The question here is different, namely, whether after the foetus is available (as for example, after a miscarriage), the foetus must be handled reverently as if it were a deceased human being, or whether it may be simply disposed of or, as this question specifically asks, whether it may be used for scientific research. In other words, does a foetus have sanctity, as the body of the dead has? If it does have sanctity, then just as there is objection to autopsy, so there would be objection to dissection of a foetus.

Although the question asked here is not the same as the question of abortion, nevertheless some of the considerations involved in the question of abortion are basic, also, to the present inquiry. These questions are: 1) Is the foetus to be considered human; that is to say, is it the body of a deceased person? 2) Does Jewish law require that the foetus be buried?

The justification for the first question arising at all is that there are religious traditions in which a foetus is deemed sacred, no matter what its age is. For example, the Catholic Church requires a Catholic nurse to baptize even the most primitive and shapeless foetus resulting, let us say, from a miscarriage. Is there, then, a similar sanctity ascribed to a foetus in Jewish tradition?

As to the possible sanctity of the foetus, the question asked here does not refer to the potential sanctity of the foetus while it is still in the mother's body, which would bring us back to the question of abortion. In this case there is some relevance in the question of the *age* of the foetus. For example, there is no objection to destroying a foetus that is less than forty days old (see Solomon of Skola, in his Responsa *Beth Sholomo,* Lemberg, 1878, *Choshen Mishpot* 132). But even if the foetus is older than forty days, there is a strong line in the Jewish legal tradition which does not consider the unborn child to be a separate soul (see Rashi to *Sanhedrin* 72b) and also Joshua Falk (16th-17th century) in his classic commentary *M'iras Enoyim* to the passage in *Choshen Mishpot* 425, end of his section 8: "Every foetus that does not come out or has not come into the light of the world is not to be described as a *nefesh,* i.e., a living soul."

A modern summary of the law was made by the late Sephardic Chief Rabbi of Israel, Ben Zion Uziel, who said in his *Mishp'tey Uziel,* III, 46 and 47, that after a general analysis of the subject, an unborn foetus is actually not a *nefesh* at all and has no independent life. As a matter of fact in Talmudic times, we are told that there was a place outside of the city in which people disposed of amputated limbs and where women buried their stillbirths. It is evident that foetuses were just informally disposed of (*Ketubos* 20b).

The second question involved is whether the foetus must by Jewish law be buried. This question is, of course, bound up with the preceding question as to whether the foetus is to be deemed as having been a living soul, since all human beings must by Jewish law, when deceased, be buried in the earth. This special question has received a great deal of discussion in Jewish law. Its source is the Tosefta in *Sabbath* 15:7 and the Talmud, *Sabbath* 135b. The law is summed up by Joseph Caro in his *Beth Joseph* to the *Tur, Yore Deah* 266, and in modern times by Jacob Ettlinger of Altona-Hamburg (1798-1871) in his *Binyan Zion,* #133. The overwhelming weight of authority is that a stillborn does not require burial by law.

Although there is no mandate to bury the stillborn, there is nevertheless some reason why it might be *preferable* to bury it, namely, the possibility of ritual uncleanliness. Ritual uncleanliness is generally not applicable since the destruction of the Temple. See Maimonides, *Yad Tumas Ochlin* 16:8. But it is still held to be applicable to people of priestly descent (Cohanim). Therefore there is objection in the traditional law for a man of priestly descent to study medicine if that study involved dissection of dead bodies. This question comes up, practically, whenever amputated limbs from a living patient are to be disposed of. Must they be buried or not? The clearest opinion on this question is given by the outstanding authority, Jacob Reischer of Metz (died 1733) in his *Shevus Yaacov,* Vol. II, #10. He says there is no mandate to bury amputated limbs; it is sufficient if they are put away and thus kept from contact with priests. It is not irrelevant that in the Talmudic discussion indicating that a foetus is not a separate living being, the foetus is called *yerech immo,* "the limb of the mother." At all events, we may say that when the Talmud tells us in *Ketubos* 20b that people who had limbs amputated buried the limbs and that women who had a miscarriage buried the foetuses in a certain place, that this was not because there was a *mandate* to bury these objects, but just to dispose of them and keep them out of the way because of possibly defiling priests. Hence the answer to the question asked must have this footnote: The same objection that there is to a Cohen dissecting a corpse in the study of anatomy would hold, also, with regard to his working on the dissection of a foetus, since the one objection to such handling of the foetus is a question of the Cohen's ritual uncleanliness.

Other than that one exception, one may sum up as follows: The overwhelming bulk of opinion in the law is that the foetus is not to be considered to have been a living being; that, therefore, it does not require burial. Hence we may say that the general opinion of Jewish legal tradition is that it has no sanctity and may well be used for scientific study, especially if such a study leads to the saving or safeguarding of human life, which is always a prime virtue in Jewish tradition.

35

DISINTERMENT DUE TO A LABOR STRIKE

QUESTION:

San Francisco has had for some weeks now a strike of the gravediggers. This fact has caused special unhappiness to Orthodox Jewish families because of the impossibility of immediate burial. The bodies must be stored until the strike is finally ended. Now it has been suggested by some Orthodox scholars that the bodies be buried immediately in the neighboring city of Oakland to which the strike does not extend. The only question, then, is whether it will be permissible later when the strike is over to disinter the bodies from the Oakland cemetery to rebury them in the San Francisco cemetery. (From Louis J. Freehof, San Francisco, California)

ANSWER:

THE EFFECTS of a labor strike on Jewish burial practices are multifarious. First, what about the custom or law of immediate burial? What about the practice of embalming, which is frowned upon by Jewish law and custom, but which is inevitable since refrigeration storage space is limited? Third, if the body is not buried in the ground for weeks or months, when is the process of mourning to begin? These and other questions are involved in the situation created by the strike. The question now asked is a special one, namely:

Would disinterment from the Oakland cemetery be permitted after the strike is over, for reburial in San Francisco?

There is no question that the answer must be in the affirmative. It *is* permitted. But first of all one must dispose of an apparent objection stated in the *Shulchan Aruch, Yore Deah* 363:2, namely, that it is forbidden to take a body from one city to another for burial if there is a Jewish cemetery in the city where the man died. In the first place, because of the strike there is no available cemetery in the city where the man died; and in the second place, the exceptions are given immediately in this same section of the *Shulchan Aruch*. The exceptions are: to bury the man in the land of Israel, or to bring him to the burial place of his fathers, or if before his death he asked to be taken to his home city (see Isserles).

In the present case we may assume that it would have been the desire of the departed to be buried in San Francisco, the home city, especially if there are other members of the family already buried in the San Francisco cemetery. In fact there is a famous responsum (#369) of Solomon b. Adret from Algiers which has become the classic one in all such cases: A man and his son came from Oran to Algiers for business (this was at the end of the 14th century). He became sick and told his son that should he die, he would like to be buried in his home town (i.e., Oran). He died of that sickness in Algiers but there was a war going on and the son could not take the body to Oran. As soon as the war was over they asked whether they may move the body and whether, now, in order to make it possible to move the body, they may use quicklime to hasten its decay. Solomon b. Adret gave full permission to do so.

The following, then, are the reasons why, after the strike is over, the bodies may be disinterred from the Oakland cemetery: First, due to the strike, there is no available cemetery in San Francisco. Secondly, if the man has family already buried in San Francisco, he is being disinterred to be buried with his family. Thirdly, if the burial in Oakland is a burial *al t'nai* (a conditional burial), with the understanding that the body is to be transferred later (*Yore Deah* 331:1). It was on the basis of conditional burial that Isaac Elchanan Spektor (*Eyn Yitzchok, Yore Deah* 33) gave permission for a temporary burial in a mausoleum (see *Ozar Dinim u Minhagim*, article *"Pinui Mesim"*).

36

BURIAL ON THE HOLIDAY
AFTER A STRIKE

QUESTION:

The San Francisco gravediggers have been on strike for many weeks. Over a hundred bodies have piled up in the Sinai Memorial Chapel. There are good prospects that the strike may be settled Sunday, October 3, 1971. May the bodies be buried the next day which will be the first day of Succos? (Asked by Louis J. Freehof, San Francisco, California)

ANSWER:

THERE IS ABSOLUTELY no question that the bodies may be buried on the first day of Succos. The *Shulchan Aruch, Orah Hayyim* 526:1-3, says that the only days forbidden for burial are Sabbath and Yom Kippur. If a body is ready for burial (and these stored bodies are more than ready) it must be buried on the first day of the holiday if it is ready then. The only restriction is that certain preparations may be made only by non-Jews. It is non-Jews who must sew the shrouds and make the coffin. But to put the body into the ground i.e., inter) Jews may do it even on the first day of a holiday. The *Shulchan Aruch* specifically prohibits keeping the body over to the second day of the holiday, so that Jews may be permitted to do the complete task.

Some rabbis might raise an objection that this applies to a person who died on a holiday, but that these bodies that have waited for weeks might as well wait another day. But this is a mistaken argument; there is no Jewish permission to delay the burial of a body once there is the possibility of burying it. But in the case that such a mistaken objection is raised, then for the sake of communal peace, those bodies should be buried first whose rabbis raise no such objection.

One more caution: There is no requirement for any type of mourning at the reinterment of a body. This must be considered a reinterment since the formal closing of the coffin after the funeral service weeks ago was deemed the formal burial after which mourning could begin. There is a short mourning required when a body is *disinterred*, not when it is reinterred. But some people may imagine that some sort of mourning is required. Therefore it is good to follow the procedure of the great Hungarian authority, Moses Sofer (in his Responsa *Yore Deah* 353) when at the time of a mass disinterment from a cemetery commanded by the government, he forbade anyone telling the relatives of the dead the time of the disinterment, so that the whole community should not sit in mourning. His example guides us. When the interment takes place, you are not in duty bound, in fact I would say you are discouraged, from informing the relatives.

37

WHICH BODY TO BURY FIRST

QUESTION:

A long grave-diggers' strike has caused the accumulation of about one hundred and fifty bodies in the Sinai Memorial Chapel. This strike is at last over. The question now arises whether Jewish tradition prescribes a certain sequence according to which bodies must be buried. (Asked by Louis J. Freehof, San Francisco, California.)

ANSWER:

IN THE PAST they did not have the present-day experience of a grave-diggers' strike. Therefore there is no precise statement in the law as to the order in which a large number of bodies must now be buried whose burial had been delayed till now because of the strike. Nevertheless, they knew of certain other types of delay. A body was sometimes kept over for a time in order that relatives may come from distant places, or to provide proper shrouds, etc. (Cf. *Shulchan Aruch Yore Deah* 357.) These delays gave rise to certain decisions which have some relevance to the question raised here.

The first clear source on this question is the Gaonic booklet *Evel Rabbosi* (*Semochos*), Chapter II. In that passage there is a discussion as to who would be buried first when there is more than one body awaiting burial.

At the outset the rule given is that the one that dies first is buried first; but the rule continues, that if the first body is to be delayed (for some good reason) then we may not delay the burial of the second because of the delay in burying the one that died first. Then follows a sequence of the relative importance of the people whose bodies are awaiting burial. This sequence of relative importance is carried over also in the relevant passage in the *Shulchan Aruch, Yore Deah* 354, namely, if one was an ignorant man and the other learned, you bury the learned man first; if one was a man and the other was a woman, you bury the woman first (because they believed that a woman's body decays sooner). It is questionable, however, whether the distinction of relative importance of the deceased people can be considered applicable today. It is, for example, a generally accepted rule in the law that we do not hold nowadays to the special status and privileges of a *Talmud Chochem*.

However, of all these regulations, one at least does concern us in relation to our present question. The law is that normally we would bury first the one that died first. Nevertheless if the one that died first is being delayed for some good reason, then we bury the other one first, although he had not died first. The chief responsa discussion of this is by Abraham Z'vi of Pietrikow, in his responsa *B'ris Abraham* (*Orah Hayyim* #14). (This responsum is cited also in the *Pith-che Teshuva*.) This scholar made an analogy between the burial of one of two bodies and another problem which actually was the question put before

him. Two children were to be circumcised. In the case
of one child it was a delayed circumcision because of
the child's health (i.e., this child was now, let us say,
twenty days old). The other child was in the eighth
day, the regular date of circumcision. The Mohelim
wanted to circumcise the older child first because it
was born first, but the rabbi said they were mistaken.
There is no requirement in the law that an older child
should be circumcised first. What matters here is that
the command to circumcise on the eighth day applies
now to the younger child and that command cannot be
delayed, it must be fulfilled first. He then makes the
analogy between this case and the case of two bodies
that are waiting for burial. If one body was delayed
(of the man who died first), the other body (of the
man who died second) must be buried at once (i.e.,
not to wait for the first death to be buried first) because the duty to bury is immediate.

However, even this distinction is not to be taken *too*
strictly, as can be seen from the earlier discussion of
this matter of the two circumcisions by Elijah ben
Samuel of Lublin (*Yad Eliahu,* #41). He makes the
same decision (as did Abraham Z'vi of Pietrikow
later) namely, that the child who is now in his eighth
day should be circumcised first. However, he adds that
if the older child is brought to the synagogue first
(where the circumcisions took place) then we are not
in duty bound to wait for the younger child. In other
words (if the analogy is sound between the number of
circumcisions and the number of burials) then it is
clear that the law is not too strict in either case.

Greenwald in his *Kol Bo,* page 176, also discusses this matter. He cites the opinion of Solomon Kluger of Brody, which is to the same effect as the other opinions, namely, that that body which is now due for burial must be buried even though there are older bodies waiting. (Please note that Greenwald's reference is incorrect. He says *Tuv Ta'am V'da'as,* Vol. I, 287; it should be Vol. I, 285.)

As a general guidance from the past laws cited, we may conclude that the following is the preferred procedure:

1. Whoever has *just* died (and now that the strike is over it is possible to bury him or her at once) he or she is the *first* to be buried. Their burial must not be delayed (except, of course, for legitimate reasons such as waiting for relatives, etc.). Certainly their burial must not be delayed until the stored-up bodies are buried.

2. As for the stored-up bodies, the *Shulchan Aruch,* based on "Semochos" would seem to say that those who died first should be buried first, but it is evident from the *Shulchan Aruch* itself that that rule applies *only* when the burial can be immediate. When, however, there is delay, then the order of precedence by time of death no longer holds and there is no required order of burial.

This can be seen also by analogy with the statement of *Pith-che Teshuva* to this rule in the *Shulchan Aruch.* The *Pith-che Teshuva* says that if the two bodies here discussed had both died on the Sabbath when burial was impossible, then there was no longer any precedent at all between them. Thus here, too, since burial was impossible for all these bodies at the time of their death, there is now no precedence among them.

3. In the law it was required that women must be buried before men. That was because they believed that women's bodies decayed earlier than men's bodies (see heading to the next section in the *Shulchan Aruch* and the statement of the case in the *Tur, ibid.*). This might indicate a line for our guidance. If any of the stored-up bodies are in bad condition, they should be buried first.

38

CREMATION ASHES BURIED AT HOME

QUESTION:

A congregant who intends to be cremated, desires that her ashes be buried in an unmarked grave on her own property. What is the judgment of Jewish law (and the secular law) on this matter? (Asked by Rabbi Norman D. Hirsh, Seattle, Washington)

ANSWER:

As FOR the secular law on this matter, it certainly varies from state to state, so the enquirer had better ask the authorities in his own state whether burial of ashes may be permitted in private property. But as for the opinion of Jewish law on this matter, there are a number of basic questions involved. First, is the cemetery the only place permitted to receive the burial of bodies or of ashes; or has one's private property some religious status in this matter? Secondly, while cremation is generally forbidden by Orthodox law, the question is whether, once a body has been cremated, the ashes may or may not be buried in the communal cemetery.

First, then, as to the status of the communal cemetery in Jewish law: Basically, burials in Palestine in the days of the Bible and Mishnah were all on *private* property. People bought caves and cut niches into the walls and so buried their dead. So it was with Abraham and his family, and so the custom continued as is evidenced, for example, by the discussion of the niches in a cave in Mishnah *Baba Basra,* VI, 8. Very likely the use of community cemeteries in place of private burial grounds developed in Babylon where there were no rocky caves to keep the bodies securely protected. At all events, even to this day the cemetery has no fixed status in Jewish law comparable, for example, to the status of the communal synagogue and the communal school. Members of a community can compel each other to build a synagogue or establish a school. But there is no law compelling a community to have a cemetery. In fact, many small communities in Europe did not own cemeteries but transported their dead to the cemetery of a larger neighboring community.

The fact that the communal cemetery has no actual legal status simply means that they exist as an established custom and are only a legal requirement to the extent that an established custom becomes a legal requirement. But, of course, this dubious situation indicates that a man's personal property still has a status in this regard which has never been abolished. (For references as to the high status of one's own property for burial, see *Modern Reform Responsa*, page 257.) Thus, if a body were to be buried on one's own estate, the civil law might not permit it, but Jewish law cannot well prohibit it.

This brings us to the question of cremation. When the practice of cremation developed about a century ago in Germany, Rabbi Meyer Lerner of Hamburg, published a whole book, *Chaye Olom,* marshalling the opinion of many contemporary authorities that cremation is against Jewish religious law and, in fact, when that sin has been permitted, the ashes be not buried in the cemetery. However, other authorities took the opinion that the ashes *should* be buried, and David Hoffman in *Melamed L'Ho-il, Yore Deah* 113, has a compromise opinion and says that it is not obligatory to bury the ashes in the cemetery but it is not forbidden to do so.

Thus there is some doubt in the law whether the ashes may be buried in the cemetery and, depending upon the Orthodoxy of the community, it is a question whether the ashes would be *permitted* to be buried in the cemetery. It might therefore even be deemed preferable to avoid the dispute and bury the ashes on one's own property. Of course if we are referring to a Reform congregation, which does not object to the burial of ashes, then it is a matter of choice; and in that case, one can merely say that there can be no objection in Jewish law against the burial of ashes on one's own property.

However, one warning must be given: If the fashion of cremation spreads, and if the burial of the ashes in one's own property likewise becomes rather prevalent, then the status of the communal cemetery which is an important part of communal life, might thereby be endangered. If that happens it may be wiser to prohibit any such use of private property. But unless that happens, one may sum up the law as follows:

One's own property as a burial place has never lost its status in Jewish law. The burial of ashes of cremation is to be considered permitted if not obligatory. Therefore (certainly from the liberal point of view) there can be no real objection to the planned interment of the ashes in the family's own property rather than in the communal cemetery.

39

POSITION OF THE BODY IN THE GRAVE

QUESTION:

> Is there definite Jewish law or established prevalent custom for the posture of the body in the grave and the position, the direction, in which it must be laid? (Asked by Louis J. Freehof, San Francisco, California)

ANSWER:

WITH REGARD to the posture of the body, Jewish custom is so consistent that it amounts to definite law. The Talmud in *Baba Bathra* 73b (at the bottom) mentions that the generation of the Exodus that had died in the wilderness were all buried lying on their back. In the Palestinian Talmud in j. *Nazir* 9:3 (in the regular one-volume Krotochin edition, p. 57d, the middle) the question is asked, "What is the normal way for the body to lie?" The answer is given as follows: the feet straight and the hands on the heart. This is taken to mean that the body lies on its back, straightened out. It is necessary to note this because many ancient people were buried in a crouched, womb-like posture. So this custom of laying the body on its back, straightened out, is so universally observed that it is recorded as law in the *Shulchan Aruch, Yore Deah* 362:2.

While the posture of the body is agreed upon and may be considered law, namely, that it lies on its back, straightened out, the direction in which the body is laid is not universally agreed upon, i.e., the customs differ whether the body should be laid feet to the east and head to the west, or the reverse; or whether it should be laid head to the north and feet to the south, or the reverse. In fact the custom of directions in burial varies even further than the question of the cardinal points of the compass. Abraham Isaac Glick, Rabbi of Toltchva, in his responsa Volume 3, speaks of people being buried in some communities with their feet pointing to the gate (in order to be ready to march at the resurrection of the dead at the coming of the Messiah). Whether it is a law or a local custom is an important distinction which must be made in special cases. For example, Abraham Isaac Glick (Volume 3, #83) had the following case: A woman had been buried with her head to the south and her feet to the north, which was the reverse of the direction that bodies were buried in that cemetery. The question now was: Should she be disinterred in order to rebury her in conformity with the direction of the other bodies? If it were a fixed law to bury in a certain direction, he might possibly have permitted the disinterment (although with some hesitation) but he absolutely forbade it. He gives his reason clearly, that there is no source at all in the legal literature for preferring burial in one direction rather than in another, and he says that is why the *Shulchan Aruch* (in *Yore Deah, ibid.*) when it speaks of the *posture* of the body does not at all mention the *direction* in which it should lie.

In the responsum of Yekuthiel Enzil, Rabbi of Przemzl and of Strij (responsa *Mahari Enzil,* #36 and #37) the practical question involving direction of the body was a different one and also important. A house had been built and bought by a Jew. After the house was built and bought, bodies were found buried in the grounds. If they were Jewish bodies a Cohen would not be permitted to enter the house. The questioner wanted to decide the question as to whether they were Jewish bodies or not by the direction in which the bodies were laid. He answers that there is no basis in the law for a preference of direction.

There is also, of course, the famous responsum of Moses Sofer (*Chatam Sofer, Yore Deah* 332). This is quoted fully in the *Pith-che Teshuvot* to the passage in the *Shulchan Aruch*. Moses Sofer's responsum, as do the two responsa just mentioned, also involves a practical problem. Here the problem was the following: A community needed more grave space. It had a piece of land adjoining the old filled-up cemetery. But the shape of this unused land would necessitate changing the directions of the rows from the directions followed in the older part of the cemetery. For example, instead of the rows running from north to south, they would in this new part of the cemetery run from east to west. Is this change of direction to be permitted? In his answer, Moses Sofer proves from the discussion of the burial cave in *Baba Bathra* 101a & b that the direction in which the body is placed in the grave makes no difference.

The matter is summed up by Yehiel Epstein in his authoritative code *Aruch Ha-Schulchan, Yore Deah* 362, in which he says that there is no basis for any preference of one direction over another. It all depends upon the local custom. Nevertheless it is important to follow the custom, whatever it happens to be in the locality. In other words, all the bodies must be buried in the direction consistent with the burying of all the other bodies in that city.

The reason for being careful to bury in the direction consistent with the local custom was that sometimes they purposely buried heretics and suicides in a direction different from the other graves. Because of this custom it might happen, at some later date, that when a body is found to have been buried in a direction different from that of the others, people might imagine that this body was *purposely* so buried because it was the body of an evil person. Such an opinion might be a grave injustice to the memory of the departed.

Therefore in the responsum from *Yad Yitzchok* mentioned above, in the case of the woman who by accident or carelessness was buried in a direction different from the rest of the bodies, he forbids (as was said above) disinterment of the body, inasmuch as the direction in which it lies is not a matter of strict legal requirement. However, in order that her memory might not be slandered in the future, he suggests that the tombstone be placed not at her head, as is usually the custom, but at her feet, so that it should appear consistent with all the other graves.

The whole question is fully discussed by Greenwald in his *Kol Bo*, p. 177 ff. To all the references mentioned above, he adds another important fact, namely, that many famous scholars had specifically asked that their bodies be buried in a direction different from that of the other graves. This in itself is proof that the choice of any special direction is not required by law.

To sum up: The law is quite definite that all bodies be laid on their back but that the custom varies from community to community as to the direction in which the body must be laid. The general feeling of the scholars is that whatever the local custom happens to be, it should be followed consistently. But even this consistency is not a *legal* requirement since, as cited by Greenwald, many great scholars specifically asked to be buried in a direction different from the rest of the bodies in the cemetery. At all events, if the body is laid on its back, then all the requirements of the law as to *posture* and *placement* have been completely fulfilled.

40

LIGHTS AT HEAD OF COFFIN

QUESTION:

At our funeral services there are usually two lights, candles or electric, burning at the head of the coffin. Is this custom based upon tradition? Must there always be *two* lights? (Asked by Louis J. Freehof, San Francisco, California.)

ANSWER:

THERE ARE MANY types of light that are used in connection with funerals and mourning: one, the seven-day memorial (*shiva*) lamp in the house of mourning; two, the annual *yahrzeit* lamp in the family dwelling; three, the candle that pious people would light on Yom Kippur in memory of their dead (the *nehoma light.*) And now, in addition, the question concerns lights that burn near the coffin during the funeral service.

The first three lights mentioned have already been discussed in various places in *Reform Responsa,* Vol. III, 14, 129, etc., but this particular question about lights at the coffin during the service is one that I have not been asked.

First let us dismiss one possible explanation for this light, namely that it is for the purpose of illuminating the face of the departed. It is contrary to Jewish tradition to look at the face of the dead (b. *Horayos* 13b) and therefore tradition is generally opposed to having the coffin open at all during services (Greenwald, *Kol Bo,* p. 36, #10). It is clear, therefore, that if these lights were for the purpose of illuminating the face of the dead while the coffin is open, it would be simply compounding a sin.

We must therefore look for another source for the lights placed near the body of the dead. Tekuchinsky (of Israel) in the first volume of his two-volume work on mourning laws, *Gesher Ha-Chaim* (*The Bridge of Life*) in Volume I, page 49, gives the Palestinian custom (which is of course followed elsewhere) as to handling the body at the time of death. He says that twenty minutes after the time of death, the body is removed from the bed where it died and placed upon the ground. Then, he says, a light is kindled near his head, or, many lights are kindled around him. Some say (he continues) that as many as twenty-six candles should be kindled around the whole body while the bystanders (usually the *Chevre Kadisha*) recite (three times) the verse from Isaiah 2:5: "O house of Jacob, come let us walk in the light of the Lord." Then again in Chapter 17, page 157 of the same volume, he deals with the question of whether these lights may be lit on *Yom Tov* if the person dies on *Yom Tov*. He answers as follows: "In those places where they are careful about lighting a light at the time when the person dies (i.e., as above) they may do so also on *Yom Tov*."

Joseph Schwartz in his book of funeral customs, *Hadras Kodesh,* in the closing section, *Likkute Dinim,* #25, also mentions the fact that we light lights by the dead. But he does not say how many lights are to be lit.

Also Greenwald, in his compendium, *Kol Bo,* page 23, says: "In many places they light candles after the person dies."

What is the purpose of these lights, except perhaps the general symbol of the verse in Proverbs 20:27, that the soul of man is a light kindled by God. It is possible that there is a practical purpose, namely, that since now the body will be washed, the lights were simply for the purpose of seing the work more clearly. This explanation is quite possible. But there is also a strange and a mystical explanation for those lights. This explanation is found in the published ethical and ritual will left by Chaim Chiskia Medini, the author of the well-known collection of responsa, *S'dey Chemed.* He speaks of handling of the body of the dead (in this case, his own body). He says that the body should be subjected symbolically to the "four species of execution" practiced by the Jewish Sanhedrin upon criminals. The purpose of symbolically subjecting the deceased to these four deaths (*arba missos bes din*) was that whatever sin the departed might have committed, he will now receive its legal punishment and he will be forgiven. Therefore Chaim Chiskia Medini asks that the following shall be done to his body: When it is being lowered onto the stone floor, that for the last handbreadth, it should actually be *dropped* onto the stone floor. This will be a symbol of execution by *"sekilla,"* "stoning." Then a candle should be lit beside his body and some of the drops of wax be allowed to fall upon his body, and that will be a symbol of the mode of execution *"serefa,"* "burning." And so through symbols of the other two deaths. This symbolization of the "four deaths" was a fairly widespread custom. Cf. *Ha-Kuntres Ha-Yechieli,* II, 46b.

Thus it would seem possible that these candles had a mystic origin besides the practical usefulness of helping in the washing of the body.

While the above may be a sufficient explanation of the custom asked about, yet after all, it would seem strange that the candle placed by the body at the time of death should be carried over to the funeral service. Actually there is a further explanation closer to being the true origin.

The Mishnah (*Berachos* VII, 6) says, "We do not recite a blessing over the light or over the spices of the dead." The Talmud (in *Berachos* 53a) discusses this and Rashi explains the "light of the dead" by saying that in order to honor the dead, they had candles as they led the body to the grave. This custom of the candles lit in the procession of the funeral is also given in the *Shulchan Aruch, Orah Hayyim* 298:12. Here, then, we have what may be the most plausible source of the custom. It was a well-established practice since Mishnaic times to have candles as part of the funeral procession, and thus it was a part of the preliminary to the procession, namely, the service in the home (or chapel).

It is to be noticed that neither in Tekuchinsky nor in Greenwald, nor in Joseph Schwartz, is there any mention of numbers of lights. As for the position of the lights, since in ancient times the candles led the procession, it is logical that they should be at the head of the coffin.

41

REFUSING TO HANDLE
AN INFECTIOUS BODY

QUESTION:

> A person died of hepatitis. It was deemed dangerous for the undertaker's men to handle the body, to wash or embalm it. Finally, at some risk, the necessary work was done to the body. But the question arose whether a *Chevra Kadisha,* which after all is not a profit-making business but a communal servant, may refuse to handle a body which is dangerous to handle. (By Louis J. Freehof, San Francisco)

ANSWER:

I HAVE MADE enquiry from Dr. Cyril Wecht, the coroner of our district (he is a member of the Temple and a friend). I wanted to know whether the authorities, the coroner's office or the hospitals, do not forewarn an undertaker if the body is dangerous to handle and whether, indeed, they do not deliver the body already sealed up in a casket and forbid the casket to be opened. If the latter is the case, then the question really never will arise. Dr. Wecht told me that there is no clear practice on the matter in our county, but he promised to write to the medical officers out west to find out whether dangerous bodies are not delivered with the warning that they are not to be handled at all. But assuming that there is no such legal warning or prohibition, then the question which is asked is a real one and must be considered.

One would have expected that there would be many such situations discussed in the law. After all, Jews lived in Europe during the great plagues which decimated the population. Among the Gentiles the bodies were just dragged away in carts, from house to house, and buried in mass graves. What did the Jews do with those Jews who died of the plague? Disappointingly enough, I have not found any reference in the legal literature to this specific situation. However, in general we have certain guide-lines.

First, it must be stated that burial is both a positive and a negative commandment (negative in the sense that it is forbidden to neglect to do so) and the duty of burial is incumbent upon all, not only the community but also the individual. If, for example, a man finds a body lying on the road, he must bury it then and there. Such a body is appropriately called *Mayss Mitzvah*. Even a priest, a Cohen, who may not defile himself with the dead, must defile himself to bury a *Mayss Mitzvah*. So, therefore, in general no communal burial society has the right to refuse to obey this Mitzvah; and in fact it would be correct to say that no Jewish undertaker, even though he is in a private business, has the right to sidestep the Mitzvah of burying the dead.

There are, however, some apparent exceptions to this general principle. The post-Talmudic compendium, *Semachos,* begins the second chapter by listing those with whose burial "we do not deal" (*En Misaskin Bo*) such as suicides, apostates, etc. But very early it was decided by Solomon ben Aderet, the great rabbi of Spain in his Responsum #763, that the phrase, "we do not deal with them" means that we do not give them special honors or dignities, but we are still in duty bound to provide shrouds and to bury them. This principle becomes the adopted law, and all bodies, even of apostates and suicides, are buried. They may be buried without special honor; they may, as in some communities, be buried by the fence, away from the other dead, but the commandment is fulfilled and they are buried.

These dangerous bodies therefore *must* be buried, but need they be handled, say, for *Tahara,* the washing, or for embalming (which is, of course, against traditional law). As I have said, there is no clear statement about handling dangerous bodies (as in the time of the great plagues). There are plenty of precedents giving circumstances under which bodies need not be washed or handled. If a man is found murdered and blood is on his clothes, he is buried as he is, in his clothes. If a woman dies in childbirth and her body is bleeding, or blood-covered, she is not washed (see Responsa *Maharil* #65 and *Yore Deah* 364:4, Isserles). In other words, it is quite possible by these precedents to say that if it is dangerous to handle the body, it may be buried without the usual washing rites.

If some of the relatives would object and say that it is not to the honor of the dead if these usual rites are omitted, I call attention to an interesting responsum by Eliezer Deutsch of Bonyhad in his *Dudoay Hasodeh,* #26, in which an honored body was not given the usual treatment and he reassured the survivors. A body was to be transported from one town to another. The law in Hungary required that it be in a double coffin (perhaps this was a plague-body) and so in this double coffin the body was buried. The surviving son complained to Eliezer Deutsch that his father was thus deprived of the usual Jewish ritual of being buried in contact with the earth. Eliezer Deutsch answered him that the purpose of direct contact with the earth was to hasten the forgiveness of sin; and a righteous man such as his father was can be sure that his sin will be forgiven even without direct contact with the earth.

To sum up, the duty to bury the dead is a basic commandment and cannot be evaded. However, not to handle the dead, not to wash the body, etc., has many precedents in Jewish law; and even the burial in a completely closed coffin may under special circumstances be justified.

42

BURIAL IN HIS OR HER CITY

QUESTION:

a) Is there any objection from the point of view of Jewish tradition to burial at night?

b) If the wife owns a lot in one city and the husband in another, is there any guidance in the traditional literature as to which city should be the place of their burial? (Question by Rabbi William Sajowitz, Pittsburgh, Pennsylvania)

ANSWER:

a) As to the first question concerning burial at night, I have answered that fully in Volume II of *Reform Jewish Practice,* p. 110 ff. The general conclusion there is that tradition is opposed to night burial unless, of course, there is a special emergency which necessitates it. If you lack Volume II of *Reform Jewish Practice,* let me know and I will send you a photostat of the responsum.

b) When the husband and wife now live away from their respective home towns, is there any traditional guidance as to where (in his or her home town) they should be buried? As far as I know there is no direct discussion of this question in the literature. There is, however, considerable discussion as to where a man should be buried, and to the extent that that is clear, it is *then* decided automatically that the wife should be buried there too. Of course if this is the wife's second marriage, then the question would arise with which of her two husbands should she be buried. I have also discussed this question (*Reform Jewish Practices,* Volume I, p. 146 ff.) and the general mood of the tradition is that she should be buried with the husband with whom she had children.

Now with regard to where the husband should be buried in relation to the wife's burial place, all the discussions concern the serious matter of distinterment. For example, let us say that the husband has been buried in a certain cemetery. Later the wife is buried in another cemetery. The children decide to buy enough land around their mother's grave to establish a family plot. May the husband be disinterred in order to be buried beside his wife in the new family plot? This question is discussed by Isaac Glick (*Yad Yitzchok,* II, 249). Of course bearing in mind the general objection of Jewish law to distinterment in general, it is understood that no body may be disinterred except for specifically enumerated reasons as given in *Yore Deah* 363. Among these reasons for which he may be disinterred is to be buried "with his fathers," that is to say, in a family plot. See the *Taz ad. loc.* The question therefore arises in this case which is mentioned, whether the wife alone, being buried in that new place, can be considered to have made it a family plot. The answer that Isaac Glick gives is that he may not be disinterred unless there are other members of the family already buried there, not the wife alone. The reverse question is discussed by Saul M. Schwadron (*Maharsham,* III, 343, and he decides that the wife may be disinterred to be buried with the husband since there are enough graves in his plot for it to be deemed a "family plot." See also *Pekudas Eliezer* (Eliezer Lev of Ungvar) #124.

Isaac Glick in the above mentioned responsum calls attention to the fact that the patriarchs all were buried with their wives. So Jacob, in Genesis 49, mentions that he wishes that Joseph arrange for his burial in Machpelah and says, "There Abraham buried Sarah, and Isaac, Rebecca, and there I buried Leah." But Rabbi Glick says that first he said, "Let me be buried with my fathers" (verse 29). In other words, it is proper that a man be buried with his wife, but primarily the important thing is that he be buried with his fathers.

There is another slight indication of preference from another point of view. We assume that in this case the husband already has a plot in one city and the wife has a plot in another city. According to the law (*Even Hoezer* 89) the husband is in duty bound to provide for the burial of his wife. But (*Even Hoezer* 118:18, Isserles) the wife is in no way duty bound to provide for the burial of her husband (his children are). Therefore it is the husband's lot which fits into the requirement of this law. Of course that is not an absolute guide in this matter because while the wife is not in duty bound to provide burial for her husband, she is certainly not prohibited from doing so.

Now, leaving out the question of disinterment, or the

question as to who is in duty bound to pay for the ground, there are some general tendencies in the law as to where a man should be buried. In the Bible (II Samuel 19:38) when David offers old Barzilai a comfortable living in Jerusalem, Barzilai refuses and says, "I will die in my own city and be buried with my fathers." So in the Talmud (*Baba Metziah* 85a) one of the rabbis died and there was a snake guarding the cave in which his father was buried, and the snake was told to get out of the way so that the son may enter and sleep by his father. In fact, so generally is it understood that a man is to be buried near his ancestors that the Biblical phrase for dying is "to be gathered to one's fathers," and indeed it is actually the established custom that a man must be buried near his father and if that is impossible, near his mother, and if that is impossible, near his grandfather. See Greenwald, *Kol Bo,* 176.

Let us assume now that both the husband and the wife are alive and the question that is asked amounts to guidance as to where they should be buried when the time comes. The answer cannot be too definite but these are the guide-lines:

First, it is preferable that a man be buried where his family is buried. That does not necessarily mean in a family plot but as near them as possible in the same cemetery. The law does not discuss any such preference in the case of a woman with regard to her family. Therefore if husband and wife are to be buried beside each other, then it is evident it must be in his city so that thus he may be buried with his fathers.

Second, if however a family lot is established

(whereas hitherto there were only single graves), then it would be preferable that both be buried in that family plot wherever it is. And if the plot is in the same city as the original grave (if one is already buried) disinterment is less objectionable, since it does not involve carrying the body from one city to another. We may say that the weight of preference is that the burial should be where the husband's family is. If neither has family in either place, then the preference is where a family plot would be established.

43

SOME BURIAL DUTIES

QUESTION:

> An Israeli widower remarried for ten years to an American Jewess died recently and was buried in the family plot in Rochester. His sons want to know whether or not it is incumbent upon them to have him disinterred to be reburied in Israel. Furthermore, if some disagreement will arise between the wife and her husband's sons, which of the two parties have the right to determine where he shall be buried? (Asked by Rabbi Philip Bernstein, Rochester, New York.)

ANSWER:

THE FIRST QUESTION is whether burial in Palestine should be deemed a duty and that therefore the sons should deem themselves obligated to have their father's body disinterred and reburied there. In *Yore Deah*

363:1 there are mentioned three circumstances under which it would be permitted to disinter a body: first, if the body was buried with the prior intention to disinter for reburial elsewhere; second, to bury in the family plot; and third, to take the body to the Holy Land for reburial. Now it cannot be said that any of these three reasons for disinterment and reburial involves a *duty* to do so. If it were a *duty* to rebury, for example, in the Holy Land, then we would have no right to have cemeteries in the diaspora. As a matter of fact, by tradition, when Messiah comes all bodies, wherever buried, will find their way to the Holy Land to be resurrected there by the Messiah; and also it is a custom to put Palestinian earth on the body (see Isserles, ibid.) which is symbolic of Palestinian burial. Of course it is deemed *preferable* to be buried in the Holy Land, based on the verse: "His land (i.e., the Holy Land) will atone for His people," (Deut. 32:43). (This traditional translation is not meant to be literal.) But although burial in the Holy Land is *preferable,* it is obviously not mandatory and the *Shulchan Aruch, ibid.,* properly says, "It is *permitted* to disinter for this purpose." So the sons are in no sense *obligated* to have the body disinterred to rebury in Israel.

The second question involved in the inquiry is the more complicated, namely: If there is a disagreement as to the question of disinterment and reburial, whose decision should be valid, the American widow's or the sons'? Perhaps the clearest answer would be based upon the analogy in this regard between English-American common law and Jewish law. In the

English-American law the widow has absolute right to determine where the husband is to be buried. If, for example, the widow is a Catholic and the husband is a Jew, then even though the husband owns a lot in the Jewish cemetery and has specifically stated in his will that he wants to be buried in the Jewish cemetery, in spite of all this the widow has the legal right to say that he shall be buried in the Catholic cemetery. Should the deceased have been a widower, then his other heirs have the right in place of his widow to determine where he shall be buried. So in our English-American law the right to determine the place of burial is bound up with the right of inheritance. The widow always inherits a certain portion of the estate and with it the right to dispose of the husband's body.

On this basis we can make a helpful comparison with Jewish law: In Jewish law the wife is absolutely not an heir of the husband's estate. When the husband dies the wife has the right to take only the sum mentioned in her wedding document (*ketubah*) and certain property which she brought into the marriage. She also has the right to be clothed, fed and housed from the estate, but she is in no sense an heir of her husband's property; only the sons are heirs. Therefore if by analogy we have a right to connect the decision as to the place of burial with the right of inheritance, then we would say that in Jewish law only the sons are the heirs (not counting special gifts that the deceased may have made) and only they have the exclusive right to determine the place of burial of their father, and the wife who is not an heir has no such right.

That this is a justified analogy can be seen from the actual facts in Jewish law on this matter. Greenwald in *Kol Bo,* p. 174, states the law on the basis of the question: Who is in duty bound to pay the expenses of burial? Naturally the one who is in duty bound to pay is the one who is responsible for the burial and, therefore, has the right to make determinations about it. He states the law that it is the sons who are responsible for their father's burial. This is implied in the statement in the *Shulchan Aruch, Yore Deah* 240:9, which states that the son must honor his father in death as well as in life, which is taken to mean that it is his duty to see about the burial. Greenwald bases his statement as to the son's right upon the responsum of Yair Chaim Bachrach (*Chavas Yair,* #139) and in turn, Bachrach bases his opinion on Moses Mintz (14th century) Responsum #53, all of whom make it clear that the son has the responsibility and privilege of burial because he is the father's heir. As a matter of fact the *Shulchan Aruch* states that clearly too. In *Even Hoezer* 118:18 the law is given as follows: If a widow after her husband's death has already collected the amount in her *ketubah,* and if after she has collected it there is no money left in the estate to pay for his burial, then even so she is not in duty bound to provide for the burial; to which Isserles adds, "Let him then be buried at the expense of the community." This opinion is based upon a number of earlier authorities such as Asher ben Yehiel, Nachmanides, Solomon ben Aderet and others.

To sum up: Burial in the Holy Land is one of the

three reasons for which disinterment is permitted, but such burial is not an *obligation*. As to who has the right to determine the place of burial, only the sons who are the heirs have that right.

44

CONGREGATIONAL CHARGE FOR FUNERALS

QUESTION:

> A Jewish man passed away in a city about a hundred miles from the nearest congregation which has a rabbi. He was not a member of that congregation. He is to be buried in this larger city but the congregation there refuses to allow its rabbi to officiate until the family pays a $100 fee in advance for the services of a rabbi. Is this proper procedure? (Asked by Rabbi Abraham I. Shinedling, Albuquerque, New Mexico.)

ANSWER:

THERE ARE A NUMBER of other questions involved which are not mentioned. For example: Does the deceased already own a lot in the cemetery of the congregation that is now charging the $100 fee? Also, is the family of the deceased able to pay the fee or does it put a great hardship on them? The latter fact would make a difference in evaluating the propriety of the practice of the congregation. To bury the dead is a *Mitzvah*. It is incumbent first of all upon the family of the deceased, and if there is no family it is incumbent upon the community to provide for his burial. See Greenwald, *Kol Bo,* p. 173, note 1. If, for example, it is extremely difficult for the family to raise that $100 and they certainly cannot pay for a lot in the cemetery, then it is absolutely wrong for the congregation to insist upon any fee at all. The body of this deceased is, as it were, a *Mays Mitzvah,* a body whom we are mandated to bury, just as much as even a priest may be defiled for a *Mays Mitzvah* if he comes across a body and there is no one but him to bury it.

But we will assume in this case that this is not a case of extreme poverty. Let us then first consider the purchase of a lot. It is the universal custom in Judaism for many centuries that the *Chevra Kadisha* (and in a modern congregation the Cemetery Committee) charges for lots. The old *Chevra Kadisha* charged more to a man who could pay more. But even the poorest of the poor should pay *something* for a lot because it is considered a virtue for a man to be buried *B'soch Shelo,* in his own property (cf. References, *Kol Bo,* p. 174, note 7). So in case this man has no lot, it is right and proper that, if his family can afford it, they should pay for a lot.

Now as to the expenses of the burial: While burial is a *Mitzvah* incumbent on everybody, the *Mitzvah* falls first on his sons and heirs. As a matter of fact, even if the father has left no inheritance to his sons, there is a strong line in the law which insists that sons nevertheless have the responsibility to provide for his burial (Minz, *Responsa Maharam,* #53 and Bachrach, *Chavos Yair,* #139). As a matter of fact, even if the man himself before he died said that he does not want any money from his estate to be used to pay the expenses of his burial, we pay no attention to such a request and exact the money from his estate to pay for the burial (*Ketubos* 48a and *Yore Deah* 348:2). It is clear so far, then, that if a man can afford it, he must be compelled to pay, or his heirs to pay, for his funeral.

The final question is: Is it right for the congregation to insure that the rabbi receive his fee from the funeral? This question involves the old and classic question, first fully discussed by Shimon ben Zemach Duran, as to the legitimacy of a rabbi receiving fees for his services (see the discussion in *A Treasury of Responsa,* p. 78 ff.). This question has changed with the changing times. If there were in the past any doubt as to the right of a rabbi to receive such fees, this doubt has vanished with the development of the rabbinate from the voluntary service of a scholar to the community to a regular profession. Now that the rabbinate is a regular profession, its status is clearly defined by the great Hungarian authority, Moses Sofer, in his *responsa, Yore Deah* 230. There he says that the questions which arose in the past as to fees no longer apply today. Today the rabbi is employed by the congregation and he is entitled to the fees as part of his livelihood.

Of course whether the congregation puts part of this fee in its own treasury and gives the rabbi the rest, whether also the fee is excessive or not excessive is not directly germane to the question. The basic fact is that a family is in duty bound by Jewish law to pay from the man's estate for his funeral, both the land and the costs of the burial. Of course if there is no money at all available, then it becomes the duty of the congregation. Otherwise the action as outlined above is in perfect consonance with Jewish practice and involves no impropriety at all.

45

FUNERAL SERVICE FOR NON-MEMBERS

QUESTION:

The practice of our congregation is for the rabbi not to officiate at funerals of non-members, unless they are the parent or child of a member. The purpose of this restriction is to encourage people to join the congregation, which is their obligation. However, the refusal to officiate for more distant relatives of our members or non-members often creates unhappiness in times of emergency. Besides, the other congregations in the city do officiate at funerals of non-members. Should we not do likewise? Or how in other ways should we change our policy, if at all? (Asked by Dr. Frederick C. Schwartz, Chicago, Illinois.)

ANSWER:

BEHIND THIS QUESTION there is a general Halachic and communal problem which has so far remained unsolved. In past centuries in Europe no distinction *could* be made between membership in the community and membership in the congregation. The two were identical and certainly so in the older communities before they grew so large as to have many synagogues. But even in such larger communities where a man might attend one synagogue rather than another, he was a tax-paying member of the community and could attend whichever of the synagogues he wished. He was not specifically a member of a congregation. That being the case, the community through its *Chevra Kadisha* (the ancestor of our cemetery committee) was obligated to provide funeral service for any member of the community.

Now the situation has changed. In America, for example, different congregations were established at different times by different people; and so individuals are no longer tax-paying members of an organized community as in Europe, but dues-paying members of a separate and independent congregation. This fact is being acknowledged as a legal fact by Orthodox authorities, because much is involved in recognizing that now the community and the congregation are no longer identical or coterminous. What is involved in deciding this general question is the following: It is a rule in the law (*Orah Hayyim* 157:7) that the synagogue building of a large community may never be sold for nonreligious purposes. The theory is that travelers, visitors from all over the world, may have contributed to the building of it and it is, therefore, the property of the whole community and even of the total Jewish people. But Moses Feinstein, the head of the Agudas HaRabbonim, in his responsa *Igros Moshe* (*Orah Hayyim* 50) faced the fact that former Jewish neighborhoods in our changing cities often become uninhabitable, and most of the membership leave the congregation almost derelict in the hands of a few. He decided that the congregation, even though a large one, is an independent entity and, therefore, can make its own decision about selling the property.

So it is in America with regard to our various congregations. They are independent entities and can make their own rules. They do not have any specific responsibilities to people who are non-members and do not contribute to the support of the synagogue. Furthermore, inasmuch as you tell me other congregations in the city do officiate for non-members, therefore any family for whom you refuse to officiate will not be left without the services of a rabbi. Whatever duty remains (due to the past history) from each congregation to non-members has been fully taken care of by the fact that they will always find congregations that will serve them.

The justification of your congregation in following the practice which is largely followed in most Jewish communities, is that among the duties incumbent upon a congregation is the duty to encourage Jewish people to support a congregation. The purpose of restricting funerals to members or close relatives is the fulfillment of this duty and it is a worthy purpose.

However, I think it would be proper on the part of your congregation to extend the list of those relatives for whom the congregation will provide funeral services when that becomes necessary. We have a test in the Halacha for deciding how close certain relatives are considered to be. Based upon the law (Leviticus 21:1-4) as to the seven relatives a priest may "defile" himself for (i.e., come in contact with the dead, which is otherwise forbidden to him) the general law is that, just as the priest, we must mourn for seven relatives: father, mother, sister, brother, husband, wife and child. I would therefore extend the list to these relatives and add to it those who own a lot in the congregational cemetery. Owning a lot in the congregational cemetery does partially support the congregation and it is bought with the understanding that in time of need, funeral services will be provided.

To sum up: The socio-legal situation of the Jewish congregation has changed. No longer are all the Jewish inhabitants of a city members of every congregation. A congregation is a separate entity. It may sell its property without question for secular purposes. It may make decisions as to which people may or may not have use of the congregational facilities and of the services of its rabbi. However, the list should be extended as indicated above.

46

FUNERAL SERVICE FOR EX-MEMBERS

QUESTION:

A Jewish doctor had been a member of the congregation for thirty years. In the last few years he had discontinued his membership. Now there are officers of the congregation who wish to deny this ex-member the right of burial in the congregational cemetery. Is there any Halachic or moral justification for this refusal? (Asked by Rabbi Joseph Gitin, San Jose, California)

ANSWER:

EACH CONGREGATION has the right to make certain restrictive rules as to non-members using the congregational facilities and the services of the rabbi. However, these restrictions should be less stringent in cases of funerals than weddings. The congregation should permit the rabbi to officiate at the funerals of non-member relatives of members.

The reason for the distinction is, first of all, a practical one. A couple can be married anywhere, in a hall or in the home; but if there are no other Jewish cemeteries in the city, then unless a grave in the congregational cemetery is made available, the funeral cannot take place. There is a further reason for the congregation to be less restrictive in its rules governing funerals.

The community has, indeed, the duty to encourage marriage, but it has no specific responsibility that this particular couple be married to each other. But with regard to a person who is deceased, the congregation has a duty to him specifically. They have a responsibility that this body be properly buried.

The specific obligation needs explanation. There is, indeed, what might be called merely a random reference to the right of the community to prohibit burial to certain classes of Jews. In the laws of ban and excommunication, *Yore Deah* 334:6, Nachmanides is quoted by Isserles as saying that if the *Bes Din* wishes to be extra strict against a man who is under the ban, they may refuse to circumcise his sons and refuse to bury him if he dies. This permission to refuse to bury a man who has been excommunicated is derived from a statement in the post-Talmudic treatise, *Evel Rabatti,* Chapter 2, where the statement is made that when criminals, people under ban, apostates, etc., die, we do not tear our garments for them, nor do we engage in any burial activity for them (*Eyn Misaskin*).

This apparent general permission to have nothing to do with the burial of certain classes of sinners has never become the rule of Jewish law. It could not possibly have become the rule because the whole law of our *duty* to bury (i.e., the *Mitzvah* of burial) is derived from Deuteronomy 21:25, where we are told that the body of the criminal who has been executed must not be allowed to remain unburied overnight. How, then, can this general commandment to bury all Jews, even sinners, be reconciled with the statement in *Semachos* (followed by Nachmanides) that we may not engage (*Eyn Misaskin*) in any burial activities for sinners? The contradiction is not a real one. All the authorities from the earliest to the latest state that what the tractate *Semachos* means by *Eyn Misaskin* is that we do not engage in any of those burial activities which *honor* the dead, such as *keriah,* eulogy, procession, but the *duty* of burial remains our duty.

There is, indeed, some discussion in the law as to whether we are in duty bound to bury an apostate. The great Hungarian authority, Moses Sofer, argues that since we have a duty to bury all the criminals as mentioned in Deuteronomy, and those criminals certainly included idolators, apostates, etc., then an apostate too should have burial in the Jewish cemetery. See all the discussion and references in *Recent Reform Responsa,* beginning with page 127, "Burial of an Apostate." (By the way, on page 130, middle of the page, the reference to *Yore Deah* should be, not 333:3, but 334:3.) At all events, let us say that the question of the burial of an apostate is still moot, but all other Jews have the right to be buried in the Jewish cemetery. Greenwald in his *Kol Bo,* page 193, states the law as follows: Every Jew, if he has not apostatized, is entitled to his place in the Jewish cemetery.

Of course, the congregation may not bury a wicked man next to a righteous man, and suicides may be buried in a separate section as was the custom in the past, usually near the fence, but every Jew is entitled to Jewish burial.

Nachmanides' prohibitory arguments mentioned

above dealt with a man actually under ban, and the restrictions mentioned in the tractate *Semachos* dealt with sinners. But the question asked here does not deal with a man under the ban (which in modern Jewish communities is not practiced anyhow) nor does it deal with a sinner. It deals merely with a non-member and a respectable citizen of the community. Now it is an established custom that people pay for their cemetery lots and it is also a custom practiced for centuries that the price charged by the *Chevra Kadisha* varies with the family. Therefore the congregation is within its rights to charge more for non-members than for members; but beyond this, it must be clearly stated that every Jew is entitled to Jewish burial, and it is the mandate of our religion (a positive commandment) that we provide such burial.

Of course the situation in our modern American communities is not quite the same as that which prevailed in the older European communities. There, there was one united community and all Jews were tax-paying members of it. There was one cemetery, and if a man were refused burial in this local cemetery, he could not easily find Jewish burial at all. But today, in our large cities there are many independent congregations and many Jewish cemeteries, and so if a man is refused burial in one, he may find burial in another. Therefore it is understandable and permissible for a congregation to make certain restrictions, to charge more perhaps for a non-member than for a member, to refuse the services of a rabbi at the funeral service except for members and their relatives. But whatever restrictions the congregation may make, the fact remains that every Jew has the right to burial in a Jewish cemetery and to bury the dead is our duty, which we have no right to evade. Certainly in a smaller community where there is only one Jewish cemetery, it may well be deemed a sin to force the family to transport the body to another city.

Finally, since this physician had been a member of the congregation for many years, he undoubtedly has close relatives who are members and also many close friends among the membership. Any refusal to bury him, besides being against Jewish law and custom, would cause grief to many who deserve consideration from the congregation.

47

BURIAL OF FALLEN ISRAELI SOLDIERS

(Questions asked by Rabbi Moshe Zemer, Tel-Aviv Progressive Congregation)

QUESTION #1:

The Israeli Army Chaplaincy has arranged for temporary burial in provisional military cemeteries in the Negev and in the Galilee for soldiers killed in action. The bodies will remain in these temporary cemeteries for twelve months and then will be transferred to permanent cemeteries near their homes. Many families feel this is a great hardship, that for twelve months they will have to go down to the Negev or up to the Golan Heights to visit the graves of their dear ones. Why is it necessary to keep them buried in these temporary burial places for a full year?

ANSWER:

THERE IS a general objection in the law to disinterring bodies altogether. The objection is primarily based upon the anecdote told concerning Rabbi Akiba in *Baba Basra* 154a. A young man (or a boy) had died. Before his death, he had sold some property from his father's estate. The relatives insisted that when the boy had sold the property, he was a minor and, therefore, the sale to which they had objections was invalid.

They asked Rabbi Akiba whether they may open the grave in order to examine the body of the deceased, to find out whether he was an adult or not. Rabbi Akiba answered, "No, you have no right (*l'navlo*) to reveal the ugliness of the decaying body." This "uglification" is the only reason in the basic Talmudic literature against disinterring a body.

After Talmudic times, other objections were developed. The most important of these is called *cherdas ha-din,* "fear of the judgment." It means that if the body is disturbed, the dead (who are presumed to be somehow conscious) will fear that they are being brought to judgment and possible punishment. This strange objection to disturbing the body is cited by Joseph Caro in his *Bes Josef* to the *Tur, Yore Deah* 363. He quotes it from the early medieval work, *Kol Bo.* He says, "The *Kol Bo* has written the reason that we do not disinter the dead to move the body from one place to another because this disturbing of the body creates a (psychic) hardship for the dead, because they are afraid of judgment (and punishment)." The proof text for this idea is the complaint of the ghost of Samuel who, when he was brought up by the witch of Endor, complained to Saul, "Why hast thou disturbed my rest?" (I Samuel 28:15)

But how long must the body lie undisturbed? The answer to this is based chiefly on the Mishnah in *Sanhedrin* 6:6. There we are told that the courts had separate cemeteries for executed criminals. Many of our burial laws are derived from the relevant criminal laws as, for example, all the laws against delay in burial.

In this Mishnah we are told that after the flesh of these bodies has decayed, the bones of criminals are taken out and buried in their family cemeteries. The reason for waiting until the flesh is gone is that it is held that once the flesh is gone, death has forgiven all sins. Hence, based upon this, no body is to be moved from its first burial place until the flesh has finally gone.

Now it is taken as a rule that it takes twelve months for the flesh to wear away and then the bones can be moved. This is the reason why the rabbinate has decided to keep the bodies in the temporary burying place for twelve months.

What concerns us is whether it is necessary as an actual legal requirement that the bodies wait out there a full twelve months for the flesh to decay. There is an interesting landmark decision on this matter in an oft-cited responsum by the Rashba, Solomon Ben Adret, #389 in his responsa. A man and his sons traveled from Oran to Algiers on a business errand. The man turned sick in Algiers and he told his sons, "If I die here in Algiers, I want you to see that I am buried in our family cemetery in Oran." He died, but the sons could not fulfill his request immediately because war had broken out and it was unsafe to travel to Oran. They buried him in Algiers. Then they came to Rabbi Solomon Ben Adret and asked him whether they may put quicklime into the grave to hasten the decay of the flesh. The Rabbi said that they may do so. This decision has been cited frequently in the law. In fact you will notice that Isserles, in *Yore Deah* 363:2, says, "It is permitted to put lime upon him in order to hasten the decay of the flesh and to bring him to the place where he had asked to be buried." And more recently than Isserles, the famous Rabbi of Metz (1870) Jacob Reischer, in his *Shevus Yaacov,* Vol. 2, 97, speaks of the case in which the government prohibited the burial in the Jewish cemetery and buried the dead out in the field. He recommends that they follow the precedent of Solomon Ben Adret to put lime on the body so that they will be able to transfer it to the security of the regular Jewish cemetery. You will notice that at the end of his responsum, he mentions what should concern us about burial in the wild Negev, namely, that animals, dogs, might root about those graves in the wilds. In fact, it has become a custom, especially among the Sephardim, to follow this practice of using quicklime. Therefore if the families will consent to this procedure, the bodies may be brought back in full conformity with the law almost immediately.

If for some reason there is an objection on the part of the family to hastening the decay of the flesh in this way, there is another reason why it is quite possible to decide that they need not wait for twelve months. Joseph Caro in 363:4 speaks of waiting for the flesh to decay in those places where they bury bodies first in caves. That is because the ugliness of the body is visible and should not be touched until the bones are clean. But what if the body is originally buried in a closed coffin? What objection is there then to moving the body? While it may be argued that there is still the objection of *cherdas ha-din,* "fear of the judgment," when the body with the coffin is taken, at least the *primary* and only Talmudic objection to seeing the ugliness of the decaying body is completely obviated. Thus, for example, Greenwald in his *Kol Bo* (p. 224) concludes that if the coffin is closed, the primary objection of *nivvul* is obviated.

There is still another strong reason why the bodies need not be kept out there for twelve months. The Talmud records that many of the scholars of Babylon were buried in Israel. Certainly there is no evidence at all that their bodies waited for twelve months in Babylon before they were buried in Israel. This is because there is special merit to being buried in the sacred soil, and that is a special privilege which should not be kept from them (see *Kol Bo,* p. 236). Especially it should not be kept from those who died to defend the sacred soil.

It is clear that if the rabbinate in Israel would *want* to decide that the bodies need not be kept out in the Negev, etc., for twelve months, they would have these three reasons for such a liberal decision: First, that the decay of the flesh could be hastened by the use of quicklime, as is well established in the law. Second, the bodies were buried in closed coffins, so the ugliness of decay is not visible and there is no *nivvul*. And third, the moving of the bodies is for the purpose of burying them in Eretz Yisrael, which should not be delayed.

QUESTION #2:

Army units are going out to search for the remains of fallen soldiers. The Army Chaplaincy has decided that on the Sabbath the *Chevra Kadisha* may not remove the remains of these soldiers. In view of the fact that fighting may break out at any moment, as well as the danger of what dogs or other animals that roam the desert may do, can we not find Halachic basis for permitting the removal of those remains lying in the open desert on whatever day they are found?

ANSWER:

THERE IS a great deal of discussion in the law as to moving the body of the dead on the Sabbath. As you correctly point out, the source is *Orah Hayyim* 311. There are various means of permitting the removal on the Sabbath, putting a loaf on the body, or carrying a child with the body. Isserles says that in this case it is permitted to ask a non-Jew to move the body. Surely there are enough friendly Bedouins or Druze who could help in this matter.

QUESTION #3:

What is the basis of the law permitting families to begin their regular mourning, even though they have no absolute proof of the death of the soldier? In other words, what is the basis of the law that they may count their "seven and thirty" (*shiva* and *sheloshim*) from the moment that they give up hope?

ANSWER:

IN *Yore Deah* 375 there is the discussion as to when people may begin the days of their formal mourning. Caro in 375:2 quotes Raba in *Moed Katan* 22a, to the effect that when the body is being buried in another city, the mourners accompany the body up to the gates of their city. When they turn away from the gates of their own city (and the body is being carried on the road to the distant city for burial) the moment that these mourners in the home city turn their faces away from the gate, even though normally mourning should not begin until the body is actually buried, these mourners may begin their "seven and thirty" days of mourning because they cannot know on what date the body will be buried in the distant city. On this basis, the Gaonic handbook *Semachos* (chapter 2, paragraph 12), says that in other cases where the people do not know when the burial will take place (as, for example, the man whose body was swept away by a river) and they do not know when, or if ever, they can recover the body for burial, then the moment the mourners give up hope (*m'she'nish'yo'ashu*), they should begin counting their days of mourning. This same precedent is followed in a tragic account given by Isaac Or Zorua in the Rhineland eleventh century: A Jewish business-man and his Gentile porter went on a business trip. He never returned home. When the unhappy family finally found his possessions in the hands of the porter, they were certain that their dear one was killed, his body thrown into the Rhine. Isaac Or Zorua uses the exact words of the tractate *Semachos* and says they should begin their "seven and thirty" from the moment of their despair (Part 2, #425). This same phrase, then, is carried over into the *Shulchan Aruch,* which says that for those whom the government does not permit to be buried, the relatives begin their mourning from the moment of their despair. This psychological test of the beginning of mourning is well established in Jewish law.

48

CAESAREAN ON A DEAD MOTHER

QUESTION:

> A mother eight months pregnant has died. Does Jewish law permit a Caesarean to be performed on her body to save the child or perhaps, even, does Jewish tradition recommend or urge such an operation? (Asked by Dr. Thomas H. Redding through Rabbi Leonard S. Zoll, Cleveland, Ohio.)

ANSWER:

THE QUESTION of cutting open the body of a mother who has died in order to remove and thus save the child is discussed as far back as the Talmud itself in *Arachin* 7a (cf. also *B.B.*142b and *Niddah* 44a). The discussion is based upon the Mishnaic law dealing with a pregnant woman who is condemned to death. Do we delay execution of the sentence until she has given birth or not? In the development of that discussion, Rabbi Samuel (in *Arachin*) extends the discussion from that of a convicted criminal to *any* woman who dies when she is near to giving birth ("a woman on the *mashber,* the birth-stool, who dies.") In such circumstances Rabbi Samuel says that we may bring a knife, even on the Sabbath (bringing a knife on the Sabbath is forbidden generally) and we may cut open her body to save the child. The discussion there in the Talmud involves the question of whether the child is alive or not and the opinion is expressed that generally the child dies immediately (or even before the mother) and therefore the Sabbath would be violated (by bringing the instruments) in vain, since the child is already dead. But Rashi says, even in the case of the "doubtful saving of life," we may violate the Sabbath; and that therefore on the *chance* that the child may be alive, we bring the knife and perform the operation.

It is exactly in this form that the law is recorded by the great legalist and physician, Moses Maimonides, in his *Hilchos Shabbas,* 2:15. He says: We perform the operation even on the Sabbath, for even when there is *doubt* whether we are saving a life, we may violate the Sabbath (cf. also *Tur ibid.* and Ephraim Margolis, *Yad Ephraim* to *Orah Hayyim* 320).

However, a new ground for doubt arises in the *Shulchan Aruch* (besides the doubt of violating the Sabbath in vain if the child is already dead). In *Orah Hayyim* 330:4, Joseph Caro gives the law according to the Talmud and Maimonides; but Moses Isserles (Poland, 16th century) says: We do not do this operation nowadays because we are no longer skilled in determining precisely whether the mother is dead or not; perhaps she is alive (i.e., in coma) and may give birth to the child naturally. However, Isserles himself in his responsa does not seem concerned with this doubt (that the mother may still be alive) and in his Responsum #40 he answers in the affirmative, i.e., that the operation should be performed.

As for the later authorities, they all are practically unanimous in favor of permitting the operation (even on the Sabbath and certainly on weekdays). What concerns these later authorities is whether or not the permission to perform this operation after the mother is dead may not imply the larger permission for autopsy in general, which Jewish law forbids except under special circumstances. Generally speaking, it is not permitted to mutilate (*l'navvel*) the body of the dead. Therefore in a discussion between Moses Schick of Ofen and Jacob Ettlinger of Hamburg (both in the first half of the nineteenth century) this matter is debated. See responsa of Ettlinger, *Binyan Zion,* I:171. Moses Schick said in this discussion (in his responsa *Yore Deah* 347) that we *may* mutilate the body of a woman to save her child; and Ettlinger says that this permission does not justify general mutilation (as in autopsy) because this operation (i.e., the Caesarean) is not really a disfiguring of the body of a woman.

Moses Kunitz of Budapest (d. 1837) in *Ha-M'zaref,* I, 101, gives almost the exact case discussed here in answer to a question asked him by Abraham Oppenheimer. The woman was pregnant for eight months when she died. A skilled doctor said definitely that she is dead and that the baby is alive. Accepting the opinion of the skilled physician, both doubts mentioned above are cancelled. The woman is definitely dead, so the doubt mentioned by Isserles that we have not the skill to be sure when a person is dead is now obviated; and the physician says that the child is definitely alive and so the doubt discussed by Rashi and the Talmud that we may be violating the Sabbath (even if this occurred on the Sabbath) for an unnecessary purpose, since the child may be dead, is also obviated. Therefore Moses Kunitz said that the physician should operate and does not even need to ask permission of the Jewish ecclesiastical court. Moses Kunitz here actually uses the word "Caesarean" and gives the origin of the term, namely, that Julius Caesar was born by such an operation.

Jacob Reischer, Rabbi of Metz two centuries ago, in his responsa *Shevus Yaacov,* I:13 at the end, not only gives permission for such an operation but ends his responsum by saying that he who performs it must be praised for doing so and his reward will be great. See also Abraham of Buczacz, *Eshel Avraham* to *Orah Hayyim* 330, who cites an authority who praises the physician for prompt action to save the child.

There is, of course, a possible complication somewhat related to this question. Since the child will die unless the operation is performed very quickly, I was asked a number of years ago by a physician whether if the mother is not quite dead but is definitely dying (for example of cancer) whether we may not make sure to save the child by performing the operation before the mother is dead, although it is certain that the operation itself will definitely put an end to the mother's life. See the discussion of this special question in *Reform Responsa,* p. 214 ff.

But this is a special form of the question and does not

apply directly here where the physician assures us that the mother is dead. See further discussion of the matter in Eliezer Spiro ("der Muncaczer") in his *Minchas Eliezer,* IV:28, and Greenwald in *Kol Bo Al Avelus,* p. 49, section 18, and p. 43 ff.

To sum up, if it is certain that the mother is dead and that the child is alive, there is no question that the Caesarean operation not only may be performed, but *must* be performed and is indeed deemed praiseworthy.

49

BEQUEATHING PARTS OF THE BODY

QUESTION:

> "Would it be in accord with Jewish tradition if we specified in our will that upon the death of either husband or wife, any part or parts of the body may be removed from the corpse and used for any patient in need of organ transplants? If there is no immediate use for the organ, it is our wish that it be preserved for future use." (Asked of and by Rabbi Louis J. Cashdan, Bowie, Maryland.)

ANSWER:

THE FIRST and basic question involved in this inquiry is the question of the permissibility of autopsy in Jewish law. Forty-five years ago Dr. Jacob Z. Lauterbach wrote his classic responsum for the CCAR on the Jewish attitude towards autopsy. He began with the statement that there is no law or regulation expressly forbidding the practice of autopsy to be found in the Bible, or the Talmud, or the *Shulchan Aruch*. Then he goes on to the fact that the great 18-19th century authorities, Ezekiel Landau (in his responsa, Part II, *Yore Deah* #210) and Moses Sofer (*Yore Deah* 336) would permit autopsy, but only when there is in the immediate vicinity a patient of whom the doctor says he may well be benefited by what will be learned from the autopsy of the dead person. Dr. Lauterbach comments on this opinion by saying that nowadays with modern communications, whatever a doctor may learn from autopsy in one city can be known almost at once in any other city; and so we may well say that patients who might be benefited by the autopsy are *always* present. And so he ends the responsum confirming the statement with which he had begun, namely, that there is no law in the classic sources that would expressly prohibit autopsy.

While Dr. Lauterbach's statement of forty-five years ago is manifestly correct, the whole traditional-legal situation with regard to autopsy has drastically changed since the time when he wrote his responsum. First of all, between the two world wars there was an increase of anti-Semitism in the medical schools of eastern and central Europe. In fact, in certain European countries laws were passed forbidding Jewish medical students the use of bodies for dissection unless Jewish bodies were delivered to the hospitals by the Jewish community. Dr. Lauterbach mentions this fact on the last page of his responsum.

As a result of this anti-Semitism some of the Jewish

burial societies (in Warsaw and in Bucharest) actually did hand over Jewish bodies to the medical schools. This action aroused a violent protest on the part of Orthodox rabbinical authorities. Especially to be noted is the literally furious reaction of Eliezer Spiro ("der Muncaczer") in his *Minchas Eliezer,* Vol. IV, #28. (By the way, Greenwald in his *Kol Bo,* on p. 41, cites this responsum as #25, which is a wrong reference.) In this responsum Eliezer Spiro speaks scornfully of the medical profession. He says that all this dissecting of dead bodies which the doctors are doing is simply willful; nothing is actually gained from it, no medical knowledge, no help for any patient. In fact in the Index at the beginning of this book, under the Index #28, he says that there would be no harm to Judaism if Jewish men did not become doctors at all, since most of them become irreligious and violators of the Sabbath.

This extreme outburst on the part of this widely respected Hungarian authority has been surpassed in recent years in the State of Israel. There Orthodox authorities have accused the physicians of the hospitals of forcing autopsy on unwilling pious families. Some doctors were actually threatened with physical harm for performing autopsies. In fact, some of the right-wing Orthodox magazines in America have gone so far as to say that doctors in Israel are making a paying business of sending parts of Jewish bodies to physicians and hospitals in other countries.

All this new bitterness on the question of autopsy is of significance to our inquiry. It means that while

Dr. Lauterbach is, strictly speaking, quite correct, nevertheless Orthodox opinion has built, since the time of his writing, upon the basis of certain Talmudic statements, a strong prohibitory attitude towards autopsy. See for example the long statement in Greenwald's *Kol Bo,* pages 40-45.

The two Talmudic grounds upon which all this anti-autopsy attitude has been built up are, first of all, that dissecting a body is *Nivvul,* an uglification, or a disgraceful handling of it. And secondly, that it is the law that a body should be buried intact and without delay. Therefore if today any Orthodox authority would be asked a question, as presented to us here, the answer would be an immediate and unequivocal negative.

However, liberal-minded people will remain unaffected by the present-day heating up of the question and will be guided by Dr. Lauterbach's judgment, that there is no real objection in the Talmud or the Codes to autopsy. Once we start from this liberal opinion, we will find that there are actually certain justifications in the traditional law for the line of action which the present inquirers have mapped out for themselves. They are as follows:

Jacob Ettlinger, Rabbi of Altona-Hamburg (1798-1871) in his *Binyan Zion,* #170 and #171, develops the now-classic objection to autopsy, namely, that it is wrong to mutilate the dead for the supposed benefit of the living. In developing his arguments he is confronted with a case given in the Talmud which clearly argues the very opposite. In the tractate *Arachin* 7a, we are told that the body of a pregnant woman who

had just died may be opened in order to save the child
to whom she was about to give birth. Is this then not
a mutilation of the dead for the benefit of the living?
Ettlinger disposes of the implications of this Talmudic
statement (which would seem to permit autopsy) by
saying that an operation upon a mother to bring forth
a child is not really a mutilation at all. We frequently
have such operations for living mothers (Caesarean
operations) and it is not to be considered a mutilation
or a shameful handling of the body. Ettlinger, in
making this answer to the Talmudic question, indicates
that if there were not a visible mutilation of the body,
then there can be no objection, or at least there is less
objection to such a dissection for the benefit of the
living. It is quite possible, therefore, in the case mentioned in this inquiry, to say that just as the child is
removed by operation without mutilating the appearance of the body of the mother, so too these various
internal organs may well be removed without a visible
mutilation of the body, and thus certainly the removal
of the organs would on this ground at least be more
or less unobjectionable. Of course, if the bodies are to
be *dismembered* for bone banks, etc., then this argument would have no validity. But if only the internal
organs are removed, and the body shows no manifest
signs of mutilation, then it well may be argued, as
Jacob Ettlinger did, that this procedure does not constitute shameful handling or *Nivvul.*

Having disposed of the problem of the autopsy mentioned in the Talmud in *Arachin,* Ettlinger then develops an even stricter opposition to autopsy than did

Ezekiel Landau or Moses Sofer. He would not even permit, as they did, an autopsy, even if there is a patient actually present who might benefit from it. Yet even though he is stricter than the other two authorities, he says that while autopsy is to be considered of course a shameful affront, *Nivvul,* to the dead, nevertheless if a man himself in his lifetime gives consent to autopsy, or even sells his body for medical use, then such an autopsy could be permitted, since a man has a right to dispense, if he wishes, with any honors or dignities to which he might be entitled. There are some scholars who object to this right of previous consent, as for example, Moses Schick in his responsa, *Yore Deah* 347-8. J. Tekuchinski (*Talpioth,* Vol. 9, 4-5, p. 58) denies that a man has a right to dispose of his own body in this way. Nevertheless, even in Israel, in the midst of all the present dispute, there are scholars who accord a man the right to permit autopsy upon his own body (Greenwald mentions this on p. 43). Hence these people who have raised the present inquiry have the right to dispense with the traditional dignities of having their bodies buried intact and immediately; and may, according to a considerable part of Jewish religious leadership, make arrangements for the autopsy on their own bodies.

But all of this deals with only one of the two objections against autopsy, namely, the prohibition of mutilating the body (*Nivvul*). There remains, however, the second basis for the opposition to autopsy, namely, that since the entire body must be buried, it is a sin to delay the burial of any part of it (larger than the size of an olive) and certainly a sin to keep certain parts from burial altogether.

However, even this objection is not completely decisive. If these organs taken from these bodies are transplanted into the bodies of living patients, they become part of these living bodies and cease to be in the category of parts of a dead body which by law must be buried. This opinion is expressed by Moses Feinstein of New York (who is the prime Orthodox authority in America) in his *Igros Moshe, Yore Deah* 229 and 230, and also a similar opinion is given by Nahum Kornmehl in his *Tiferes Z'vi,* #75 (compare discussion in *Current Reform Responsa,* p. 119 ff.).

There remains, however, one final difficulty which arises in case there are no recipients immediately available for these organs. The difficulty is that these organs will now have to be preserved until such time as they can be used. In that case there may well be a lengthy and forbidden delay of the burial of the parts of a dead body. There is, however, one possible mitigation of this difficulty. It is the opinion of Rashi (as opposed to the opinion of his grandson, Rabbenu Tam) that once a coffin is closed (*Nistam Ha-Golel*) that enclosing of the body may be considered to constitute its burial. Cf. the discussion and references in *Reform Responsa,* p. 152 ff. This is a far-reaching decision which is relied upon when a body is put into a coffin and taken away to another city; mourning can begin immediately after the enclosed body is taken away. This decision has also been relied upon when there was a grave-diggers' strike and bodies could not be buried for weeks. The closing of the coffin constitutes burial and the process of mourning can begin. That being the case, we may give consideration to the fact that these organs removed from the bodies do not just lie around. They are carefully preserved. They are kept enclosed and even sealed. Therefore we may say that this complete enclosing constitutes their burial. When they are later used and are, as it were "disinterred," they become a living part of another human body. Then, of course, they require no burial at all, being now part of a living being.

To sum up: While it is true that there is no clear prohibition in Talmud or Codes against autopsy, there has developed in recent years a strong and even bitter opposition to it. However, if the body is not dismembered but kept outwardly intact, the removal of the internal organs need not be considered shameful handling or *Nivvul.* Moreover, many authorities permit a person in his lifetime the right to make provision for autopsy on his own body, as these people are now doing. If the organs from their body are transplanted successfully, they become part of a living body, and are no longer liable to the laws of burial. Until that time they are hermetically sealed, which may be considered equivalent to burial.

50

THE VANDALIZED CEMETERY

QUESTION:

> The congregation in Poughkeepsie has been given the title to an old Jewish cemetery which has not been used for over seventy years. The neighborhood in which the cemetery is located has become a slum. It is impossible to keep the cemetery decent. It is constantly being desecrated. It would cost a great deal of money to shield this cemetery from abuse and, even so, it is doubtful whether any effort could succeed. Besides, there is possibility of neighborhood urban renewal and it will be difficult to keep the cemetery anyhow. What should be done in this case? (Asked by Rabbi Henry Bamberger, Poughkeepsie, New York.)

ANSWER:

THIS TRAGIC situation is, alas, not new. It has arisen time and time again in the past. In Europe, frequently the ruler of the neighborhood would send his cattle to graze in the Jewish cemetery. Such a case is mentioned by Israel Isserlein (14th century), in his *Terumas Hadeshen,* #284. This was deemed to be a particularly offensive desecration, with the cattle trampling over the graves and befouling them, and especially because the Talmud specifically forbids grazing cattle in the cemetery (*Megilla* 29a). Worse than that, sometimes the government would want to run a new roadway through the cemetery. Sometimes, still worse, the government would want to repossess the cemetery. All these situations came up again and again, and the question always is, what can we do, how much effort should we expend in the attempt to overcome these various threats?

Isserlein himself suggested that the congregation should not tax itself too heavily in order to bribe the officer of the king to keep his cattle out of the cemetery. After all, it is not the Jews themselves who are committing this desecration. As for the second situation, this arose in the city of Cracow, where some of the rabbis, including Moses Isserles, are buried (cited by Moses Feinstein in his *Igros Moshe, Yore Deah* 247). Of course, great effort should be expended to prevent, if possible, so permanent a desecration, but what if it fails? And what to do when the ruler repossesses a cemetery entirely? In the latter case, of course, there is no recourse other than disinterment. In fact, Moses Feinstein suggests disinterment in the case of the old cemetery in New Orleans which was in the same state as the one in Poughkeepsie, mentioned in the question. He suggests that disinterment is the only permitted solution (*Igros Moshe, Yore Deah* 246) and he prescribes that while all the bones taken out of the old cemetery need not be put in separate graves and may be put in one large grave, nevertheless they should not be mixed up with each other, but kept separated by ridges of earth or stone.

This solution (i.e., disinterment) is of course the optimum solution, for once the bodies or the bones are removed, there is no sanctity left in the land from which they were removed. The land is then considered *Karka Olom,* the world's earth, the use of which cannot then be prohibited for any ritual reason.

Nevertheless, although Moses Feinstein's suggestion is basically the best, it entails many difficulties. If the cemetery has not been used for almost seventy years, the bones, while they still exist, may well be scattered and unrecoverable. In this regard it must be remembered, also, that disinterment is always a cause for sorrow. In traditional law a person must sit on the ground as in *Shiva,* for a whole day while the bones of his close kin are being disinterred (*Yore Deah* 403:1). In fact, Moses Sofer, in the case in Budapest where the whole cemetery was taken away from the Jewish community, actually forbade the *Chevra Kadisha* to make public the date and the hour of the disinterment, so that a large portion of the community should not need to sit on the ground as in *Shiva* (*Chatham Sofer, Yore Deah* 353).

Perhaps the best thing to do under the circumstances would be, first of all, to remove all the tombstones and to set them up in a special place in the existing protected cemetery. Thus the memorial of the departed will not be forgotten. Secondly, if there are traceable descendants of those buried in that old cemetery, they should be gathered in a meeting and asked to decide whether they are content with the preservation of the tombstones, or would wish also that the bones be disinterred. The chances are that they will be content with leaving the bones rest, since they will very likely consider that it is to the honor of the dead not to disturb their bones, and much is permitted in Jewish legal tradition if it is for the honor of the dead. Finally, the community can do what Rabbi Moses Goldberg of New Orleans suggested in his question to Moses Feinstein, namely, that a layer of earth three-hand-breadths or more be spread over the entire cemetery. Moses Feinstein rejects this; yet it is, nevertheless, a *possible* suggestion, since when a layer of earth that thick (three-hand-breadths, or according to the *Shulchan Aruch,* six-hand-breadths (*Yore Deah* 362:4)) is laid down, the rights of those already buried below have been fully protected, since, if need be, new bodies may then be buried over the old graves. While it is debatable that such an earth-covering would cancel the sanctity of the old cemetery, at least the rights of those buried in it would be completely provided for. One thing more, however, must also be provided for, if possible, namely, to see to it by all means available that if the area is taken over in an urban renewal, the possibility of which is suggested in the question, then this particular section of land should never be dug up for foundations for houses (which would disturb and scatter the bones of the dead) but should become one of the open areas converted into a park, and the very trees and grass would be an evidence of respect to those who sleep below the surface.

51

FAMILY DISAGREEMENT OVER CREMATION

QUESTION:

A Jew had died and left instruction in his will that his body is to be cremated; but the next of kin, either for religious or other reasons, wish to have a burial instead. Whose wish is to be carried out? (Asked by Rabbi John D. Rayner, Union of Liberal and Progressive Synagogues, London, England.)

ANSWER:

THERE IS a Talmudic maxim which, under ordinary circumstances, should guide the family. The maxim found in *Gittin* 40a and *Taanit* 21a is as follows: "It is a *Mitzvah* to carry out the intentions of the dead." In the Talmudic discussion and in the *Shulchan Aruch* (*Even Hoezer* 54; *Chosen Mishpot* 252:2) this principle is applied to the disposition of the property left by the deceased. However, the maxim is also used in a more general sense than that. For example, when a man says he does not want a eulogy spoken, or if he says he does not want *Kaddish* said for him, his wishes are to be fulfilled. See the full discussion in *Recent Reform Responsa,* p. 110 ff. (If the book is not available to you, let me know and I will send you a photostat of the responsum.)

However, it will be observed in this responsum that

there is a definite limitation placed upon the maxim to fulfill the will of the dead. We may grant a man's wish not to have a eulogy or *Kaddish* because eulogy and *Kaddish* are for the honor or the atonement (respectively) for the dead; and a man has the right to say that he does not want these privileges. But if, for example, he had expressed the wish that his survivors should not mourn for him (*Shiva* and *Sheloshim*), this wish must *not* be carried out, because these periods of mourning are religiously incumbent upon the survivors and he has no right to expect his wish to be fulfilled when his wish contravenes the law.

On this basis the question would seem to be easily answered, namely, since cremation is contrary to Jewish law, the man's wish contravenes the law and may not be carried out. This would be the instant decision of an Orthodox rabbi.

However, since the question is put by Liberal and Reform rabbis to a Liberal or Reform rabbi, the question and the answer cannot be so clear-cut. While Orthodox opposition to cremation has occasionally gone so far as to refuse the burial of the ashes (though some permit this) and while some authorities have gone even further to prohibit any services for the person who has been cremated, the Central Conference of American Rabbis decided early (*CCAR Yearbook* 1892, p. 43, cf. *Jewish Encyclopedia,* Vol. IV, p. 344) that we will not refuse to officiate at a cremation. This decision leads us to look a little more closely into the status of cremation in Jewish law.

The fact of the matter is, there is no clear-cut prohibition of cremation in the Talmud. Of course, the presumption is that cremation was not practiced very much, if at all, first because earth burial is simpler and, secondly, because in Mishnaic times at least they knew that cremation was a Roman custom and, therefore, to be avoided as idolatrous.

The Orthodox agitation against cremation actually began about a century ago, when cremation became an ideal that was agitated for through many societies in the western lands. When one studies the arguments adduced (in the last century) against cremation, one can see that they are forced. For example, burning the body would be tantamount to a denial of bodily resurrection. The patriarchs all made arrangements for their burial. So, clearly, that was the only proper way of disposing of the body. (The best statements of the Orthodox case against cremation are in Lerner's *Chaye Olom* and Greenwald's *Kol Bo,* p. 53 ff.) A good article giving the permissibility of cremation is to be found in the Central Conference *Yearbook* for 1891-2, by Schlesinger, p. 33 ff. However, it is to be noticed that Solomon Ben Adret in his Responsum #369 permitted the putting of quicklime on the body, which would burn up the flesh so that the bones could be transported to another city in fulfillment of the wishes of the dead. In fact, Isserles gives this as a law, that we may put quicklime on the body if the deceased had left a request that his body was to be buried in another city (see *Yore Deah* 363:2). Of course, it must also be noted that Joseph Caro in *Yore Deah* 362:1 does speak of burial in the earth as a *Mitzvah.*

The situation, therefore, is as follows: While cremation is not well-established as a classic prohibition, nevertheless in the last century it has become an established decision and mood of Orthodoxy that cremation is forbidden. If we are dealing with Orthodox people, we should take this mood as a fact and respect it. If, then, the family *is* chiefly Orthodox, we would be inclined not to fulfill the wish of the dead. But if the family is chiefly Liberal, then we consider the fact that the prohibition against cremation is not a firmly rooted one and that Reform rabbis have long since decided to officiate at cremations. Surely if we officiate at a cremation, we cannot refrain from fulfilling or encouraging the fulfillment of a man's wish for this type of disposal of his body.

The decision then in this case must depend upon the mood prevailing in the family. If the family is not definite about it and asks our advice, we should urge them to carry out the Talmudic maxim: It is a *Mitzvah* to fulfill the wishes of the dead.

52

VISITING THE CEMETERY

QUESTION:

A man from Hartford, Connecticut, visiting his father in Milwaukee, decided also to visit his mother's grave in the Milwaukee cemetery. It was *Chol Ha-Moed* of Passover. When he returned from the cemetery, his father rebuked him, saying that he should not have visited the cemetery during this period. Was he right? What rules govern visiting the cemetery? (Asked by Rabbi Harold Silver, Hartford, Connecticut.)

ANSWER:

THIS FAMILY INCIDENT involves a rather important question. When is it proper and when is it improper to visit the cemetery? And are these rules a fixed and an authoritative part of Jewish traditional law?

This question, like many other questions of popular observance, involves a number of larger questions. The first is: Are the laws of visiting the cemetery to be deemed Biblical law (which is the most authoritative) or only rabbinical law in elaboration of the Bible (*M'd'Oraisa* or *M'd'Rabbanun*)? The second question is: Is this, altogether, a question of law, or is it a question merely of popular custom (*Din* or *Minhag*)? If it is only *Minhag,* then there is this further question:

Is it a well-established or widespread *Minhag* (in which case it would be deemed as authoritative as law itself) or is it merely a local *Minhag?* All these questions need to be settled in all cases where there is a dispute with regard to any observance, in order to know how strictly the observance must be followed.

As soon as one looks at the question of visiting the cemetery, one finds an astonishing vagueness as to the observances and a curious variety. In almost every case where the visiting is mentioned, it is mentioned with the words, "It is a custom in some places to visit on this and this day," etc. In some places it is a custom to visit on *Erev* New Year and *Erev* Yom Kippur. (This custom is traced to Frankfurt; mentioned by the recorder of Old Frankfurt customs, Yosef Ometz). In some places the cemetery is not to be visited during the month of Nisan. Some Cabalistic sources (mentioned in the name of the Ari) say that a woman in her period should not visit the cemetery. The variety of customs indicates in itself that the entire question of cemetery visiting is not really in the realm of law, but only in the realm of custom, and not too widespread a custom either. The best proof of this fact is that you do not find in any of the codes any worked-out listing of the days in which the cemetery may or may not be visited.

If that is the case, the best thing to do is to go back to basic principles and decide the question involved here on more general grounds. The basic question involved here is derived from the Talmud. The Talmud, in *Taanis* 16a, describing the ritual on the fast days (referring to the special fast days called in case of drought) says that among other observances, people visit the cemetery on these fast days. To which the *Tosfos* comments and says, "That is why we visit the cemetery on the Ninth of Av." This comment of the *Tosfos* on the Talmud establishes a general rule for us, namely, that the proper time to go to the cemetery is on fast days or, in general, at penitential times; hence *Erev* Yom Kippur, Ten Days of Penitence, etc. We may also derive the reverse rule that we may not visit the cemetery on days of happy holidays; so not on the Sabbath, nor on the *Yom Tov*.

This reasoning, however, leaves the specific question of *Chol Ha-Moed* somewhat open. Is *Chol Ha-Moed* holiday enough to make cemetery visitations improper? After all, we do have funerals on *Chol Ha-Moed* (but perhaps that is because a funeral cannot be long postponed). On the other hand, it is a generally observed rule not to have weddings on *Chol Ha-Moed,* so as not "to mix one joy with another." So *Chol Ha-Moed* is enough of a holiday to say, perhaps, there is justification for the custom not to visit the cemetery then. But this is not really well-established. If you look in the *Shulchan Aruch* (*Orah Hayyim* 548) where the laws of *Chol Ha-Moed* are given, there is no mention at all of prohibiting cemetery visiting; and if you look in the *Yore Deah* (401) where the law of mourning is given as it applies to *Chol Ha-Moed*, there is no mention there either. So in general we may say affirmatively, there is a custom to go to the cemeteries at penitential times, the Ninth of Av, the month of Elul, the Ten Days of Penitence, *Erev* Rosh Hashonah and *Erev* Yom Kippur. As to the days, then, on which we may not visit the cemeteries, we may say on Sabbath and holidays and *possibly,* also, on *Chol Ha-Moed.*

But a clear proof that all this is only *Minhag* is to be found in Greenwald's well-known handbook, *Kol Bo,* page 166, who quotes an authority, *Mishmeres Shalom,* (Shachne Tcherniak) to this effect: If a person has a sick person at home and he wants to go to the cemetery to pray in his or her behalf, he may go even on *Chol Ha-Moed,* the New Moon and the Sabbath.

So the whole matter is based on custom. While generally we may say that it is preferable not to visit on *Chol Ha-Moed,* nevertheless if the son came halfway across the country for a brief visit, he certainly may violate this custom and visit his mother's grave on *Chol Ha-Moed,* as he would have been permitted had he a sick person to pray for at his mother's grave. His father should not have rebuked him, unless, of course, what he really wanted was for the son to prolong his visit and then he could go to the cemetery after Pesach.

53

EXCHANGING A TOMBSTONE

QUESTION:

A surviving child desires to exchange the tombstone on her father's grave, presumably for a more elaborate one. She states that the proposed second tombstone conforms to a request that her father had made. Is it permissible to make such an exchange? (By Rabbi L. Winograd, McKeesport, Pennsylvania)

ANSWER:

IN GENERAL it is deemed praiseworthy in the legal tradition to fulfill a behest of a departed parent. The Talmud in *Taanis* 21a states it as a principle that "it is a *Mitzvah* to fulfill the command of the departed." This *Mitzvah* applies not only to the disposing of his estate, but also to matters relating to the funeral and to the grave. However, there is a definite restriction as to such requests. No request may be fulfilled which is contrary to the law. Thus, if a man says: "Do not have any funeral eulogies for me," this request must be fulfilled because the funeral eulogy is for the honor of the dead and he may, if he wishes, say he does not desire that honor. But if he says, "Do not bury me in the ground," this request may *not* be fulfilled because it is contrary to the law which requires that the body be buried in the ground.

Now assuming that the father had requested or expressed a wish for some other type of tombstone than the one that is already on his grave, may this wish, namely, to substitute another tombstone, be fulfilled? Is it permitted to exchange a tombstone once it is on the grave? The question involves the status of the tombstone: Is it an integral part of the grave (in which case it may not be removed since it belongs, as it were, to the dead) or is it merely a convenience for the survivors so that they may easily find the grave? If it is merely the latter, then the survivors may do with the tombstone what they wish. They may take it down, put up another, or sell the old tombstone, since it is theirs and does not really belong to the grave. This basic question as to whether it is an essential part of the grave or not, was discussed with relation to another tombstone question in *Current Reform Responsa,* p. 149 ff. But since the question asked here is really a different one than is discussed there, it needs to be gone into once more.

Greenwald, in his compendium on funeral practices, *Kol Bo,* p. 385, leaves the matter unsettled as to whether a tombstone may be exchanged. The reason for his uncertainty is that the earlier sources are in themselves divided on the larger question as to whether the living may consider the stone as theirs and may therefore benefit from it. Most of the discussion in the earlier sources is dealt with by Joel Sirkes ("The Bach") in the *Tur,* 364. And so Isserles to the *Shulchan Aruch* (the same reference) leaves the discussion open, saying: Some forbid the living to sit on the tombstone, but some differ, i.e., it is not quite settled whether the tombstone belongs to the grave and therefore the living may not benefit in any way from it.

Interestingly enough, almost precisely the same question that is asked here was asked centuries ago and is referred to by Azulai in his *Birke Joseph,* to *Yore Deah* 342. A widow was dissatisfied when she saw the tombstone that had been put on her husband's grave. She therefore ordered a larger tombstone but wanted to turn in the smaller tombstone for credit on the cost of the larger tombstone. This was forbidden, namely, to turn in the smaller tombstone for credit, but there was no objection to her exchanging it for a larger tombstone, for that was for the honor of the dead.

So actually there is no real objection to substituting a larger tombstone. The real question is: What may be done with the first tombstone which has been removed? Since there is a large body of opinion among the scholars that the stone actually belongs to the grave and that, therefore, the living may not benefit from it, there is a strong limitation as to what must be done with the original stone. This specific question has come up frequently. For example, the community of Budapest had to evacuate a cemetery (on which they had only a lease) and they were left with tons of tombstones. It would have been too expensive to transport them to the new cemetery. Besides, where should they be placed there? (Cf. *Responsa Maharsham,* Swadron II, 122.) A similar question arose in Italy: Because of a lack of cemetery space, tons of earth to a considerable depth were spread to cover all the old graves so that bodies could be buried in the newly placed earth. The old tombstones therefore were not even visible. Perhaps they should have been left there buried, but they were removed from the graves before the new earth was put in. So again there was a question of what to do with the old tombstones. See Isaac of Aboab (Venice, 1610-1694) in his *D'var Samuel,* #342. Also Menachem Azariah da Fano, Responsum #56 (Rabbi in Venice, 16th century). The answer usually is given that the stones may not be used for private benefit (just as the aforementioned widow could not turn it in for credit) but may be used for the benefit of the cemetery or other communal causes.

Therefore the family, in the question asked here, may substitute a new stone, but the old stone cannot be sold. It may be given to some poor family to be rechiseled for the use of their graves, or it may simply be buried somewhere else in the cemetery.

In *Ha-dorom* for Nisan, 1970, there is a responsum on emptying out a cemetery by Rabbi Chaim D. Regensburg, pp. 28-35. He comes to the same conclusion with regard to the tombstones and mentions that Isserles, *Yore Deah* 364a, gives two opposite opinions as to whether it is permitted to have benefit from a tombstone.

54

A CONVERT AND JEWISH BURIAL
(Ruth's Vow)

QUESTION:

Since Ruth said to Naomi, "Where thou diest I will die, and there will I be buried," it is evident that Ruth felt that a vital element in her conversion was that, after her death, she be buried beside Naomi (i.e., in a Jewish cemetery). If that is so, why is Jewish burial not mentioned among the requirements put to a candidate for conversion? Should not a convert who promises loyalty to Jewish commandments be asked, also, to promise that he or she will be buried in a Jewish cemetery? (Asked by Rabbi Fredric Pomerantz, in behalf of a group of colleagues gathered at a meeting in Columbus, Ohio.)

ANSWER:

THE PASSAGE in Ruth 1:17 in which Ruth describes her full conversion as involving the intention to be buried among Jews (or by the side of Naomi) has been used in the rabbinic literature as a basis for a number of conclusions regarding the laws and customs involved in the process of conversion. Therefore the question asked her is quite justified.

In fact, the earlier verses of the dialogue between Naomi and her two daughters-in-law are used as a comment on conversion. In verses 8, 10, and 11, Naomi says three times, "Return to your homes, my daughters." From this threefold statement of Naomi, it is concluded (Ruth, *Rabba* II, 16) that we should not be too hasty to accept proselytes, but we should reject them three times at first (thus testing their resolution).

Now, as to Ruth's statement, "Where thou diest," etc., the comment in the Talmud and the Targum (b. *Yevamos* 47a and b) is rather a surprising one. Ruth's statement, "Where thou diest . . ." is taken to be Ruth's response to a previous statement by Naomi; a statement not actually given in the Bible, but understood as having been said. Naomi says, in effect, that the law requires that a candidate for conversion be warned that he should be careful before he accepts Judaism; since once he accepts Judaism, he will be obligated to observe many commandments which he is not now obligated to observe, and if he violates them, he will (in the case of some of the commandments) be liable to the penalty of death. So the Targum and the Talmud (*Yevamos* 47b; also, Samuel de Useda in his commentary *Iggeres Shemuel* to the passage) say as follows: "There are sins for which the law ordains four types of death, stoning, hanging . . ." etc. This warning as to the penalties involved in the violation of the law is understood to have been given by Naomi to Ruth; to which Ruth now says, "I will risk these penalties of death." Then Naomi says further, "The Beth Din has two separate cemeteries for those who are thus condemned to death" (m. *Sanhedrin,* VI:5); to which Ruth says, "I am willing to take the chance that if I sin, there will I be buried."

Thus, the traditional comments on Ruth's statement are all more or less Aggadic. Her statement is not directly used as the Biblical source for an actual commandment, namely, that a convert must promise to be buried in a Jewish cemetery. Actually, Ruth's statement could not possibly be used as the Biblical basis for any such commandment. When Ruth made her statement, she was still a Moabite Gentile. How, then, could her personal intention be made the foundation for a law in Judaism? If it had been Naomi who said, "You will be buried by my side," one might assume that Naomi, a Jewess, was revealing Jewish law. But no such conclusion can be derived from a statement, however lovable, of an unconverted Moabite Gentile.

Besides, is there actually, as a matter of fact, such a commandment, namely, that a person must promise to be buried in a Jewish cemetery? Of course, once a person is dead, no commandment is incumbent upon him any longer, since "the dead are free from the commandments" (b. *Shabbas* 30a). But it might be said that while a person is still alive, it is his duty to provide for his Jewish burial; but even that is not so. It is, of course, a *custom* for a person to provide for the future and buy a grave (see *Kol Bo Al Avelus,* p. 174) and that custom is based upon the statement of Rabbi Elazar in Leviticus *Rabba* 5:5. But this worthy custom is not a commandment. No Jew commits a sin if he fails to buy a grave or provide for his Jewish burial.

There is, of course, a commandment involved in providing burial. That commandment is not incumbent upon the man himself, but upon his survivors. The *Mitzvah* of burying is a real *Mitzvah,* based on the verse, "Thou shalt bury" (Deuteronomy 21:23 and *Sanhedrin* 46b). In other words, Ruth, or any other convert, is not obligated to provide or to promise Jewish burial for herself, but her Jewish survivors *are* so in duty bound.

Furthermore, even if the "worthy custom" of providing for one's own burial were deemed to have attained the force of an actual Mitzvah, even so it should not be required specifically as a promise by the convert. The laws of what is to be required of a convert are mentioned in *Yevamos* 47a and given in detail in *Yore Deah* 268:1 and 2. There are only two of the important commandments mentioned in order to caution the candidate of the risks he is taking if he violates them after his conversion. These two commandments refer to forbidden food and the Sabbath. Then the Talmud and the *Shulchan Aruch* specifically say: "We mention *some* of the commandments" (*Miktsas Mitzvos*) "and we do not go into detail as to the various commandments" (*Eyn M'dak't'kin*). Of course, the candidate must promise in general that he or she will obey *all* the commandments, but it is quite sufficient if only one or two crucial commandments are mentioned as illustrations. We are not in duty bound to go through the whole list.

To sum up: While the story of Ruth is used as Aggadic material dealing with the process of conversion, the actual *commandments* involved are not based upon it. Nor *could* they be based upon it because

Ruth spoke as a Gentile and her noble resolve could not be made the basis of Jewish law. As for the commandment itself (of Jewish burial) it is the duty of the *survivors* to provide it; but it is only a "worthy custom" for the person himself to make provision for it. Hence it could not be *required* of a proselyte. It is not required of born Jews. Finally, the laws as given in Talmud and *Shulchan Aruch* insist that we mention to the candidate that we only mention a few of the commandments and not all of them.

Of course, it is conceivable that at some future date increasing numbers of converts may ask to be buried in Christian cemeteries, in the lot of their Christian family. If this situation arises, it might lead us to cast doubt upon the sincerity of their conversion. But, actually, in twenty years I have received only one enquiry regarding such a request. So, for practical reasons as well as for the Halachic reasons mentioned above, we should not demand a promise of consenting to Jewish burial as a prerequisite to a conversion. We take for granted that a convert who is reborn as a Jewish child (*Yevamos* 22a) will receive Jewish burial.

55

COPYRIGHTING BOOKS

QUESTION:

Is it right, according to Jewish legal tradition, to photo-stat or Xerox and sell books that have been published by other publishers? (Asked by Bernard Scharfstein, KTAV Publishing House, New York.)

ANSWER:

WHAT CAN PROPERLY be called copyright to a publisher was in the form of *Haskamos* printed by the rabbi of the city or the district. These *Haskamos* actually began with the age of printing when, you might say, publishing in the modern sense began. How it started is not quite clear. Ludwig Blau, in a brief but important statement in the old *Jewish Quarterly Review*, 1898, page 175, believes that it started with the Pope. (By the way, Eisenstein, in the *Ozar Yisroel*, has a fine article on the subject of *Haskama*, but gives a wrong reference at the end of the article, i.e., *JQR*, 1897; it should be 1898.)

The purpose of the *Haskama* was twofold. The first was to give an author permission to print. This was to avoid the danger of unworthy books being broadcast. This type of *Haskama*, therefore, was equivalent to the

Catholic *imprimatur,* i.e., that the books deserve printing.

The second purpose of the *Haskama* was to protect
the publisher against his book being pirated by other
printers. Usually the rabbi or rabbis forbade any other
printer to reprint the book for ten years from the date
of the original publication. Sometimes it was for three
years and occasionally for *more* than ten years, but ten
years was the usual period of protection to a publisher.
In other words, this second purpose of the *Haskama*
was not *imprimatur,* but actually copyright.

Generally *Haskamos* for an important or an expensive book were given by three or four rabbis. Wolf
Heidenheim (1757-1832) who made and published the
first scientific edition of the Machzor and its Piutim
(the well known Roedelheim Machzor) received copyright (*Haskamos*) from the rabbis of Amsterdam, Rot-
terdam, London and Frankfurt. In spite of these
Haskamos, a publisher in Vienna announced that he
would republish this Machzor together with Heidenheim's commentary. Whereupon Phineas Halevi Horo-
witz, the Chief Rabbi of Frankfurt, issued a proclamation addressed not only to the pirating publisher, but to
the entire Jewish community everywhere. This proclamation in Hebrew and Judeo-German is published at
the back of the 1832 edition of Heidenheim's Machzor
and reads in part as follows:

> Warning to our brethren of the house of Israel to keep
> their hands away from the Machzorim being printed in
> Vienna . . . It is commanded in the name of our rabbi
> that a man has declared in open print that he will reprint

the Machzorim of Wolf Heidenheim, to protect which our rabbi had given an Haskama and Cherem, that they are not to be republished (by any other publisher) for twenty-five years . . . and therefore the rabbi now proclaims that no one small republish these Machzorim and also that no man shall subscribe for them, and also (this in large type) whoever shall buy them shall be subject to the anathema (Cherem) and be punished as was Achan (who violated the Cherem proclaimed by Joshua, Chapter 9).

From this proclamation published by one of the leading rabbinical authorities of the early nineteenth century, it would seem that the sin of violating the copyright Cherem applies even to the people who buy (and presumably read) the pirated book.

The great outburst of responsa on the question of copyright *Haskama* occurred at the beginning of the nineteenth century with regard to the Talmud printed in Slavita. The publishers in Slavita received a *Haskama* for ten years. Before the ten years were over, other publishers in Vilna and Grodno started to publish the Talmud. The Vilna and Grodno publishers justified their right to publish, even though the ten years' copyright of Slavita was not yet over, by arguing that the Slavita publisher had sold out his entire stock and, therefore, although the ten years had not passed, the *purpose* of the *Haskama* was fulfilled, his investment and his labor were amply repaid.

Of all the responsa on this cause celebre, the clearest is that by Moses Sofer, in his responsa *Choshen Mishpot* 41, in which he gives clearly the reason for protecting a publisher; namely, that if he were not protected, he would never invest his money and labor, and thus the study of the Torah would be more difficult for lack of availability of books.

Now the question might be asked: While it is clear that a second publisher is forbidden to republish during the lifetime of the first publisher's *Haskama,* suppose, however, the first publisher published without a *Haskama;* is there any prohibition to a second publisher to republish? The answer must be "yes," it would be forbidden, if not legally, at least morally. The rabbinical *Haskama* did not *create* the rights of the first publisher; it merely recognized them. Therefore the money and labor invested by the first publisher gives him an inherent right to be protected against piracy, even if he has no formal *Haskama.*

But, alas, the rabbis did not have the powers of the state to punish legally the infringement of copyright. They made up for their lack of enforcing power by very stern language of threat (of Divine punishment). Unfortunately, that did not always help. Books were often pirated whether they had *Haskama* or not.

It is certainly morally wrong to destroy the investment in money, time and labor of a publisher by pirating his book. The rabbis attempted to prevent this sin by their *Haskamos,* but were not always successful.

Two further questions, nowadays, are involved in this matter. One: Would the following be considered an infringement of the Jewish ethics governing copyrights? Suppose a school Xeroxes a book, not for the purpose of selling the Xerox copies (which would obviously be a violation of the copyright) but merely for the purpose of use by the students in the school. Since the Xeroxed books are not sold, is this action to be deemed unethical? The second question involved is whether the laws of the state governing copyrights, have any validity in Jewish law according to the principle of *dina d'malchusa dina* ("the law of the government is deemed valid by Jewish law").

First, the question of whether Xeroxing not for sale is to be deemed a violation of Jewish ethics governing copyrights: Of course, the old *Haskamos* speak only of the prohibition of *printing* (*D'fuss*) for a period generally of ten years, in order to protect the original publisher and to encourage men to go into the publishing business so that books be available for students. Now, if a second publisher would plan to pirate the book, he must set up type and buy the paper, etc. Since he must go to considerable expense, then the fact that there is a rabbinical copyright prohibiting the piracy, this would-be pirate was often discouraged and gave up his plans. But now with the modern method of Xeroxing, a book can be so easily copied (without setting type, etc.) that the whole process of book piracy has become very tempting.

To answer the question whether such Xeroxing is to be deemed "piracy," one can only judge by the *intent* of the law (i.e., the ethics implied in the *Haskamos*). The *Haskama* was clearly for the purpose of protecting the original publisher, to give him a chance to make an adequate profit, so that people would find it worth their while to enter into the publishing business, and thus books would be available for students. Judging by the basic *purpose* of the copyright, this Xeroxing certainly is a violation. If, for example, a large school is involved and three hundred copies have been Xeroxed, the author and the publisher have certainly been subjected to considerable potential loss. Three hundred fewer copies are sold. This surely is a violation of the intent of the *Haskamos*.

Of course, the situation involved could be still more definitely answered if there were a law against Xeroxing large numbers of a book without permission of the publisher. It may well be that the copyright laws have not yet taken cognizance of the modern easy way to book piracy. But let us say that a bill will be introduced in Congress and a law passed preventing large-scale copying of a book without permission of the publisher or the author. One is inclined to think that such laws already exist because many of the copyright statements back of the title page prohibit the copying of the book or parts of it by *any* method without permission. The question which concerns us is whether these laws, those already in existence and those that will be passed governing Xerox copying, are to be deemed valid in Jewish law by the principle of *dina d'malchusa dina* (first enunciated by R. Samuel in *Gittin* 10b).

The validity in Jewish law of the principle of *dina d'malchusa dina* is subject to certain definite restrictions. First of all, it never applies to ritual or spiritual laws. If, for example, a government would prohibit *shechita* (as, indeed, had frequently happened) we are not bound to accept that government decree, but should resist it as much as possible. The government decree is valid in Jewish law *only* in civil law, matters of money, contracts, etc. So in general it would apply to the financial rights of the publisher and author to be prevented from unfair piracy.

But it is important to note that even though in *general* the principle of *dina d'malchusa dina* applies to civil law, certain rabbinical authorities have restricted its applicability even further. Some authorities say that it applies only in civil matters of *public* concern such as taxes, the roads, law and order, etc., but does not apply to the private sector even in civil matters. Thus, according to this opinion, a private debt between two people would be governed by Jewish law and not by public law, since it is not a matter of *public* concern.

But this restricting of the principle to civil laws in the public domain is contraverted by great authorities as, for example, Solomon Ben Adret, the great rabbi of Spain in the thirteenth century. He discusses this matter in his responsa (Volume II, #356) and says that the secular government has the right (i.e., according to Jewish law) to pass laws, not only in the public sector, but even in the private sector "in order that the people should not come into quarrels and bitter disputes." In other words, Rashba anticipates the purpose of law as given in the prologue of the Constitution of the United States, "to insure domestic tranquility." This opinion of the great Spanish rabbi is echoed by the great Ashkenazic scholar, Solomon Luria. In his *Yam Shel Shlomo* (*Baba Kamma* 6:14) he says that if the government did not pass laws governing private debts, etc., general social chaos would ensue. And, in fact, the various decisions of Isserles in the *Shulchan Aruch* reflect this point of view, namely, that the laws apply even in private civil matters. See Isserles, *Choshen Mishpot,* 3:4, 68:1, 74:7, 162:1, etc.

The situation is, therefore, clear. The ethics of the Jewish copyright *Haskama* means to protect the author and the publisher, and thus encourage them to continue their work. The technique of the pirate republishing is immaterial. If by any technique the publisher and the author are deprived of the sale of hundreds of copies, the intent of the *Haskama* is definitely violated. Furthermore, if the public law prevents, or will in the future prevent, such unauthorized republication, even if the results are used in a school and not for sale, then that public law *will* be applicable in Jewish life by the principle of *dina d'malchusa dina.* This piracy cannot be deemed a purely private matter between individuals, with regard to which some authorities believe the law of *dina d'malchusa* does not apply. It is certainly a matter of public order and decency and, besides, most of the later authorities agree that even if this situation be deemed a private one involving two individuals, nevertheless, the law of *dina* applies.

I suppose it would not be considered worthwhile discussing the action of one poor scholar who copies a book just once for his *own* use, as to whether this would be prohibited. But there is no question that large-scale copying for the use of a school, for example, is definitely against Jewish religious ethics for the reasons mentioned above.

56

TO DISSUADE A WOULD-BE SUICIDE

QUESTION:

How much effort does our religious tradition require of us to prevent a person from suicide? By words only, or even by force if necessary? (Asked by Rabbi Allen S. Maller, Culver City, Calif.)

ANSWER:

As FAR AS I KNOW there is no clear mention in the legal literature of the duty to exert strong effort to dissuade or prevent a person from committing suicide. Nevertheless it is possible to answer the question asked here by way of analogy and by developing the implications of existing law.

First it must be clearly understood that in this regard Jewish tradition is diametrically different from that of the Romans and the Japanese, among whom suicide was considered under certain circumstances virtually only a private matter. In Jewish law suicide is considered a most heinous offense. In fact, one may judge with what horror it was looked upon that in the long and often bloody history covered by the Bible there are only three clear suicides, Saul, his armor bearer, and Achitophel. Another indication as to what horror suicide aroused all through Jewish history, Bible and post-Bible, can be seen from the law governing the burial of suicides. The strict letter of the law as given in *Semachos* II is that we do nothing with regard to the funeral of suicides (*Eyn Misaskin Bohem*); but immediately the law as it developed came upon various ways of removing the stigma of suicide from the person who died. If the man was afraid, or if he changed his mind or, as some say, even if he repented at the last moment, he was said not to have committed the crime of suicide. Even as strict an authority as Moses Sofer (Resp. *Yore Deah* 32b) permitted such a man's relatives to observe full mourning for him so that a respected family would not have to bear the stigma of suicide (cf. *Recent Reform Responsa,* p. 114 ff.).

This shameful crime of suicide is considered analogous to murder. The Scripture in Genesis 9, verse 6, speaking of murder, says: "He who sheds the blood of a man, his blood will be shed by man." And in the previous verse, 9:5, it says: "I will seek your blood from yourselves," which the Talmud (*Baba Kamma* 91b) says means a prohibition against suicide. See Rashi to the passage, and also *Midrash Rabba,* Genesis, Chapter 34:13. The term used in the Talmud for doing oneself harm and suicide is *Chovel,* which means "to damage" or "to harm," and the Talmud says: Just as a person may not harm (*Chovel*) another person, so he may not harm (*Chovel*) himself. This is exactly equivalent to the legal phrase "felo de se," a felony against oneself.

Now there is a great deal of clear law about the efforts which must be expended to prevent a person harming others (*Chovel*). The law is given in detail in the *Shulchan Aruch, Choshen Mishpot* 425. There we are told what great efforts must be made to prevent a person harming another (*Chovel*). If he is pursuing somebody to harm him or to kill him, you must pursue after him. You must stop him somehow or other, even if you injure a limb of the potential murderer, or even if your pursuit to save the victim results in the death of the murderer.

Clearly, then, we may make this analogy: Since the law uses the term "to harm" (*Chovel*) for suicide as it does for murder, and thus considers suicide equivalent to murder, it seems clear that we may make the same effort to prevent a man from suicide as we must make to prevent him from murder. Of course in his case, we avoid harming him in our efforts to save him.

So far our discussion of our duty toward would-be suicides was based upon a general consideration, namely, that since in Jewish law we are in duty bound to prevent a man from doing damage to another man, it would stand to reason that we are equally in duty bound to prevent a man from committing the sin of doing fatal damage to himself. However, beyond this general consideration, there are also some specific legal statements in the Halacha which bear more directly on the subject.

It might be mentioned at the outset that there is an interesting responsum rather closely related to the subject in the *Or Ha-Mizrach,* the magazine of the Orthodox Zionists, the Mizrachi, for Tishri, 5772. Rabbi Judah Gershuni reports that he received the following question from a religious Israeli soldier at the Suez Canal. Israeli soldiers encamped along the canal are forbidden by army orders to swim in the canal because of the danger from Egyptian snipers. Nevertheless many soldiers ignore the order and go swimming in the canal. Thus they are wilfully endangering their lives. The Orthodox soldier therefore asks this question: Is he in duty bound religiously to go to the rescue of those soldiers who are wilfully risking their lives?

Since these soldiers are certainly not seeking death but surely hope to avoid it, this question is not precisely one dealing with would-be suicides. Nevertheless because they are wilfully putting themselves into danger, the religious problem of whether to rescue them or not comes very close to the question of suicide. In his answer Rabbi Gershuni cites virtually all the relevant Halacha. It would be well for our purposes to go over the legal material and see what conclusions it leads us to.

The basic commandment involved here is the statement in Leviticus 19:16: "Stand not idly by the blood (i.e., the bloodshed) of your neighbor." The Talmud (in *Sanhedrin* 73a) on the basis of this verse says that if you see a man drowning or being attacked by a wild beast or by robbers, it is your religious obligation to come to his rescue, as Scripture commands: "Stand not idly by," etc. This obligation has become one of the regular 613 commandments. In the *Sefer Hachinuch* it is commandment 237, and in the *Shulchan Aruch* it is in *Choshen Mishpot* 426.

Joseph Babad (19th century) wrote a large commentary on the *Sefer Hachinuch.* This commentary, *Minchas Chinuch,* has become a standard legal reference book. In his supplementary notes (*Kometz Mincha*) Joseph Babad comes to the conclusion that although the commandment, "Thou shall not stand idly by," impels us to come to the rescue of any one in danger, this duty does *not* apply when a person willfully and of his own accord puts himself into danger. As his reason for this conclusion, that the duty to help does not apply to suicides, he uses an inference based upon which proof texts are used and which are not used in the Talmud in the passage in *Sanhedrin.*

Yet actually there is another and a firmer ground for Babad doubting the duty to rescue a suicide. It is as follows: The duty to ransom captives is one of the prime obligations in the law. Cf. *Shulchan Aruch, Yore Deah* 251:1: "There is no *Mitzvah* greater than that of ransoming captives." Nevertheless, the Mishnah (*Gittin* IV:9) says that if a man *sells himself* as a slave, we should *not* rescue him. The Talmud in *Gittin* 46b says that we *do* ransom him the first or second time because he might have sold himself because he was under some duress (poverty, etc.) but if he sells himself the third time, then his intention to enslave himself is clear and we are not in duty bound to help him further. But even so, we should ransom his children.

However, an opinion exactly contrary to that of Joseph Babad is given by the premier 13th-century authority, Meir of Rothenburg. In his responsa collection (ed. Budapest, #39) there is an especially interesting responsum because it deals with the ransoming of captives. He himself had been captured and held for ransom, and remained in prison for the latter part of his life. The Jewish communities would have raised money to ransom him, but he did not permit them to do so because he feared that the authorities would then imprison other leaders and force the community to ransom them. However, in cases of captives and ransom which did not involve the danger of mulcting the Jewish community, but were a private matter for private ransom money, he was of course strongly in favor of ransoming captives (as the commandment requires). This responsum of his concerns two Jewish men who were held for ransom. "A" got enough money to ransom them both. After they were free, "A" asked "B" to pay his share of the ransom money. "B" refused, saying he did not ask nor want to be ransomed, and so refused to pay. Meir of Rothenburg decided this dispute by saying that "B" was in duty bound to pay, even though he said that he was unwilling to be ransomed. He concludes this responsum by saying that we must rescue a drowning man even if he cries out, "Do not rescue me" (I want to die). In other words, Meir of Rothenburg took the stand that we must rescue a person even if he does not want to be rescued; even if he wants to be a suicide.

Faced with these two opposite opinions (that of Joseph Babad and Meir of Rothenburg), Rabbi Gershuni has no decisive answer for the pious Israeli soldier. But he wisely makes a practical compromise. The soldier who would want to rescue these swimmers can approach carefully and quietly and be in minimum danger. It would therefore be permissible to expose himself to *minimum* danger in order to save others who were in *maximum* danger.

We might come to a similar conclusion. To put it pictorially: If the would-be suicide is standing on the ledge of the twentieth story of a building and threatens to jump, you are not required to risk your life by going out on the ledge also. You may stand in the window, or on the ledge near the window and hold on, but certainly you must make an effort to dissuade him. In this we follow the great authority, Meir of Rothenburg, that it is our duty not to "stand idly by" when a man is trying to commit suicide. We must try to save him even though he shouts, "I want to die," etc. But on the basis of the dubieties mentioned above, we are not in duty bound to endanger our own life. Nevertheless we are still in duty bound to obey the commandment, "Stand not idly by," and must make earnest efforts to save him in spite of himself.

57

GARNISHEEING WAGES

QUESTION:

> If the court orders the wages due to an employee to
> be garnisheed, and the employer is Jewish, has the em-
> ployer the moral and religious duty to resist the court
> order, since the Bible prohibits withholding the wages
> of an employee? (Asked by Rabbi Joshua O. Haber-
> man, Washington, D.C.)

ANSWER:

THE BIBLE is specific in prohibiting the withholding of
wages due to an employee (see Leviticus 19:13 and
Deuteronomy 24:16). If, for example, the employee is
a day-by-day laborer, he must be paid on the very day
that his work is finished. This law is developed in full
detail in the Talmud in *Baba Metzia* from 110b to
112b; and based upon the Talmud, the law is discussed
fully by Maimonides in his *Yad,* in the laws of "hiring"
(*S'chiros*), Chapter 11. Then it is dealt with in the *Tur,
Choshen Mishpot* #339 and the same reference in the
Shulchan Aruch.

There are certain circumstances under which even
the strict Jewish law does not deem it a sin to withhold
wages. According to some opinions it is no sin to do
so in the case of agricultural labor (evidently because

the farmer himself gets his money only after the harvest. See the *Tur*.) Also, if the workingman knows beforehand that his employer has no money except on market-days, then in that case, the employer is not liable for his delay till the market-day. Finally, the employer is never liable if the employee does not demand his wages. This is clearly stated in *Baba Metzia* 112a and in the *Tur* and in the *Shulchan Aruch* 339:10.

So it may well happen that the employee, whose wages are garnisheed by the law, may well appreciate the fact that his employer cannot violate the court order; and knowing that fact, he does not make the futile gesture of demanding his wages. Thus if he does not demand it (for whatever reason) the employer has committed no sin under Jewish law if he withholds the wages.

As to the moral principle involved, that may depend upon what sort of debt it is, for the payment of which the wages are now being garnisheed. In the Commonwealth of Pennsylvania, for example, we have no garnisheeing of wages, except for the support of children and a wife (also for income tax). If it is to support children and wife, how could it be considered unethical for the employer to help in their support in this regard?

There is another ethical consideration involved. The sin denounced in Scripture actually involves two sins: a) the workman is deprived of what he has justly earned and b) the employer dishonestly keeps (permanently or for a time) money belonging to the worker. But in the case of the garnisheeing of the wages to pay a debt (to a third party) while it is true that the workman is deprived of his just due, the employer at least does not have the use of the money withheld. It goes to satisfy the debt designated in the writ.

But actually the whole question is theoretical. The garnisheeing of the wages comes to the employer as a court order which he cannot fail to obey without legal penalty. The fact that he is compelled to obey the court order has special relevance in Jewish law. In all matters of civil law (such as these) the principle of *Dina D'malchusa Dina* applies, "The law of the land is the law." In such cases it is the duty (the *Jewish* duty) of the employer to obey the law. This principle of *Dina D'malchusa Dina* does not apply in ritual or spiritual matters. A decree to violate Jewish law in such matters should be resisted even to martyrdom. But the decrees of a secular court in *civil* matters are laws which (by Jewish law) we are bound to obey. Therefore the employer has no moral or *religious* right to pay the man his wages.

58

RABBINICAL TENURE

QUESTION:

Is it a fact that a cantor or a rabbi or other such person employed by a congregation for more than a certain number of years is entitled to be supported by that congregation for the rest of his life, albeit he need not be continued in that official capacity? (Asked by Rabbi Joseph Glaser, New York.)

ANSWER:

THE QUESTION really amounts to this: Is there such a thing as automatic rabbinical tenure, analogous to the situation which prevails in American universities, namely, that if a teacher is reappointed to the faculty for a number of years, he arrives at the stage that is described by saying "he now has tenure;" that is to say, he can no longer be discharged?

To which extent this is applicable to the rabbinate cannot be answered simply. The reason why the question is somewhat complicated is due to the fact that up to the end of the Middle Ages, the rabbinate was not a profession at all. It was a voluntary, unpaid public service. A learned man would serve the community as a judge, settling disputes, preparing divorce documents, and answering problems of kosher and trefe, etc. This was his occupation but not his livelihood. He was a businessman. If he was occasionally paid, this was in recompense for the time taken away from his business (*s'char b'tayla*). But even so, certain authorities were indignant at the fact that even in those pre-professional days, the Rabbi took payment for preparing divorce documents, etc. (cf. *Current Reform Responsa*, p. 199 ff.).

Even in those days (when the rabbinate was no more than a voluntary devotion on the part of a learned man) even then, the congregation had certain responsibilities as to this volunteer's tenure. The general principle involved here is: We may raise the man in sanctity but not lower him (the phrase is used in *Berachos* 28a). This phrase was used to mean that once a man was given a position of dignity by a community, he could not be deposed from it unless, of course, for cause.

However, since being the rabbi was really not a profession, and although protected against being deposed from his sanctified status, nevertheless he had no monopoly; in those days, any other scholar could come into the community and serve it in a rabbinical manner. Most of the disputes on this question are cited by Moses Isserles in his note to *Yore Deah* 245:22, dealing with the rights of other scholars to come to the city and perform rabbinical functions. This statement of Isserles ends with the statement that if it is the custom in the community to supplant the rabbi with another, they may do so. At this stage, then, there was no such thing as tenure; cf. the classic case of this situation in *A Treasury of Responsa*, p. 61 ff.

But as the centuries passed, the rabbinate became a profession and a man was engaged with a fixed salary to serve the community as rabbi. The status therefore was new and the rights were different. Most of the rights of the rabbinate in the new professional situation are described by Moses Sofer, the great Hungarian authority, in a number of places, but most fully in his responsa, *Orah Hayyim* 205 and 206.

In these responsa he takes the trouble to explain away Isserles' statement that where it is the custom for the congregation to supplant one rabbi with another, they may do so. Moses Sofer explains that this statement of Isserles is based on the *Kol Bo,* which describes the situation as it was in those days (before the rabbinate was a profession) when there were many men who could serve the community as cantor or rabbi. In those days it was the custom to alternate the cantoral and rabbinical honors from one man to another and, therefore, they could make a change whenever they wanted to do so. But now the situation is obviously different.

In his responsa, *Orah Hayyim* 205 and 206, Moses Sofer says in general that it is unheard of for a rabbi to be removed when the term (usually three years) specified in his contract is over. He discusses the term "three years" (sometimes five years) put into the usual rabbinical contract. The reason for it is not actually to limit the rabbinical term of service; really it is based upon the rule in *Choshen Mishpot* 333:3 in Isserles, namely, that since a Hebrew slave in ancient times was indentured for six years, no one should engage himself for a period equal to that, or he ceases to act like a free agent. In practice, the term limit means that the rabbi, if *he* wishes, may leave the community after three years are passed; but it does *not* mean that the community has the right to discharge him after that term, which is after all only a formalized limit. Even if there is presumptive ground of misbehavior on the rabbi's part, even so it is doubtful whether he can be deposed. If there is a specific understanding written into the contract that *both* sides may terminate it after three years, then it is possible that he may be removed from office. But even that is debatable if anyone raised objection to it.

So strong is the concept of rabbinical (and cantoral) tenure in the law that there is considerable opinion that the rabbi's son, if fit for the office, has the preeminent right over other candidates to succeed his father. See the responsa, *Shem Aryeh,* by Aryeh Balchover, *Orah Hayyim* #7.

To sum up: The general principle that "we do not degrade in holiness" (*En Moriddin Bakodesh*) stands against removal of any appointee of a congregation for sacred work. Such removal was possible, however, in the early days when the rabbinate was not a profession. After it became a profession it is unheard of that a rabbi be removed after the formal term of three or five years mentioned in the rabbinical contract has passed. As for the subsidiary question, whether he must still be supported, when he can no longer serve the community due to age or sickness, this is not discussed, as far as I know, in the literature. But the presumption is that if he is not to be deposed, he cannot be allowed to starve.

There is a full article on this subject in the latest volume of *Encyclopedia Talmudis,* Vol. 14, column 347 to 357. The article gives all the opinions from scholars of all periods. Many of those (not all of them) who date from the time preceding the professionalizing of the rabbinate, believed that the rabbinate had no tenure (no *Chazakah*). Those of the modern centuries, in which the rabbinate had become a profession, almost unanimously hold that the rabbinate has tenure (*Chazakah*) and even the right to bequeath the position to a son if the son is worthy.

INQUIRIES

1

Inquiry

QUESTIONS FROM ISRAEL ON PROSELYTISM

Mr. Asher Maoz
6, Ahuzat Bait Street, 6th floor
Tel Aviv, Israel

Dear Mr. Maoz:

I shall be glad to answer your letter of July 29, but it is not possible to give a simple and direct answer to each of your questions in the order you presented them. The reason this is difficult is that some of the questions require an explanation of the basic philosophy of the Reform movement and it would be misleading simply to say "yes" or "no." This situation applies especially to Question 1, to what extent does proselytism by a Reform rabbi meet the requirements of the Halacha as to: a) Circumcision (*Brith-Mila*); b) Baptism (*Tevila*); c) Acceptance of the commandments (*Kabalat Ol Mitzvoth*). If I answered simply that we do not a) or do b) or c), I would fail to explain the reason for our basic attitude in such matters.

The attitude of Reform Judaism on ceremonial commandments is that they are secondary to the moral and

doctrinal commandments. So our emphasis in proselytism is as follows: We do not *require* as absolute
prerequisites either circumcision or *Tevila,* but lay
great emphasis on the instructions. This should not
surprise you, for it is possible according to the *Halacha*
to conceive of a conversion without circumcision or
the *Mikvah,* because this was the very subject of the
debate in the Talmud (*Yevamoth* 46a) where some of
the authorities believe that a proselyte is a full proselyte even without circumcision or *Mikvah.*

But the debate in the Talmud is not the real reason
for our practice. It is our general philosophy that the
ethical and philosophical meaning of Judaism is more
essential than the ceremonial. Therefore we may correctly say that less emphasis is placed upon circumcision and *Mikvah* and more on the instruction. That is
to say, it is not the mood of Reform to *abolish* the first
two rituals. Some rabbis require it, some do not. In
some countries the Reform movement requires it and
in some countries it does not. In ceremonial matters we
avoid strictness; but on the third element, namely, the
instruction, we put our great emphasis. In this regard,
if I may say so, our method of accepting proselytes is
superior to that of Orthodoxy. In Orthodoxy instruction
is comparatively minor, although it is indeed required.
With us it is major. Most large congregations have a
class of proselytes whose instruction will last a half
year or even a whole year; and as you may well imagine, while we teach the various home ceremonies which
the candidate will observe (such as Friday night lighting of the candles, etc.) our main emphasis in this long

instruction is on Jewish history, Jewish teachings, Jewish ethics. Forgive this long answer. A short answer would have been no answer at all.

Now with regard to your other questions, some I will answer simply "yes" or "no," but with others I will give you a specific case in which your question came up and how it was answered.

2. Proselytism for material purposes, etc.: We examine the candidate carefully to make sure that there are serious and worthy motives leading to the desire to become Jewish. However the difference between us and Orthodoxy is this: Theoretically, but not actually, in Orthodoxy if a person comes to be converted for the purpose of marrying a Jew, this is deemed *unworthy*, but with us, we consider that the desire to establish a home of unified spiritual mood is a worthy motive. We do not consider that if a candidate desires to be married to a Jew that this is unworthy at all. I am enclosing the relevant section, which I will mark "A" from the report of the Central Conference of American Rabbis on "Mixed Marriage and Intermarriage," *CCAR Yearbook* LVII, 1947. This also answers Question 3.

4. Attitude towards a proselyte and a Cohen: Reform Judaism has abolished all differences in religious standing between Cohanim, Leviim and other Jews. We are all deemed equal. Therefore Question 4 has no meaning for us.

5. A proselyte continuing with his non-Jewish spouse: We would consider this wrong for the reason indicated in a responsum which I wrote a few years

ago, which was published in the CCAR *Journal* and
is found in *Current Reform Responsa,* p. 215 (see
appendix B).

6. Could a minor proselyte without his parents?
No; we would not break up a family. With the consent
of his parents, certainly. This is already mentioned in
the Talmud in *Ketuboth* 11a.

7. As to the status of a minor who did not prosely-
tize while his parent did, we have made a new provision
for children whose parents have become Jewish. The
change is in accordance with our general principle:
Since the ceremonials of circumcision and *Mikvah* are
not as important to us as the instruction, we have decided that if such parents wish their child to be Jewish
and enter him into our school, when he graduates (or
is confirmed, usually around the age of fourteen) this
is deemed with us to be full and official conversion of
the child (see appendix C).

8. To answer this question I must first answer 13e:
Is there supreme Halachic authority in Reform Judaism? No; the Central Conference of American
Rabbis and our other organizations, such as the Union
of American Hebrew Congregations, etc., are voluntary organizations for consultation and mutual guidance. We have at the Conference a Responsa Committee of which I have the honor to be Chairman. My
decisions in answer to questions are made according to
what seems to me a balance between the attitude of
the *Halacha* and the needs of modern times. The decisions are meant for guidance and not for governance.
We respect the *Halacha* as an expression of Jewish

spiritual thought and feeling for two thousand years, and we follow it whenever we deem it possible to do so.

Now, therefore, the question of No. 8: The Conference is opposed to the marriage of a Jew with an unconverted non-Jew. Nevertheless there are a few rabbis who do officiate at such marriages. They are a small minority. Even this few do not officiate indiscriminately, but only under special circumstances as, for example, if the couple are both old people or if they had been married already in the civil courts and the husband is going overseas to serve in the Armed Forces, etc. So your question deals only with a few special cases and we have not yet come to a conclusion as to what the status of such children should be.

9. Should the laws of proselytism be changed according to the principle of *Hora'at Sha'ah?* We think so. That is really the mood of Reform Judaism, but the motive for change must be a serious one.

10. Could a non-Jew become a Jew other than by proselytization? No.

11. Differences in Israel and abroad: My *personal* judgment is that proselytization should be made easier in Israel because the whole environment is Jewish and it is almost inevitable that a home in which one member is a convert will be a truly Jewish home.

12. Is Judaism a nationality or a religion or both? The question would make more sense in eastern Europe than in the western democratic countries. In eastern Europe as, for example, in Soviet Russia, historic groups are considered separate nationalities. In

western democratic nations each person is an individual. A nation is composed of individuals of equal status. There is no separate grouping of nationalities.

Nevertheless our sense of historic unity and our brotherly bond with the state of Israel is deep and real. The best description of Judaism according to the feeling of most Reform Jews is that we are a religion and a family with all the intimate relationships which the word "family" implies. This is in accordance with the spirit of Jewish law. A convert is converted not merely to a religion, but to a real kinship. He or she may now marry a Jew and is always part of the Jewish family. In fact, the historic phrase that a convert is like a new-born child is an exact expression of somebody being reborn (*Yevamoth* 22a).

13a, b, b-1: In actual practice only a rabbi officiates, but according to Jewish law, if necessary a non-rabbi can conduct a conversion. I am appending a responsum that I gave on this question to the congregation in Bombay.

13c. The authority or *Semicha* of a Reform Rabbi: Orthodox rabbis have no legal authority either. The true *Semicha* ceased in the third century. What is called *Semicha* today in Orthodox life is really *Hatarat Hora'ah,* the right to teach. In other words, it is exactly equal in status to a graduation diploma. The Reform rabbi has the same rights as an Orthodox rabbi, the right conferred upon him by his education and his acceptance by a congregation. No rabbi in the world has any greater authority.

This should answer 13d, since there is no actual legal

authority anywhere in the rabbinate, Orthodox, Conservative or Reform. I would answer "yes" to d, but an Orthodox rabbi does not recognize the status of any other type of rabbi. 13e is already answered.

14. The relation of a proselyte to his former neighborhood and family: Technically speaking, they do not exist for him; but as the Talmud says, he would then justly complain that he has left a nobler sanctity for a lower one (*Yevamoth* 22a). Hence in many ways traditional law recognizes the relationship that remains between the proselyte and his family. Practically the problem comes up in questions of whether proselytes should say *Kaddish* for their Gentile fathers. This has been answered affirmatively in Jewish law. I enclose an answer I have given to this question (appendix E).

15a. I do not know of this occurring often, but it did occur at least once, and I am enclosing a responsum on the question. A proselyte attains an indelible allegiance to Judaism and can never throw it off again.

I do not know any statistics regarding 15b or c and 16. My own experience has been that in many cases, proselyte women especially become more earnestly Jewish than many of their Jewish-born friends.

17. Is conversion *Reshut* or *Mitzvah?* This is an open question in Jewish law, and as far as we are concerned in the Reform movement it is still debated among us. For example, the Union of American Hebrew Congregations a few years ago passed a resolution that we should go out and seek converts. In other words, it is a *Mitzvah*. The Central Conference of

American Rabbis has not yet passed on this matter. As I say, it is still an open question.

Please let me know when you have received these answers and if there are other matters that you want me to discuss, do not hesitate to ask me.

2

Inquiry

EXTRA SHROUD FOR COHEN

QUESTION:

> A family arranging the funeral for their deceased parent (?) asked that in addition to the regular shrouds in which he was wrapped an extra set of shrouds should be put in the coffin since the man was a Cohen. Is there any traditional justification for this request? (Asked by Louis J. Freehof, San Francisco, California.)

ANSWER:

THE QUESTION of the number and the arrangement of the traditional shrouds is not one which has clear legal definition. It is based upon tradition which only since the Middle Ages has made itself concrete and fairly definite. In Talmudic times there was a great deal of variation in the arrangement and the number of the shrouds (*tachrichim*). This can be seen, for example, from the statement of Rabbi Hezkiah asking that when he dies: "Do not put *too many* shrouds on me" (Jerushalmi *Kelaim* 9:4) and also by the fact that Rabban Gamliel had noticed that the people were going to too much expense in arranging special shrouds for their dead. He purposely, although a man of wealth, decreed that only linen should be used for himself and thus put an end to the extravagance (b. *Moed Katan* 27b).

Gradually, apparently under Cabalistic influence, the number of shrouds were developed and became fixed, on the theory that the soul was to be nobly clad as the body was. At all events, the *Shulchan Aruch* itself has very little to say on the matter. *Yore Deah* (352) merely says: "We do not use expensive shrouds for anybody," and that the custom is to bury in white shrouds. The later handbooks on funeral customs already give details of a developed and fixed custom. These details, for example, are to be found in Greenwald's *Kol Bo Al Avelus,* p. 91 ff., and also in the best modern Palestinian handbook, the two volumes *Gesher Ha-Chaim* by Tekuchinski and his son (in Vol. I, p. 102). In Greenwald the regular eight *tachrichim* are mentioned and described in detail, and there is even greater detail in Tekuchinski.

Now, is there any distinction made between classes of people as to the number or the type of *tachrichim* that should be put upon them? As to that, there is only one clear legal dictum: In discussing the question as to what funeral arrangements may be omitted with regard to a wicked person, Joel Sirkes (the Bach) to *Tur, Yore Deah* 362, said that with regard to a wicked person the *tachrichim* may be omitted. Otherwise there is no requirement in the law for special treatment for special people.

Nevertheless, there *is* a difference, if not in law, at least in custom, at all events in Palestine. Tekuchinski, giving the details of the *tachrichim,* begins by saying that there are eight of them and a ninth additional one for a Cohen. The additional one is an interesting addition. This ninth garment is a pair of gloves, because in the holiday services the Cohen raises his hands in blessing. When during his lifetime the Cohen raised his hands to bless the people, it was the duty of the Levite present to pour water over the Cohen's hands before he went up to the *Duchan.* Hence, according to Tekuchinski, if there is a Levite present among the *Chevra Kadisha,* it is he who puts the gloves on the hands of the dead Cohen and all present recite the priestly blessing, "May the Lord bless you and keep you . . ." etc. That is all there is with regard to a Cohen.

To sum up: The whole matter of the number of *tachrichim* is a matter of custom, not of law, since the *Shulchan Aruch* gives no enumeration and description. There is no special privilege except in this one case of Palestinian custom mentioned by Tekuchinski. As for putting a whole additional set of *tachrichim* in the coffin of the priest, I have found no record of it in any of the sources.

3

Inquiry

OATH OF OFFICE

QUESTION:

The Governor of Pennsylvania is a Jew. It is said that he did not take his oath of office with his hand on the Bible, but with his hand on a volume of the Talmud. Is there any traditional justification for this action? (Asked by Rabbi Frederic Pomerantz.)

ANSWER:

THERE IS no such thing as an oath of office in Jewish law. The only instance where there is something like an oath of office is found in the Mishnah, *Yoma* 1:5, in which on Yom Kippur the High Priest swears that he will not make any variation in the proper ritual. The Talmud explains that this oath was needed to prove that the High Priest was not a Sadducee; but there was no such thing as an oath of office other than this one incident of the High Priest.

The regular oaths that Jewish law knows are the oaths between litigants, and usually it is the defendant who makes the oath. These litigation oaths were not taken with any special object like a Bible touched by the hand, etc. Such ceremonies involving Bibles, etc.,

were introduced by the Christian authorities to degrade
the Jews. Jewish law knows nothing of holding a Bible
or any other book, when the litigant takes the oath.

Please see *Responsa Literature,* p. 140 ff., where
there is a description of the answer given by Ezekiel
Landau (1713-1793) Rabbi of Prague, to a question
relevant to this inquiry. He was asked officially by the
imperial officer in charge of such matters to refute the
charge that some Jews feel religiously justified in giving
a false oath in the Government Courts because when
they take the oath, the *Sefer Torah* which they hold is
a spoiled one (*posul*), i.e., unfit for synagogue use.

Landau answered that we Jews are commanded not
to swear falsely even if we do not hold a *Sefer Torah*
in our hand. The holding of the book has nothing to
do with the validity of the oath. He then lists the
various oaths listed in Scripture and shows that in no
case is there any mention that it is necessary to grasp
a Torah or any book while taking the oath.

However, in the case of the present inquiry, it would
have aroused unfavorable comment, or at least surprise, if the Governor took the oath of office without
the Bible. These unfavorable comments can easily be
avoided, since it is a fairly well-established custom that
men being sworn into public office bring their own
home Bible for the ceremony. In that case, the Gov-
ernor-elect can bring either a Hebrew Bible, or the
Jewish Publication Society translation. But actually,
according to the Jewish tradition and conscience, the
absence or presence of a book at the taking of an oath
makes no difference at all.

4

INQUIRY

GRANDSON AND GRANDFATHER

QUESTION:

The Talmud mentions the duties of a father to a son (first chapter of *Kiddushin*) and the duties of a son towards a father. The clearest enumeration of these duties are in the Tosefta to the first chapter of *Kiddushin*. The question asked is the following: Do these duties, or similar duties, apply also from the son to the grandfather and from the grandfather to the son? (Asked by D. B., Pittsburgh, Pennsylvania.)

ANSWER:

IT IS NOT definitely fixed in the law that the respective duties of father to son and son to father apply also between grandson and grandfather. This indeterminacy is noticeable in the careful phrasing of Isserles in his notes to the *Shulchan Aruch, Yore Deah* 240:24. He says: "Some say that the duties do not apply from grandson to grandfather but I do not agree with this opinion, except insofar as it is a man's duty to honor his father more than his grandfather."

The "some say" refers to a great scholar who lived in Italy a century before Isserles, namely, Joseph Colon (the Maharik) in his responsa, *Root* 30:2. The Maharik says that there is no such duty as honor due from the grandson to the grandfather; in fact, since a grandson may testify in court in a case involving his grandfather (which he may not do in a case involving his father), that proves that they are substantially not really kin, at least insofar as the duty to do honor is involved. As for the fact (he continues) that the grandson may say *Kaddish* for his grandfather, that proves very little since a man may say *Kaddish* for anyone who is dead. But Isserles in his own responsa (#118) says that the grandson says *Kaddish* for his grandfather but, of course, the honor due to his father comes first; and in the responsum Isserles uses the same argument that you used to me when we spoke on this matter, that since the son takes his father's place, he also therefore must honor his father's father.

All of this indicates that just as a son has duties towards his father, so we may say a grandson has duties to his grandfather. But the real question is: Is this dutifulness reciprocal? In other words, does the grandfather have duties to the grandson as the father has to his son? The general tendency of the law is to answer this question in the affirmative. Joel Sirkes (the Bach) to the *Tur* (same reference) takes the point of view of Isserles, that the duties are reciprocal. His argument is as follows: In Jacob's dream, God Himself says, "I am the God of your father Abraham" (but Abraham was Jacob's *grandfather*), and Jacob himself, in his last days in Egypt, speaks of God "of my fathers Abraham and Isaac" (Genesis 28:13 and

48:15). So God Himself and Jacob, too, refer to a grandfather (Abraham) as "father." Then Sirkes says that since the Talmud says that a grandfather must teach his grandson Torah (if the father dies or neglects his duty) it is inconceivable that the duty should not be reciprocal, and that the son is in duty bound to honor the grandfather. What the Bach refers to is the discussion in *Kiddushin* 30a on the verse in Deuteronomy 4:9: "Thou shalt teach them to thy sons and thy grandsons." There the Talmud discusses the grandfather teaching the grandson (in the case of a certain scholar named Zebulon, son of Dan). A further reference with the same tendency is in *Shevus Yaacov* (Jacob Reischer of Metz, 18th century) II, #94.

We may sum up as follows: that as to the relationship between grandson and grandfather, the law is not as sharply defined as in the case of the mutual duties between father and son. But the tendency of the law is that these mutual duties do indeed carry over the two-generation gap.

5

INQUIRY

PLANTINGS OR FLOWERS ON THE GRAVE

QUESTION:

What is the Orthodox objection to the use of plantings or flowers on the grave? (Asked by J.S.)

ANSWER:

THE MISHNA, in *Berachos* 8:6, speaks of the incense which was used around the body of the dead, but there is no mention of flowers or plants on the grave. As a matter of fact, none of the codes has any mention of prohibiting plants or flowers on the grave. There are, of course, discussions about trees in the cemetery, as to whether if cut down their wood may be sold; or whether if they over-arch the graves a Cohen may walk under them. But there is no mention at all in the codes of people planting flowers or shrubs or bringing flowers to the grave. Even the Responsa Literature has nothing about it until about a century ago; and from the sparse discussion of the question in the Responsa, it is evident that the whole objection arose as a reaction to modernism.

As far as I know, the first full recorded responsum

on the question was by Eliezer Spiro ("Der Munca-czer") in his *Minchas Eliezer,* Vol. IV, Responsum 61. Here he cites, also, the manuscript responsa of a predecessor in Muncacz. From his description it is perfectly clear that putting flowers on the graves was a custom picked up from the environment by certain modern-minded Jews, and it is primarily on this ground that Spiro objects to it. He says that the rabbis issued a decree against this new habit of putting flowers; he cites such a decree in Budapest and he even heard there was such a decree in Vienna before the community came into the hands of Jellinek and Guedemann (who were *modern* Orthodox). It is natural, therefore, that the objection should first be voiced in Hungary, where modernism and Orthodoxy were organized into national parties, as it were, and opposed each other as such.

Eliezer Spiro now proceeds to search out arguments against the custom. First, he says it is an imitation of Gentile practice and, therefore, forbidden. Also, since rich people can afford to put flowers or plantings on the graves, it violates the rule (*Yore Deah* 352:1, based on *Moed Katan* 27b) that there must be no distinction (in the shrouds) between rich and poor, and this would apply also in this case to the flowers. The rich graves would be decorated; the poor graves would be bare. Another objection would be that the flowers would rapidly fade, and this is a violation of the prohibition against destroying things needlessly (*Bal tashchis*). And finally, the fragrance of the flowers brings pleasure or gratification to the onlookers and it is forbidden to have any benefit (*Hana'ah*) from the body or the grave of the dead.

We may say, however, that since this objection to flowers was instituted by an authoritative rabbi, and since this objection has become widespread now for over a century, it must now be considered an authentic *Minhag,* which has the power of law in Orthodox life.

It is noteworthy that Greenwald, in his fine compendium, *Kol Bo,* p. 168, merely says quite mildly, *"Yesh limnoah lintos. ."* ("It is advisable to refrain from planting . . .") Furthermore, when the Chaplaincy Committee (composed of Orthodox, Conservative and Reform Rabbis) was asked whether it is proper to decorate with flowers the graves of military dead on Decoration Day, they answered in the affirmative, on the ground that the true objection is to permanent planting, and as for the flowers, they are not primarily for the *Hana'ah* of the living, but for the honor of the dead (*Kevod ha-mass*). See *Responsa in Wartime,* page 50.

6

INQUIRY

SPICES AND PASSOVER

QUESTION:

A lady preparing a cookbook of Passover foods was told that garlic is prohibited on Passover. Is this prohibition a firm one or may she include, as she wishes to, garlic in some of the Passover recipes? (Asked by Rabbi Kenneth Segel.)

ANSWER:

I KNOW of no specific prohibition of garlic on Passover although there are some general prohibitions under which some might want to include the prohibition of garlic. The Mishnah (*Pesachim* 2:8) says that one shall not put flour into horseradish or mustard, because these strong condiments will leaven the flour that is put into it. So if it is done the mixture must be eaten at once before it leavens. The *Shulchan Aruch, Orah Hayyim* 464, says that if mustard *and other spices* are wet, i.e., mixed with water, it will leaven flour which is put into it; therefore such a mixture must be eaten at once before it has time to leaven. To which Isserles adds that it has become our custom to eat no mustard at all on Passover, just as it is our custom not to eat peas and beans on Passover.

The objection to peas and beans on Passover is mentioned in *Orah Hayyim* 453. Caro says they are actually not prohibited, but Isserles says it is our Ashkenazic custom to prohibit them. The *Tur* gives a reason for this Ashkenazic custom, namely, that the flour made from peas, etc., can be confused with flour made from wheat, which must be guarded against leavening.

So the state of the law seems to be that one must be careful with mustard and other spices, to eat the mixture of them with flour at once, before it leavens. Whereas the Ashkenazic custom is to make sure and not eat mustard at all on Passover. You will notice that Isserles does not speak of prohibiting *other spices,* but some people may well have included other spices in the prohibition and considered garlic as one of the other spices.

As a matter of fact, this is exactly what has occurred. Many people did get the notion that among the spices which were forbidden for the reasons mentioned above, garlic must be included. So there is a well-established custom among people not to eat garlic on Passover. However, the scholars deprecate this popular prohibition. Joseph Teomim, whose *P'ri Megadim* is the most voluminous commentary (on commentaries of) the *Shulchan Aruch,* says in the subdivision "Eshel Avraham," *Orah Hayyim* 464, that he does not know any basis for this objection to eating garlic on Passover, but he advises not to tell the ignorant that it is permitted. This caution is according to a well-known principle in the law, not to get the uneducated into the habit of non-observance. If they consider something prohibited, it is not wise to tell them it is permitted (even though it actually *is* permitted). However, Joseph Teomim adds that educated people may, if they wish, eat the garlic in private. So, too, Abraham Danzig, the famous codifier, says in his *Chaye Adam,* 127:7 (at the end) that there is *no* reason for this prohibition and it should be permitted outright. A full discussion of this whole matter is found in Gedalye Felder's *Yesode Jeshurun,* Vol. 4, p. 212.

So you may tell the lady who inquired that there is, indeed, a folk notion that garlic should not be eaten on Passover, but that the great authorities say that there is no ground for such a prohibition. Tell her to include the garlic in her Passover recipes. If some ignorant people complain, she can brush them aside with the statement that the *P'ri Megadim* and the *Chaye Adam* are on her side.

7

INQUIRY

EARTHQUAKES

QUESTION:

What is there in Jewish tradition, Biblical and post-Biblical, dealing with the phenomenon and human experience of earthquakes? (Asked by Rabbi Philip Bernstein, Rochester, New York.)

ANSWER:

CONSIDERING the fact that Palestine and the whole Asia Minor area are in an active earthquake zone, it is remarkable how little study has been made of the reverberation in Hebrew literature of this shocking experience. For example, the encyclopedias have only one article, namely in the *Jewish Encyclopedia*. Even the larger and thorough German encyclopedia (*Judaica*) has not a single article on the subject. Yet the subject deserves study because it is evident that the deeply disturbing experience of having lived through an earthquake has left a definite mark on Biblical literature.

First of all, great earthquakes were remembered for a long time. The Prophet Amos's sermons begin with the dating: "In the reign of King Uzziah two years before the earthquake." This must have been a tremendous earthquake because the Prophet Zachariah, two hundred years after Amos, still recalls that event and Zachariah (14:5) says: "As ye fled in the days of King Uzziah before the earthquake." The experience is so deeply moving that the Bible associated earthquakes with the manifestation of God Himself. Psalm 18:8, speaking of God's coming, says: "And the earth shook and trembled and the foundations of the mountains were moved." And at the manifestation of God to Elijah, there was an earthquake (I Kings 19:11). In the description of God's destruction of Nineveh, the earth is described as "quaking" (Nahum 1:5). In fact, in many of the prophetic descriptions of coming catastrophe, the image of earthquake is used as a metaphor for an irresistible invading army.

Isaiah 5:25: "And He stretched forth His hand and the hills did tremble."

Jeremiah 4:24: "I beheld the mountains and lo they trembled and all the hills moved to and fro."

As a matter of fact when Isaiah describes the manifestation of God in the Temple in Isaiah's consecration vision, he says: "And the posts of the door were shaken at the Voice of them that called." Surely he had an earthquake experience in mind.

The experience with earthquakes continued as a living experience in the literature. The Mishnah in *Taanis,* Chapter 3:4, speaking of the various calamities for which the shofar must be blown and a public fast proclaimed at once, mentions the falling of houses. The Talmud *ad loc.* explains this to mean: Not weak houses, nor houses built at the bank of a river, but strong houses when they unexpectedly fall, that is a reason for the proclamation of a public fast. Also the Rambam in Chapter 2 of his "Laws of *Taanis*" also explains it must be strong houses that fall. And on the basis of the Rambam's and the Talmud's statement the well-known commentator, Lipschitz (*Tiferes Yisroel*) says that the Mishnah means houses which collapse because of the shaking of the earth; and he uses also the German word for earthquake, "Erdbebung."

As a matter of fact, it is definitely recorded as a law in the *Shulchan Aruch, Orah Hayyim* 576:4, that for earthquakes and tornadoes that crush houses, a public fast must be called at once. I have also seen a reference to the famous systemizer of Halachic rules, Malachi Cohen (17th century) in Livorno, who, after a destructive earthquake in Italy wrote a book entitled *Shifche Toda* (*Grateful Thanks to God*) which contained a ritual of thanks that the community of Livorno was unhurt by the earthquake.

The Mishnah in *Berachoth* 9:2 has a special blessing to be recited when an earthquake comes. It is the blessing "Whose power fills the world."

The word used in this Mishnah for "earthquake" is not the usual word *Ra'ash,* but the word *Z'vo-os* which means "shaking," and the Talmud (*Berachoth* 59a) discussing this, uses the word *Giha* which means "rumbling of the earth."

This is an interesting subject although references to it in the literature are scattered. The people of Israel taught all of nature to speak the language of faith: the passing seasons, the trees, the flowers and the rain. Surely, then, the searing experience of an earthquake must have moved them deeply and expressed itself in religious moods and ideas. It would be a valuable study to collate all the Biblical uses of the verb and noun, *Ra'ash,* and clarify the subject of the Biblical reaction to the experience of a massive earthquake, how it affected the concept of God's manifestations on earth and expressed itself in the Biblical literature.

8

INQUIRY

ASKING PARDON OF THE DEAD

QUESTION:

What is the origin of the custom to ask pardon of the dead; and also the origin of the variant of this custom seen among Jews from Alsace to touch the foot of the dead when asking pardon? (Asked by Rabbi Andre Zaoui, Jerusalem.)

ANSWER:

ALTHOUGH asking pardon of the dead is a well-known custom, it cannot be considered a religious *require-ment.* That is to say, if this were omitted in any funeral, it could not be said that something essential was omitted. I looked through Greenwald's well-known handbook, *Kol Bo Al Avelus,* and *Ta'amey Ha-*

Minhagim and I could not find a single reference to this custom. Then I looked through Tekuchinsky's *Gesher Ha-Chayim,* which speaks chiefly of the customs in Jerusalem. As far as I could see, Tekuchinsky mentions only an incidental variant of asking pardon of the dead. It is in Volume I, page 138, and is as follows: The custom in Jerusalem, when the body is brought to the cemetery, is to lead it around in seven circles (*Hakofos*). On *Erev Yom Tov,* these *Hakofos* are omitted. Tekuchinsky says that when the body is lowered into the grave, we should ask pardon for omitting this mark of honor. This, of course, is not really what you are asking about. You are speaking of the custom in which the family and all the other people present at the cemetery ask pardon of the dead. Since apparently it is not a requirement, but only a custom, how did the custom arise? It is not too difficult to trace.

In Mishna *Yoma* VIII, 9 we are told that the Day of Atonement will forgive sins between man and God. But the Day of Atonement will not forgive sins between man and man, unless he first appease his neighbor. That is, if he has insulted his neighbor, God will not forgive him unless he asks pardon first of his neighbor and his neighbor forgives him. Thus the custom arose that on *Erev* Yom Kipper, people who feel they have offended each other, ask for forgiveness.

But then the Talmud raises an interesting question (b. *Yoma* 87a and j. *Yoma,* near the end): Suppose the man whom you have insulted has died? How can you get forgiveness from him? The Talmud says (in both places) that you should go to his grave and ask forgiveness of him. This statement of the Talmud becomes the law. Maimonides in *Hilchos Teshuvah*, II:11, gives this as a law, and the *Shulchan Aruch* gives it as a law in two places, in *Orah Hayyim* 606:2 (in the laws of Yom Kippur) and also in *Choshen Mishpot* in 420:38 in the law of injury (note of Isserles). See also the large note of Moses Rifkes (*Be'er Ha-Golah*) (ibid.). This asking of forgiveness of the dead could take place any time, even years after the person had died. But one can easily see how the custom developed to ask pardon at the deceased insulted person's funeral. The Talmud says (b. *Shabbas* 152b): "Everything that is said in the presence of the dead, the dead will hear and know until the grave is filled up." Therefore the custom of asking forgiveness is generally observed while the body is in the cemetery but still not yet put into the grave.

But to ask a man who has insulted another to beg for forgiveness is a much different matter than to expect *everybody* present, including the family, to ask for forgiveness. How the custom spread to everybody and the family is, perhaps, in the realm of psychology. It may be the frequent sense of guilt that has caused the custom to spread to innocent people who had not offended the dead at all. Thus Levinsohn, in his *M'korey Ha-Minhagim*, #93 at the end, merely says: "And so we need to ask forgiveness from him. Because it *might be* that we did something improper or hurt his honor." Joseph Schwartz in *Hadras Kodesh* has no mention of this custom, except that a widow, before remarriage, should visit her husband's grave, ask pardon of him, and thereafter never visit his grave again (21:4).

As for the custom you have seen among Alsatian Jews to touch the foot of the dead when asking forgiveness, again it is difficult to trace strange folkloristic habits. I might guess the following explanation: The *Be'er Hetev* to *Orah Hayyim* 606:2 says: The man who asks forgiveness of the dead should be barefoot. Maybe the people, remembering something about barefootedness, think that to touch the bare foot of the dead is sufficient. Or there may be another explanation. There is a well-known phrase in the rabbinic literature: "I am dust under the feet of so-and-so." (Lev. *Rabba* 2 end) When somebody disagrees with the opinion of another authority, he apologizes, or begs pardon for doing so, and uses this phrase, "I am dust under his feet." Perhaps that too is the origin.

But in general you are right in referring to the custom as "macabre." It certainly is. It really amounts to asking a loving family, in the cemetery at the time of their greatest sorrow, to make a gesture which is a public declaration that they have reason to ask pardon for some injustice or unkindness done to their beloved dead. This is generally quite untrue and may even do psychological harm to the survivors for many years. But, then, there are many macabre things that folklore has added to funeral observances.

To sum up: As far as I know, it is not a requirement anywhere for all present including the relatives to ask forgiveness of the dead. The custom developed from asking forgiveness at first at *Erev* Yom Kippur from

the dead whom one may have insulted or hurt. From
that it spread.

9

INQUIRY

THE FALASHAS AS JEWS

QUESTION:

> The Chief Rabbinate of Israel has influenced the Israeli
> government to refuse the Falashas any recognition as
> Jews (and therefore they are not eligible to the priv-
> ileges of the Law of Return). The rabbinate argues that
> the religion of the Falashas is primitive and that they
> have neither *get* nor *kesuba*. Evidently, therefore,
> their legitimacy is in question. This is the same problem
> faced by the Bene Israel of Bombay who are residents
> in Israel today, namely, doubt as to their legitimacy. The
> questioner, Rabbi Zaoui of Har El in Jerusalem, and
> representative of the World Union for Progressive Ju-
> daism in Israel, has recently visited Ethiopia. He met
> many Falashas and found them eager to settle in Israel
> as Jews. The question is, from the point of view of
> Liberal Judaism, should they be considered Jews or
> not? (Asked by Rabbi Andre Zaoui, Jerusalem.)

ANSWER:

THE ORTHODOX rabbinate in Israel is very exclusionary
in its policies. If it had full power, it would certainly
prefer to restrict the status of being a Jew only to
Orthodox Jews or those born of Orthodox Jews. It is

fighting now to rescind the law which admits the validity of conversions conducted by Reform rabbis outside of Israel. It is also excluding a Jewish brother and a sister from the right of marriage to other Jews on the ground that they are *mamzerim,* i.e., born after a re-marriage which followed a non-Orthodox divorce. On that basis, the Orthodox rabbinate could exclude a large proportion of the loyal Jews of Europe and America, if it dared. Also, (mostly on the question of doubt as to the *get* being fully Orthodox) they would exclude Karaites and Samaritans and any other group about whose bills of divorce they could raise doubts.

Against such inflexible exclusiveness, there is no use arguing. It simply represents a stage in the history of the nation of Israel which we can only hope in the name of our fellow Jews will some day be outlived. But of course, from the point of view of Reform Judaism, the situation is entirely different. We face the reality of modern life and we accept the validity of a civil divorce. To us a woman divorced in the courts is truly divorced and her children by a subsequent marriage are legitimate children. But of course our liberal point of view has no significance to the Ortho-dox rabbinate and they have the overwhelming religious power in the State of Israel today.

But perhaps the Orthodox rabbinate might be influ-enced by the opinion of one of the greatest authorities (*poskim*) in Jewish legal history. I refer to David Ibn Zimri, the Radbaz. The Radbaz was born in Spain in 1479 and died in Safed, 1589. Yes! He lived to the age of one hundred and ten! His main career was

Chief Rabbi of Egypt for forty years. Having been Chief Rabbi of Egypt for forty years, he is a better authority on the true nature of the Falashas and their Jewishness than any other single Jewish authority. He has a long responsum on the Falashas. It is found twice in the collection of his responsa, Volume IV, #219, and Volume VII, #9. You can find it in either place.

The question involved in the responsum had to do with a Falasha woman who fled from Ethiopia after a war in which she says her husband was killed. She came to Egypt and is now a servant (or a slave) in the house of a Jew. Her Jewish master had sexual relations with her and she gave birth to a son. The question now concerns the status of her son. His status depends upon whether she is to be believed when she says that her Falasha husband had been killed. If she is to be believed that she is truly a widow, then this son, Reuben, is legitimate and he may marry a Jewess.

In the entire discussion there is not the slightest doubt expressed either by the questioner or by David Ibn Zimri that the Falashas are to be considered Jews. The questioner says as follows: "It is clear that they are of the seed of Israel, of the tribe of Dan which dwells in the mountains of Ethiopia." And David Ibn Zimri in his answer says, "There are three groupings in Ethiopia: a) Mohammedans, b) Christians, and c) Israelites of the tribe of Dan."

And, of course, David Ibn Zimri also discussed their type of Judaism. He says: "Since they follow the Bible and not the Talmud, they are virtually the same as the Karaites, and what applies to the Karaites and their rights to marry with Jews, also applies to these (whom we now call Falashas)." He says, of course, that the Karaites and these people of Ethiopia do not have proper *gittin* or *kiddushin,* but, he says, since they are not eligible to witness, their marriages are as illegal (from the strict Talmudic point of view) as are their divorces. Therefore, never having been legally married, according to Jewish law, their divorced women are not *Eshes ish* and, therefore, their children cannot be *mamzerim.* Hence, he says, if these Karaites (and Ethiopian Jews) will declare their comradeship (*chaverus*) to our Judaism, we may marry with them.

The modern Orthodox rabbis in Israel must surely admit that there is no greater rabbinic authority than this famous rabbi of Egypt, who knew the Karaites and the Falashas better than any other rabbi. In his opinion, they are Jews from the tribe of Dan, and if they express their loyalty to Judaism, we may without question include them in our community.

These Falashas, according to your testimony, are eager to be a loyal part of the Israeli community; and that, according to the greatest authorities, should be quite enough.

Combined Index for "Reform Responsa" (I), "Recent Reform Responsa" (II), "Current Reform Responsa" (III), "Modern Reform Responsa" (IV), "Contemporary Reform Responsa" (V)

Abortion and German measles: II, 188

Adoption: I, 32, I, 200
  baptism of adopted child before, II, 97
  by Cohanim, V, 145
  children of mixed races, III, 196
  two problems, V, 86

Aguna: I, 86

Answers:
  to CCAR Journal, III, 214
  to Israel on conversion, V, 269
  to Social Security Office, III, 209

Apostate:
  attitude to, IV, 169
  burial of, II, 127
  daughter of, I, 192
  Kaddish for, II, 132
  priest (Cohen) I, 196
  reverting, I, 195; II, 120
  Shiva for, III, 181
  status, II, 120

Ark:
  open during services, V, 37
  standing, while open, V, 38

Artificial insemination: I, 212, 217

Ashkenazim:
  age at Bar Mitzvah, III, 70
  Chanukah lights, I, 25

Athletics and sports: III, 231

Autopsy:
  increased polemics, V, 216

Baptism:
  by Jewish nurse, II, 67
  child before adoption, II, 97

Bareheadedness:
  see Toupee, IV, 302

Bar Mitzvah:
  and quarreling family, V, 27
  at age of twelve, III, 70

divorced father, I, 33
error in reciting Torah blessing, IV, 56
Gentile stepfather, III, 91
in legal literature, V, 27
of uncircumcised boy, III, 107
retarded child, II, 23
Sabbath afternoon, I, 37; II, 19
stepfather called up, I, 32
Sunday, I, 35
Yom Kippur, I, 38

Bas Mitsvah: II, 19

Bastardy: I, 201, 203
  Karaites, III, 186

Birth Control: I, 206

Blood from the dead: III, 242

Body:
  bequeathing parts of, V, 216
  infectious, refusing to handle, V, 181
  lost at sea, I, 147
  position of in grave, V, 172
  preparing on Sabbath, I, 126
  remains to science, I, 130; IV, 278
  which to bury first, V, 165

Brain:
  injury of, IV, 192

Breaking glass at weddings: II, 182
  Jacob Z. Lauterbach, II, 183
  Hillel Posek, II, 186
  see also, Wedding

Breast feeding: II, 226
  kinship affected by, IV, 308

Bride:
  pregnant, V, 64

Bridegroom:
  impotent, IV, 121
  not seeing bride, I, 182
  soldier wearing sword, IV, 116

Bride's veil: III, 188

301

Burial:
  arrangement of graves, I, 156
  burial without family or Kaddish,
    IV, 274
  Christian cemetery, I, 140
  Christian funeral, rabbi partici-
    pating, III, 175
  crypts, IV, 254
  delayed, I, 150
  enemies, side by side, I, 136; II, 61
  family crypts, IV, 254
  in his or her city, V, 185
  in Israel, without talit, IV, 271
  infant in grave of parent, II, 139
  Jewish, of a convert, V, 240
  mass burials, III, 169
  men and women side by side, IV,
    260
  mother's ashes in son's grave, III,
    145
  non-Jews in Jewish cemetery, III,
    155
  of cremation ashes at home, V,
    169
  of fallen Israeli soldiers, V, 205
  of pet animals, III, 165
  of suicides, V, 254
  on festivals, I, 49
  on holiday after a strike, V, 163
  sequence of, after a strike, V, 165
  sinner, burial of, II, 131
  some duties, V, 189
  three day delay, V, 189
  tombstone in absence of body, III,
    141
  see also, Cemetery
Bowing and kneeling:
  on Yom Kippur, IV, 79

Caesarean operation:
  on a dead woman, I, 213; V, 212
  on a dying woman, I, 212
  Maimonides discusses, I, 216
Candle lighting:
  at Kol Nidre, V, 60

Candles:
  in home on Yom Kippur, custom,
    V, 62
Cantor:
  reciting Tefilah with, IV, 18
  serving as rabbi, III, 211
Cemetery:
  alignment of graves, III, 132
  Arlington, I, 141
  eternal flame, IV, 249
  first grave, III, 138
  municipal and Jewish sections, I,
    161
  of defunct congregation, IV, 240
  outright possession preferable, II,
    148
  section in general cemetery, II,
    144
  Sefer Torah carried into, II, 43
  synagogue near, II, 41
  vandalized, V, 224
  visiting the, V, 232
  see also Burial, Tombstone
Chanukah: I, 29
  lights, I, 25; IV, 90
  non-linear arrangement of lights,
    IV, 87
  Shamash ("servant") IV, 90
Chaplain's insignia:
  Hebrew letters on, V, 120
Chaverus, promise of: II, 123
  Ethical Culturists, III, 183
  Jews raised as Christians, III, 217
Chevra Kadisha: I, 128
Child named:
  after Gentile grandparents, IV,
    134
  after deceased person, IV, 136
Children:
  Christian service, attendance at, I,
    115
  Christian Sunday School, II, 59
  Christmas celebration at school,
    I, 112
  custody of, I, 33, 200, 209; III,
    193

Children ("Sons") of Noah:
I, 89, 110, 114, 116; IV, 71
Christian cemetery:
body of Jew to, III, 163
convert buried in, V, 151
memorial services in, I, 143
officiating for Christians, III, 175
worshiping in, I, 144
Christians:
not idolators, IV, 71
officiating at funerals of, III, 175
relatives memorialized, IV, 226
Sefer Torah, called to, II, 49
"Sons of Noah," IV, 71
substituting for on Christmas, V, 131
taught Torah, V, 47
temple organ used for Christian hymns, II, 47
Christmas:
celebration of in school, I, 112
Church:
use of synagogue building, V, 44
Church membership and conversion: I, 82
Circumcision:
anesthetic for, III, 103
before eighth day, I, 90
child of unmarried mother, III, 100
children of mixed marriage, IV, 165
Christian surgeon, I, 93, 111
dead child, I, 96
Jewish adult, I, 100
naming of orphan, II, 91
naming when circumcision is delayed, II, 94
on eighth day, I, 38
son of Gentile wife, II, 99
who may circumcise, I, 105
Coffins: I, 155
lights at head of, V, 177
wife's ashes in husband's coffin, IV, 237
wooden nails for, II, 153

Cohen:
adoption by, V, 145
extra shrouds for, V, 276
Competition, unfair: IV, 281
Confession:
for the dying, I, 124
knowledge of a crime, III, 205
Congregation:
English name for, I, 78
expulsion from, III, 84
Gift Corner, I, 51
meeting on the Sabbath, I, 24
membership of mixed couple, II, 63
Seder, I, 55
social hall, I, 75
Succah, I, 60
Contributors:
changing purpose of gift, IV, 138, 229
criminal contributors, III, 52
listing names of, II, 203
Conversion:
a married woman, I, 85
and church membership, I, 82
answers to Israel on, V, 269
conducted by layman, III, 96
dubious, V, 136
incomplete, IV, 154
insincerity of, IV, 157
indelible allegiance, II, 126
infants, III, 80
man, when family remains Christian, III, 215
of Negroes, II, 83
preconverts and Sabbath lights, III, 88
questionable, II, 78
Reform attitude to, IV, 157
reverting proselyte, IV, 159
unprovable claim to, II, 87; III, 219
without marriage, I, 87
woman, when children remain Christian, III, 110
see also, Miscegenation, II, 83

Convert:
  and Jewish burial, V, 240
  buried in Christian cemetery, V,
    151
  surname of, IV, 148
Cremation: IV, 269
  ashes buried at home, V, 169
  bodies donated to science, IV,
    278
  family disagreement over, V, 228
  wife's ashes in husband's coffin,
    IV, 237
Cryobiology: III, 238
  see "Freezing of Bodies"
Crypts:
  as family burial places, IV, 254
Curtain, Ark: I, 62

Dead:
  blood, using of, III, 242
  clothes and shoes of the, I, 175;
    II, 149
  pardon asked of, V, 293
  shoes for the, II, 149
Death:
  body lost at sea, I, 147
  child before Bar Mitzvah, I, 167
  dates of, II, 148
  determination of, IV, 188
  donating body, I, 130; IV, 278
  euthanasia, I, 118
  hastening of, I, 118, 215; IV, 201
  Kaddish for unmarried child, I,
    167
  last hours, IV, 195
  postponement of, IV, 188
  presumption of, II, 107
  time of despair, II, 105
Deconsecration:
  of old synagogue, V, 9
  of synagogue in large city, V, 10
Dedication:
  of a synagogue, V, 9
Disinterment:
  due to labor strike, V, 160

Divorce:
  father, natural, and Bar Mitzvah,
    I, 33
  father, obligation, I, 33
  for doubtful marriage, V, 82
  daughter, custody of, III, 193
Dog:
  burial of, III, 165
  seeing-eye dog at services, III, 74
Drugs, psychedelic: III, 247
Duchan: I, 41
Dues:
  synagogue, nonpayment of, IV,
    179
Dying patient:
  Caesarean operation for dying
    woman, I, 212
  infant, naming of, IV, 223
  informed of condition, I, 122
  kept alive, I, 117; terminal, IV,
    197
  organ transplants, III, 118
  requests no funeral, II, 110

Earthquakes: human experience of,
    V, 290
English name for congregation: I, 78
Eternal flame: in cemetery, IV, 249
"Ethiopian Hebrews": III, 112
Etrog:
  frozen, III, 26
  last year's: III, 48
Eulogy: I, 27
  for a Christian, I, 145; III, 175
  for a suicide, II, 119
Eunuch (saris): I, 27
Euthanasia: I, 118
Excommunication, laws of: IV, 180

Falashas as Jews: V, 297
Falasha woman: II, 85
Fallen Israeli soldiers:
  temporary burial of, V, 205
Fasting: if Torah dropped, V, 117
Father's name forgotten: V, 32
Feebleminded, sterilizing the: V, 74

Festival, burial on: I, 49
Foetal material: study of, V, 155
Foundling: "son of Abraham," V, 34
Freezing of bodies (cryobiology): III, 238
Funeral:
    Christian, rabbi participating, III, 175
    congregational charge for, V, 193
    double, II, 138
    for those lost at sea, II, 104
    mass burial, III, 169
    requests no funeral, II, 110
    services for ex-members, V, 200
    services for non-members, V, 196
    service in synagogue without body, IV, 274
Funeral folklore: I, 174; II, 148

Gambling:
    for synagogue, III, 56
Garnishee of wages: V, 260
Gentile:
    bridesmaids, I, 190
    Kaddish for, II, 132
    musicians, I, 191
    obstetrician, I, 111
    officiating at funeral of, III, 175
    officiating at marriage of, I, 186
    visitors and the Kaddish, IV, 62
German measles: II, 188
    see also, Abortion
Get, modern: V, 3
God's Name:
    destroying, III, 29
    embroidered on ark curtain, III, 22
    icing on cakes, III, 20
    painted on wall, III, 30
    printed on stationery, III, 224
    spelled "G-d," II, 50
Grandson and grandfather:
    mutual duties between, V, 281
Grave:
    alignment of, III, 132
    depth of, IV, 230

    mother's ashes in son's grave, III, 145
    of Oriental Jews covered with flat stone, II, 142
    plantings or flowers on, V, 284
    position of body in, V, 172
    vacated, re-use of, I, 132
    visiting another, I, 176

Halloween masks, etc.: III, 93
Hatred, avoiding: II, 72
Hebrew letters on chaplain's insignia: V, 120
Homosexual congregations: V, 23
Homosexuality: III, 236

Infant, dying, status of: IV, 223
Israel:
    Jewish religion in: II, 76
    questions on proselytism from, V, 269
    visit to, V, 69

Jewish nurse, dying Catholic infant: II, 67

Kaddish:
    adopted son, I, 26
    after study, II, 18
    apostate, Gentiles, II, 132
    as legal duty, I, 166
    CCAR Yearbook 1957, II, 138
    congregational, II, 27
    customs, III, 179
    for a child, I, 165
    for first wife, I, 162
    for Gentile, II, 136
    for Gentile parents, IV, 63
    three steps backward, II, 217
    with Gentile visitors, IV, 62
    various types, I, 32
    worshiping alone, II, 14
Kol Nidre:
    candle-lighting at, V, 60
    United Jewish Appeal at, V, 57

Law:
    civil, I, 7
    guidance, not governance, I, 22
    Reform and Halacha, III, 4
Lights:
    at head of coffin, V, 177
    Chanukah, I, 24; IV, 90
    eternal light *(ner tamid)* III, 8
    memorial at home, III, 129
    pre-convert and Sabbath lights,
        III, 88
    Sabbath, I, 24; on table, IV, 91
Loaves:
    Sabbath, pre-sliced, IV, 95

Mamzer: IV, 104
Marranos: I, 80, 86, 195; II, 121
    converted to Judaism, II, 121
    woman raised as Christian, III,
        217
Marriage:
    barren wife, II, 155
    bride's veil, III, 188
    civil mixed, II, 65
    doubtful, divorce for, V, 82
    Ethical Culturists, III, 183
    Karaites, III, 186
    pregnant girl, V, 103
    Reform marriage and Orthodox
        aspersions, II, 194
    remarriage to first husband, II,
        163
    two Gentiles, I, 186
    with half-aunt, IV, 100
    without *chalitza,* III, 221
    without license, V, 98
    woman raised as Christian, III,
        217
Marrying the sterilized: V, 78
Mausoleums:
    communal, I, 158
    private, I, 159
Membership, mixed couples: II, 63
Memorial candles for Yom Kippur:
    III, 14

Memorial, Christian relatives: IV,
    226
Memorial lists:
    on Sabbath, III, 178; IV, 24
    whether to shorten, IV, 24
Memorial service:
    in Christian cemetery, I, 143
    on Sabbath, I, 26
Memorial windows:
    changing names on, IV, 138, 229
Menopause: II, 219
Menorah:
    and the Two Tablets, IV, 37
    as floor decoration, I, 68
    made from Torah ornaments, III,
        19
    made from metal Torah rollers,
        III, 37
    non-linear Chanukah menorah,
        IV, 86
Midwifery: I, 188
Mirrors, covering of: I, 179
Mixed couple:
    temple membership, II, 63
Mixed marriage:
    CCAR attitude to, IV, 112
    circumcision of children of, IV,
        165
    Cohen and child of, II, 158
    on temple premises, IV, 108
Money matters on Sabbath: I, 47
Mourning:
    dates of, in different time zones,
        IV, 243
    delayed burial, I, 151
    dishes returned, I, 178
    for stillborn and infants, I, 166
    greeting mourners, III, 156
    when body lost, I, 147, 150
Museum case, Torah in: V, 110
Music in synagogue:
    organ and Christian, II, 47
    secular music, III, 33

Naming child of unmarried mother:
    V, 91

Negroes:
see Races
New Testament:
rabbi reading, IV, 73

Oath of office: V, 279

Pants suit, lady's: V, 123
Pardon asked of the dead: V, 293
Passover:
spices prohibited, V, 287
Patient:
terminal, allowed to die, IV, 197
which to save, IV, 203
Physician:
atheistic, I, 109
Christian, I, 93
divine emissary, I, 119
Jewish, I, 106
Pidyen ha-Ben: V, 28
Plants or flowers on grave: V, 284
Posul Torah in Ark: V, 114
Pornography: III, 240
Prayerbooks, burning of: I, 71
Priest (Cohen):
apostate, I, 196
community composed of, I, 40, 41
marrying daughter of mixed mar-
riage, II, 158
Prohibitions, Biblical and Reform:
IV, 102
Proselyte:
accepted into family, IV, 162
born anew, I, 84
indelible allegiance of, IV, 162
pregnant, IV, 143
reverting, IV, 159
Proselytism:
questions from Israel on, V, 269
Prostration, on Yom Kippur: III, 49
Protest, halting religious services as
a: IV, 82

Rabbi:
participating in Christian funeral,
III, 175

reading or responding to passages
in New Testament, IV, 73
Rabbinate:
fees and salary, III, 199
questions from Social Security,
III, 209
Rabbinical Tenure: V, 263
Race:
adopting Mulatto children, III, 196
"Ethiopian" congregations, III,
112
mixture of, I, 200; II, 85
Reconversion, of ex-nun: V, 141
Red Cross, identification card of:
IV, 175
Redemption (*Pidyen ha-Ben*): V, 29
father's right absolute, V, 30
Reform attitude to conversion: IV,
157
Roses, grafting of: II, 222
Rosh Hashonah, two days in Israel:
IV, 286

Sabbath:
caterer working in synagogue on,
III, 225
communal business planned on,
V, 58
congregational meetings on, I, 46;
see also, Congregation
eighth day Passover, III, 42
Gift Corner open, I, 51
hiring musicians, II, 35
lights, I, 24; on table, IV, 91
loaves, presliced, IV, 95
memorial service, I, 26
money matters on Sabbath, I, 47
New Year Shofar, II, 36
reading memorial list on, IV, 24
school dance on, II, 32
wedding on, II, 167
Sabbath candle:
composition and size of, V, 49
Sabbath candlesticks:
weekday use of, V, 53
Samaritans: I, 64

Seder:
  congregational, I, 55
  wine, types of, III, 43
Sefer Torah: See Torah
Services:
  dog, seeing eye, III, 74
  interfaith, IV, 69
  halting, as a protest, IV, 82
  lengthened on Yom Kippur, V, 59
Shofar:
  New Year Sabbath, II, 36
Shroud, extra, for Cohen: V, 276
Sinai, stones from, for decalogue
    tablets: IV, 40
Social hall of synagogue: I, 75
Soldier:
  Israeli, entering synagogue with
    rifle, IV, 119
  wearing sword at wedding, IV, 117
Spices:
  which prohibited for Passover use,
    V, 287
Statuettes in synagogue: V, 127
Status Quo group, Hungary: I, 82
Stepfather at Bar Mitzvah: I, 32
Sterilization of feebleminded: V, 74
Sterilizing husband: I, 206
Succah, congregational: I, 60
Suicides: II, 114
  burial of, V, 254
  CCAR Yearbook, 1959, II, 120
  Dr. Jacob Z. Lauterbach, II, 114
  eulogy, II, 119
  failed, II, 117
  great stress, II, 117
  noble martyrdom, II, 116
  to dissuade, V, 253
Surgical transplants: III, 118
  pig's heart valve, IV, 217
  trans-sexuals, IV, 128
Synagogue:
  Bagdad, I, 61
  building used by church, V, 44
  collecting pledges through civil
    courts, II, 206
  gambling for, III, 56

  gift to, IV, 140
  gifts from criminal, III, 52
  in joint building with Unitarian
    Church, V, 18
  in large city, deconsecrated, V, 10
  near cemetery, II, 41
  old, deconsecrated, V, 9
  orientation, I, 66
  permanent ownership of, V, 20
  portrait bust in, IV, 184
  rabbis contributing to building
    fund, II, 215
  regulations, two questions on, IV,
    179
  sale of to Black Muslims, V, 13
  sanctity of unfinished building, II,
    210
  secular music in, III, 33
  social hall of, I, 75
  statues in, V, 127

Table, Sabbath lights on: IV, 91
Talit:
  bride and groom under, IV, 294
  for the dead, IV, 269
  in Reform service, IV, 46
  women wearing, IV, 52
Tefilah, reciting with a cantor: IV,
    18
Tombstone:
  anywhere in cemetery, II, 109
  at the head, II, 143
  behalf of living, II, 109
  exchanging a, V, 236
  Hebrew, I, 169
  in absence of body, III, 141
  location of, II, 141
  name missing on, II, 107
  repossessing tombstone, III, 149
  secular date, I, 168
  uniformity of, I, 154
Torah:
  ark closed, I, 435
  auctioning of, III, 60
  blessings, errors in reciting, IV, 56
  blind people called to, III, 75

calling people to without name and Hebrew patronymic, V, 33
carried, how, III, 38
carried into cemetery, II, 43
Catholic priest, reading from, IV, 76
Christians, II, 49
covers, white, III, 25
decorations, III, 18; IV, 31
eighth day of Passover, III, 42
fasting if dropped, V, 117
in jails and asylums, III, 77
in museum case or ark, V, 110
in procession, IV, 14
on Friday, IV, 14
ornaments of, IV, 31
ownership of, V, 104
posul, in ark, V, 114
reading translated verse by verse, V, 40
rollers, III, 36
taught to non-Jews, V, 47
unworthy man called up for, III, 62
white mantles, III, 25
woman called up for, I, 40
Toupee:
bareheadedness, IV, 302
Transplant of pig's heart valves: IV, 217
Trans-sexuals, surgery for: IV, 128

Unitarian Church:
in joint building with synagogue, V, 18
Jewish member of, II, 56
United Jewish Appeal at Kol Nidre: V, 57

Wages garnisheed: V, 260
Wedding:
borrowed ring, II, 178
breaking glass, II, 182-3, 186
Gentile bridesmaids, I, 190
groom not seeing bride, I, 182
in temple, I, 198
on Hoshana Rabba, II, 170
Moses Isserles and Sabbath, II, 169
on Ninth of Av, II, 173
Saturday before dark, II, 167
soldier wearing sword at, IV, 116
sound taping of, II, 53
without license, V, 98
see also, Marriage
Who is a Jew: II, 73
Wine:
congregational Kiddush, II, 27
types of wine at Seder, III, 43
Woman:
returned to first husband, II, 163
wearing pants suit, V, 123
wearing *talit,* IV, 52
wearing wig, III, 227
Women called to Torah: I, 40

Yahrzeit:
observance of, IV, 30
secular date for, I, 168; II, 17
Yizkor: I, 164
during first year, I, 177
prayer developed on three festivals, IV, 25
Yom Kippur:
Bar Mitzvah, I, 36
bowing and kneeling on, IV, 79
memorial candles on, III, 14